the indian
media business

the indian media business

(second edition)

vanita kohli-khandekar

foreword by peter mukerjea

Response Books
A division of Sage Publications
New Delhi/Thousand Oaks/London

First published in 2003
This revised second edition published in 2006 by

Response Books
A division of Sage Publications
B-42, Panchsheel Enclave
New Delhi 110 017

Sage Publications Inc	**Sage Publications Ltd**
2455 Teller Road	1 Oliver's Yard
Thousand Oaks	55 City Road
California 91320	London EC1Y 1SP

Published by Tejeshwar Singh for Sage Publications India Pvt Ltd, phototypeset in 11/13pt AGaramond by Star Compugraphics Private Limited, Delhi and printed at Chaman Enterprises, New Delhi.

Library of Congress Cataloging-in-Publication Data

Kohli, Vanita.
   The Indian media business/Vanita Kohli.
       p. cm.
   Includes bibliographical references and index.
1. Mass media—India. I. Title.

P92.I7K64   302.23'0954—dc22   2006   2006014388

ISBN: 0-7619-3469-3 (Pb)   81-7829-650-0 (India Pb)

Production Team: Anupama Purohit, R.A.M. Brown and Santosh Rawat

to
suman kohli
and
sreekant khandekar

contents

list of figures

list of figures

9

foreword

The Indian Media Business as a book the second time round—with chapters on the Internet and Telecommunications—is an interesting course correction. I am delighted that Vanita has decided to include them.

Back in the 90s, we used to talk about convergence. That convergence is already here. But our policy makers have failed to grasp this occurrence and continue to think about media as 'information and broadcasting.' What we need is an industry framework that will create employment opportunities to bring broader economic and social progress. This costs money and we don't have a lot of that. The government needs to allow private capital but too often red tape and restrictive policies make it impossible to invest. The Indian media business can and will flourish at a much faster pace than what has already been achieved provided we follow the example set by the now world class IT and Telecom sector.

That is why it is good that Vanita has gone into some detail on Telecommunications and the Internet. Reflect on what India has achieved in mobile telephony. We add up to 2 million new subscribers a month and pay the lowest prices anywhere in the world. This has happened by applying the right levels of regulation and FDI (Foreign Direct Investment).

Currently, up to 74 per cent FDI is allowed in telecommunications and 100 per cent in the Internet. Compare that to media. The FDI cap in news is 26 per cent, FM Radio is 20 per cent, DTH is 20 per cent, and cable 49 per cent. Media needs to be seen in exactly the same light as telecom and the Internet and it will grow at, perhaps, an even more rapid pace than telecom and IT.

The Government should nonetheless be given credit for refusing to back away from the reforms that were already in motion, as some observers thought would be the case after the 2004 elections. Some progress has been made in the past year in promoting foreign investment and establishing a value-added-tax (VAT) among other things. The prime minister has established an investment commission to attract foreign capital; is meeting CEOs from various multinationals and has promised to clear hurdles they may be facing.

None of the above would be of any use if we did not have a large consumer base. The big change from the earlier edition of this book is that the declared/

reported number of TV households (45 million consumers) has crossed the 100 million mark with cable and satellite homes crossing the 60 million number—a growth of 40 per cent since the last research report two years ago. During this time there has also been the launch of several new newspapers and magazines all aimed at Indian consumers who are increasingly looking for a slice of the good life. One way in which this attitude manifests itself is borrowing to buy big-ticket items. Such consumers challenge the myth that Indians are averse to credit. The role of media in all of this is unquestionable and as a business we have such a long way to go. Progress is being made, albeit slowly.

In conclusion Vanita's book outlines and details various aspects of the wonderful catalytic industry which can, if given the freedom to operate, create millions of new jobs and help uplift each Indian's ambitions and perspective on what they can achieve for themselves and the country.

Peter Mukerjea
CEO, Star Group (India)

preface

The first time I wrote this author's note in 2003, I knew exactly what I wanted to say. This time I am not sure. *The Indian media business* has been a success as far as I can make out. It is a textbook in several institutes of mass communications. There have been scores and scores of calls and e-mails from students, investment bankers and other people from India and other countries. They have read the book and wanted to ask a question or two. I have been offered several consulting projects and have even been asked to become an investment banker myself. So the book has hit the target audience it was meant to: students, investors, analysts, or anyone outside the business of media and entertainment in India, who wants to understand its construct and dynamics.

Yet this time round I am not sure. This second edition is different in many ways. There are two new chapters—one on the Internet and the other on the telecom industry. Based on feedback many of the charts and graphs have been redesigned, or done away with. The writing is much crisper. Hopefully there are fewer errors of English or facts. The last edition had me cringing in several places, my apologies for that.

That is not all that is different. What has changed is the importance that the government, investors or society now attach to media and entertainment. 2005 was in many ways the year in which the industry grew in stature. It is a long way from becoming something that befits the largest democracy in the world. But now I can say, that it is well and truly on its way. This edition and successive ones will try and capture that growth and its texture.

As usual write to me at *vanitakohli@hotmail.com* for any feedback.

acknowledgements

My heartfelt thanks to the following people for sharing their time and insights with me. Without them this book would not have been possible:

Ameen Sayani—radio professional • Ashni Parekh—media lawyer • Amit Khanna—Reliance Entertainment • Ajay Sekhri—chartered accountant • Ajay Shanghavi—Metalight Productions • Arpita Menon—Lodestar Media • Apurva Purohit—Radiocity • Amrit Shah—film industry veteran • Ashok Mansukhani—Hinduja TMT • Anup Jayaram—ABP Private Ltd. • Ajit Balakrishnan—Rediff.com • Ashok Desai—ABP Private Ltd. • Ajay Gupta— ABP Private Ltd. • Bhaskar Ghose—former I&B Secretary • Bala Deshpande— ICICI Venture • Bharat Kapadia—*Divya Bhaskar* • Cyriac Mathew—*Mid-Day* • Chandan Mitra—*The Pioneer* • Dinyar Contractor—*Satellite & Cable TV Magazine* • Deepak Nanda—investment banker • G.S. Randhawa—Press Information Bureau • G.K. Krishnan—Aaj Tak • Gita Ram—Synovate • G.P. Sippy—Sippy Films • Hemant Mehta—IMRB • Harish Bhimani—radio professional • Hormuzd Masani—Audit Bureau of Circulations • Jagjit Kohli—Broadband Pacenet • Jaideep Chakraborty—ABP Private Ltd. • Katy Merchant—ex IMRB • Kanchan Sinha-Amarchand Mangaldas • L.V. Krishnan—TAM Media Research • N. Murali—*The Hindu* • Nitin Gupta—Ernst & Young • Namrata Datt Ernst & Young • Mohan Nair— Maharaja TV • Roop Sharma—Cable Operators Federation of India • Mr. Saxena—Press Institute of India • Mammen Mathew—*Malayala Manorama* • Maneck Davar—Spenta Multimedia • Mohan Mahapatra—ex Virgin Music • Meenakshi Madhvani—Spatial Access • Mahendra Swarup—Times Internet • Pradeep Guha—Diligent Media • Pratap Pawar—*Sakal* • Pradeep Chanda— consultant • Prashant Maheshwari—ABP Private Ltd. • R.S. Narayan—ex Star India • Radha Namboodri—AIR Mumbai • Ramesh Lakshman—RLC • Raj Singh—Activemedia • Rajesh Jain—emergic.org • Rajesh Kanwal— *agencyfaqs!* • Sreekant Khandekar—*agencyfaqs!* • Sankara Pillai—ex-ORG— MARG • Shyam Malhotra—Cybermedia • Satish Shenoy—formerly with IL&FS Bank • Sameer Kale—CMCG Consultants • Shobha Subramanyan— ABP Private Limited • Sanjay Chakraverti—WPP Media • Sevanti Ninan— Media columnist • Shravan Shroff—Shringar Cinemas • Suresh Thomas— Crescendo Music • Sunil Lulla—BCCL • Shashi Gopal—Magnasound • Supran Sen—Film Federation of India • Siddharta Dasgupta—FICCI • Sanjeev Sharma

—Nokia • S.C. Khanna—AUSPI • Sunil Rajshekhar—BCCL • Sanjiv Agrawal—Ernst & Young • Siddhartha Mukherjee—TAM Media Research • Tariq Ansari —Mid-Day Multimedia • Viney Kumar—IDBI • Vinod Mehta—*Outlook* • Vijay Dixit—AIR Mumbai • Vikas Joshi—*Dainik Jagran* • Yash Khanna—Star India • Yogesh Radhakrishnan—ETC Networks • Yogesh Shah—ETC Networks

My special thanks to the following people for giving me the professional and logistical support to research and write this book:

Aveek Sarkar, Niranjan Rajadhyaksha, Prosenjit Datta, Avinash Celestine, Sheril Dias—ABP Private Ltd. • Mangesh Borse, Vandana Borse—Symbiosis Advertising • Yogendra and Namita Arora • Vijaya Khandekar, New Delhi.

why media matters

It is time for business.

Investors have poured in over Rs 20 billion into the Indian media and entertainment (M&E) industry over 2004 and 2005. Some of the biggest private equity deals and initial public offers (IPOs) in this sector, in Asia, are being inked in India. Reliance-Adlabs and Nimbus-3i are recent examples. Across the business, in multiplexes, digital theatres, publishing, direct-to-home broadcast services (DTH), film production and distribution, television software, and several other areas investors are parking their money and sitting back to wait for the market to deliver.

Will it?
In 2003, when I wrote this section, the question was, 'why media matters?' Just two years later in 2005 it is 'can it now deliver' on all the 'potential' we talked about. All the debate and discussion on M&E has moved beyond the basic numbers. It is now about how this potential will show up in profits and dividends for retail investors, in a good internal rate of returns for private equity investors, in higher market capitalisation for the stock markets. Investors have bought the growth story that media companies were selling. Now it is time for the industry to deliver on the harshest measure of potential—actual returns. I am betting that it will.

There are many things that could trip it and I shall get into that soon. But the reasons why it will deliver are in large measure linked to why investors want a share of the Indian media action.

The first is democracy. It allows us to read, write, make, watch, and listen to whatever we want. It gives investors a range of options and the market a depth, unlike other Asian markets. There are too many restrictions on media ownership in China. In print or TV most investors make do with joint ventures with state-owned enterprises. So far China has seen very little strategic investment, and almost nothing in content. Strong controls mean that except for cheap action films or historicals, the Chinese entertainment industry cannot try its hand at anything else. A Balaji Telefilms or UTV Software kind of listing is unheard of in China.

As a result it has a yawning demand-supply gap in content. For every 10 hours of Chinese films or TV programmes needed, there is only an hour available. Therefore all the investment that foreign media companies made in infrastructure—theatres, television distribution systems—is lying about without getting 'monetised' as investors put it. The heads of two of the world's largest media companies recently went on record on China's lack of democracy and how it limits investors' ability to make money in media and entertainment. Both Rupert Murdoch chairman of News Corporation and Richard Parsons of Time-Warner say that India is where the action will be (see Figure 0.1).

Figure 0.1: The Indian Media Business

Segment	Revenues (Rs billion) 2005
Television broadcasting	185
Press	95
Films	79.67
Music	15
Radio	3.6
Local media	
Outdoor	12
Events	8
Local print	12
Rural media	5
Others	5
Total	**420.27**

Note: (i) Cable advertising is included in the figure for the broadcasting industry. (ii) The figure for outdoor differs from Lodestar Media's numbers because it includes estimates of outdoor advertising that is not routed through ad agencies.

Source: Lodestar Media, PricewaterhouseCooper's Global Entertainment and Media Outlook 2004–08, *Satellite & Cable TV* magazine, *Businessworld* and estimates.

They are also saying it because for both these companies and others, the Indian market has started delivering some results. That brings me to the second reason why investors are flocking to M&E—profits and returns.

More than 70 per cent of NewsCorp's Asian revenue comes from Star India. Time-Warner's Turner Broadcasting has had a successful run in India with Cartoon Network and CNN among its other brands. On the back of rising advertising and pay revenues, operating margins for a bulk of the listed M&E companies have risen by anywhere between 15–100 per cent over the last three years. Deccan Chronicle, Shringar Cinemas and several others have seen their market capitalisation grow 2–3 times since they raised money through an IPO. Private equity investors, usually the toughest of the lot, too are getting what they want. GW Capital sold 14.9 per cent of its 26 per cent stake in Shringar Cinemas (bought in 2000) to Temasek in 2005. It made exactly what it makes on an investment in any other sector: a 30–33 per cent internal rate of return. This is a big difference from 2000, when the sector titillated investors, only to disappoint.

So, democracy without a growing economy or a huge population of young and middle-aged people with more time and money to spend on various media would have meant little. Mix them all up and M&E has the potential to become to the Indian economy what telecom already is—a beacon of the strong economic fundamentals of India and its rising spending power as a nation full of young consumers.

There is a third factor that embellishes the first two. Just like economic liberalisation happened in 1991, M&E liberalisation began in the truest sense of the word, only in 2003. That is when regulation freed publishing to get institutional money; DTH licences were issued. Add multiplexes, and radio liberalisation. The media sector is finally free to talk to investors.

As a result, every part of the industry is ready to build scale and realise its potential. Film companies have been 'professionalising' for over five years now, publishers are expanding all over the country, broadcasters have more options like DTH and broadband to sell television signals, and radio is finally free of licence fees.

And capital is reaching out to these at just the right time.

That is why the industry will deliver.

Sure the industry is still small by global standards. At Rs 420 odd billion or over $9 billion it is a tiny fraction of the global market that is estimated to touch $1,375 billion in 2005.[1] But if you took a look at the annual reports of the media majors the markets that are growing fastest, albeit on a small base, are the Asia-Pacific ones. And within Asia-Pacific, India is one of the most important markets from a growth perspective for most of them.

Having said that the fact remains that the deal sizes are small—anywhere between Rs 0.5–5 billion. The HT Media IPO, ranked among the 10 largest in Asia in 2004 and 2005, is still one-tenth that of the largest media IPO in Asia in that period. The deals in telecom are gargantuan by media standards. The Bharti-Warburg Pincus deal, which pushed Indian telecom to the forefront, got a respectable $1.1 billion for Warburg against the $300 million it spent. That is almost four times the total money that has come into media and entertainment in 2004 and 2005. So the size of the action relative to say telecom, arguably the only comparable sector, remains small.

---

[1] According to PricewaterhouseCooper's Global Entertainment and Media Outlook 2004–08. See Figure 0.1 for a break-up of the Indian media business by segment.

That is because the business itself is terribly fragmented. Its Rs 420 billion size means little, since most of it is splintered in tiny bits. Even the fifth largest media company in the world, News Corporation is more than twice the size of the Indian M&E business. Also it is the smaller companies that are coming to the investors. The larger, more profitable ones such as Bennett, Coleman & Company (BCCL), Sony or Star India, have not yet looked at raising outside capital. But what could really trip this growth are not limitations of size. As investment comes into the business, scale is being built. What could stop it is regulation.

If democracy works to India's advantage, the ad-hocism of its media policy is a letdown. In radio, the most local of all media, private operators are not allowed to broadcast news. That hampers seriously its ability to make money. In DTH foreign investment is limited to 49 per cent. That is a serious restriction of capital for a project that could cost anywhere between Rs 10–20 billion. Consider that cable and DTH are about media infrastructure needed to monetise the pay TV market in India and there is actually an argument to incentivise it. Policymakers have to learn to separate infrastructure from content. Infrastructure is about capital play. In China that distinction is made, to the advantage of the country. Most firms are free to list abroad and raise foreign equity in non-content businesses.

The big fear, especially among broadcasters and film companies in India, is what the minister for information and broadcasting is going to change next. There is also the threat of content regulation looming. Plus there is the new downlinking policy, which specifies that private sports broadcasters have to share their signals for events of 'national importance' with state-broadcaster Doordarshan. Funnily enough these events are largely cricket, not healthcare or education related. The government's desire to continue to protect a broad-caster that has already lost billions of taxpayer rupees is evident.

However as they gain in size and lobbying power media companies will learn to tackle the bogey of regulation better.

The other factor that could trip growth, in either of the segments is the fact that all media is booming at the same time (see Figure 0.2, 0.3 and 0.4). Unlike in the US where newspapers took off, then radio, then TV, then the Internet and so on, India is seeing a simultaneous boom in all media. It will intensify. This leaves very little space for each segment to grow at its own pace. However, this could only have short-term impact before things settle down.

What will this round of expansion mean? Competition, mergers and acquisitions and the birth of media conglomerates. Currently the only serious contenders for that title are—Zee Telefilms and Sun TV.[2]

---

[2] Zee own a large broadcast network with national and regional brands, a DTH platform, a cable distribution company, a film production arm and is a partner in a newspaper

The biggest most important change this round of capital infusion will bring is a move towards greater dependence on pay revenues. That is because much of the investment is coming into media infrastructure, where the gaps are the biggest. Currently the ability to deliver and make money from one of the most prolific content industries is limited. So investment into the delivery mechanisms—the digital theatres, the multiplexes, the broadband pipes, the satellites for DTH and the set-top-boxes for pay TV—will change the industry for good. It will bring in more variety in the ways media and entertainment reaches consumers, in the form it reaches them in, and in what they pay for it. As this variety increases consumers' willingness to exercise choice and to pay for what they want will increase. Recently the balance in the US market shifted from ad-dominated media to pay-dominated media. That means more consumers chose and paid for what they wanted to read, listen or watch, rather than consuming ad-subsidised media.

In India, that stage is many years away. But the process has begun. In TV consumers have had their fill of ad-subsidised channels, for over a decade. Now, millions of up-market homes are looking forward to DTH so that they can watch exactly what they want. In films, consumers are already paying an average of Rs 50–100 for a ticket. As ticket prices in multiplexed small-towns go up, that will rise further. Conversely in radio consumers may not be willing to pay, since they haven't yet had their fill of ad-financed radio offering the variety that say TV does.

All the major factors that had to be in place are already there. Now it is up to media companies to make the most of it.

It is indeed, time for business.

Figure 0.2: We Spend a Lot of Time on Media, Everyday

Weekdays

		2000	2001	2002	2003–04	2005
Press	No of readers (in millions)	232	233	231	252	360
	Time spent in minutes. All India 12+	32	31	30	29	35
TV	No of viewers (in millions)	333	343	350	370	386
	Time spent in minutes. All India 12+	113.9	110.4	112.4	107.9	106.4
Radio	No of listeners (in millions)	122	105	101	138	153
	Time spent in minutes. All India 12+	64	63	66	80	80
Internet	No of users (in millions)	3	5	8	12	12
	Time spent in minutes. All India 12+	65	65	66	58	60

(*Figure 0.2 continued*)

company. Sun owns the dominating broadcast network in the four southern states, large chunks of cable distribution in the same region, two newspapers, a magazine and has a DTH licence.

(*Figure 0.2 continued*)

Sundays/Holidays

		2000	2001	2002	2003–04	2005
Press	No of readers (in millions)	223	225	222	261	370
	Time spent in minutes. All India 12+	35	34	32	31	37
TV	No of viewers (in millions)	334	349	357	376	390
	Time spent in minutes. All India 12+	139.2	129.4	129	124.4	122.2
Radio	No of listeners (in millions	120	104	103	131	149
	Time spent in minutes. All India 12+	67	65	68	81	83
Internet	No of users (in millions)	2	4	6	10	11
	Time spent in minutes. All India 12+	68	66	69	57	59

Source: Hansa Research and IRS.

Figure 0.3: . . . And We Spend a Lot of Money on It Too

Expenditure by Media (Rs million)

Year	TV	Press	Radio	Cinema	Outdoor	Internet	Total
1991	3900	10690	680	70	1584		16924
1992	3950	13250	590	80	1080		18950
1993	4960	15550	680	90	1632		22912
1994	8480	22390	1020	100	2152		34142
1995	13450	27350	1340	90	4064		46294
1996	19750	30470	1130	110	7072		58532
1997	25840	31280	1360	410	8800		67690
1998	33670	35030	1400	500	10512		81112
1999	39410	39240	1450	620	11200		91920
2000	44390	43160	1460	700	6400		96110
2001	45640	43250	1760	790	6400	300	98140
2002	47170	44240	2110	790	4392	500	99202
2003	50940	46890	2270	820	5488	540	106948
2004	58020	60348	2769	984	6860	702	129683
2005	67460	79290	3600	1160	9940	1229	162678

Share of Expenditure by Media (Figs in %)

Year	TV	Press	Radio	Cinema	Outdoor	Internet	Total
1991	23	63	4	0	9	0	100
1992	21	70	3	0	6	0	100
1993	22	68	3	0	7	0	100
1994	25	66	3	0	6	0	100
1995	29	59	3	0	9	0	100
1996	34	52	2	0	12	0	100
1997	38	46	2	1	13	0	100
1998	42	43	2	1	13	0	100
1999	43	43	2	1	12	0	100
2000	46	45	2	1	7	0	100
2001	47	44	2	1	7	0	100
2002	48	45	2	1	4	1	100
2003	48	44	2	1	5	1	100
2004	45	47	2	1	5	1	100
2005	41	49	2	1	6	1	100

(*Figure 0.3 continued*)

(*Figure 0.3 continued*)

80% share still with TV and Press

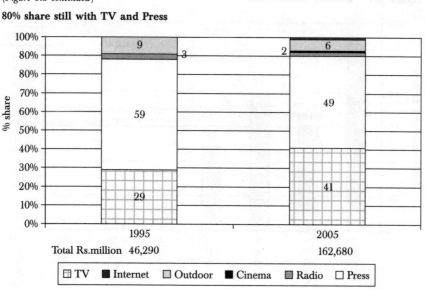

Share of expenditure by media.

TV grows, Print and Cinema losing reach

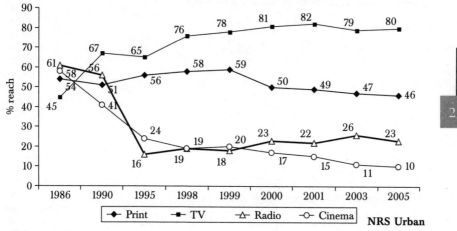

All figures in %

Source: Lodestar Media.

Figure 0.4: Getting Connected

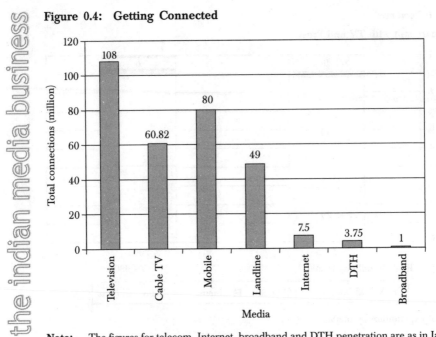

Note: The figures for telecom, Internet, broadband and DTH penetration are as in January 2006. Those for television and cable TV are for September 2005.

Source: TRAI, TAM Media Research and estimates.

1 press

Indian print is finally living in the future

JAMES AUGUSTUS HICKY, a 'rambunctious and irreverent Englishman', gave India its first newspaper in January 1780.[1] The weekly *Bengal Gazette*, also known as *Hicky's Gazette*, was a rag of sorts with gossip about English society in Bengal, the centre of the British East India Company's existence at that time. More than a year later in June 1781, he was in jail for defamation. Undaunted, Hicky edited his paper from jail and his audacious column continued to appear. After a second prosecution in 1782, his press was confiscated and his career as an editor came to an end.

If that seems like an unpromising beginning for India's publishing industry, it wasn't.[2] Here was an Englishman with the impudence to question the governor general and chief justices appointed by his own country. Hicky symbolises in many ways that essential element of a vibrant print industry—freedom. Combine that with the other element—that of government censorship and control. Across the developed and developing world, the history of the press is littered with examples of governments trying to browbeat, scare, cajole and bludgeon the freedom that the Hickys of this world want—to write what they think—for the people who want to read it.

In the end, this freedom survived. It did so partly because there was a business in selling books, periodicals, newspapers, pamphlets, fliers and other such material to people. It survived because people paid good money to read them. It thrived because other people—advertisers—paid even more money to reach the people reading them. This happened in spite of government attempts to choke newsprint supplies, to cut off power to newspapers or to censor them outright, as for example, during the Emergency (1975–77). While the numbers

---

[1] Jagannathan, N.S., 1999.
[2] Throughout this chapter publishing refers to the Indian newspaper and magazine industry. It does not include books.

for the early part of print's growth in this country are difficult to come by, we do know almost 200 years after *Hicky's Gazette*, in 1980, publishing was estimated to be an Rs 1.5 billion industry.[3]

More recently, in 2005, Indian publishing generated about Rs 95 billion in revenues in advertising (ad) and subscription revenues. It is a poor show from a 225-year-old industry. The relatively younger television industry clocked over Rs 185 billion in revenues 2005.[4] If just advertising revenues are considered, then TV has almost half the national ad pie, is growing at a faster pace, is more global in outlook, and is more professionally managed. Print's share of the national ad pie, on the other hand, has reduced from over 70 per cent to just below 50 per cent in 2005 (see Figure 0.3). It remains, largely, an owner-driven, small, proprietorial kind of industry.

Why has print fallen behind? If 'the essence of this business is speed', as Mammen Mathew, publisher of *Malayala Manorama* puts it, print has had plenty of time to dominate and become a huge industry. After all, it has had a 179-year headstart ahead of TV. Is it true then that print doesn't have a future? That it is a medium past its prime and in genteel decline? That it simply doesn't have the fight needed to take on competition from television, radio or the Internet for the consumer's time?

When I last wrote this chapter in 2002, that is what it looked like. Print looked like any boring, pre-liberalisation business that kept seeking protection. In 2005, it looks like it is actually shedding its old skin and learning the rules of the new game in media. What's more, it seems to be beating television at it. There are three things that have forced this change. One, in 2004, after many years, print actually gained in ad revenues over TV. Two, across the country young blood has been taking over the business. From Malayala Manorama in

---

[3] This includes advertising only.

[4] According to the First Press Commission's report in 1953 the print industry was Rs 110 million. This figure was for 127 dailies which submitted their figures to the commission. It included advertising revenue of Rs 50 million and circulation revenue of Rs 60 million. The figures are for the year 1951. The 1981 figure is an estimate based on 'The Managerial Crunch in the Fourth Estate', *Businessworld*, June 8–21, 1981. The source for number of newspapers is the website of the Registrar of Newspapers in India or RNI. In March 2005 a total of 60,374 titles were registered with the RNI according to a circular issued by the ministry of I&B. However since the total circulation of these is not available, I am going with the figure for 2003–04. While the registered newspapers and periodicals stand at 58,469 in 2003–04, the revenue figure is relevant only to the roughly 990 odd publications which are members of the INS or the Indian Newspaper Society. The industry revenue figure and the one for the US market is sourced from PricewaterhouseCooper's Global Entertainment and Media Outlook 2004–08. These are estimates for 2005. They differ from the graphs that Adex India has collated since Adex' numbers are for 2004 and only for a limited sample.

Kerala to Jagran Prakashan in Uttar Pradesh, almost every major publishing company in India has seen younger managers, usually the sons, nephews or heirs of the publishers taking over. Many of them have been educated abroad and want to grow their businesses. It was a young Samir Jain who took over an ailing Bennett, Coleman & Company (BCCL) in 1986 and transformed it into India's largest and most profitable media company. Expect such transformation to happen in almost every major Indian publishing house soon. Three, the rules were changed in 2005 to allow foreign institutional investment into print. That makes it easier for financial investors to pick up shares in publishing companies. This increases the liquidity or tradability of the shares of a listed print company. That in turn makes it easier for private equity investors or others to exit from the company when they want to, something they couldn't do earlier.

As a result, after decades of inaction there is a buzz about print media. Over Rs 10 billion of capital has come into the sector over 2004–05. Investors who have always wanted to invest in print are finally asserting themselves. They see a steady circulation and therefore dependable ad-revenue business. However, for many it goes beyond plain circulation growth. There is the potential of one of the youngest markets in the world. There is also the promise of being in one of three markets in the Asia-Pacific region where newspaper circulation and readership is growing along with China and Singapore.[5] Then there are the revenue possibilities from other media. Almost every major publisher is trying to get into either TV or radio besides launching new editions and attempting different languages. There is also the money to be made from websites and from mobile phone companies looking for news or 'content'. Much of this optimism about publishing has driven some of the larger media deals in recent times.

The first big one came about in 2003 when Henderson Asia Pacific Equity Partners picked up an over 19 per cent stake in HT Media for about Rs 1 billion. Others like *Business Standard-Financial Times* and *Dainik Jagran-Independent* followed. It was Hyderabad-based *Deccan Chronicle's* primary issue in 2004 that gave the market a big impetus. Deccan Chronicle Holdings had a target of Rs 1.3–1.5 billion. It raised over Rs 1.49 billion from an issue that was oversubscribed 9.5 times. In August 2005, HT Media raised Rs 4 billion and made it to the top ten media IPOs in Asia over 2004 and 2005. This gave HT Media a valuation of Rs 24.95 billion—over 90 times the profit it made in the financial year ending March 2005.

There will be several more such rounds of capital. These will fuel more expansion, mergers and acquisitions and other activity. As the capital is spent and businesses grow, the landscape of the publishing business is bound to change.

25

---

[5] PricewaterhouseCooper's Global Entertainment and Media Outlook 2004–08.

But if print is to have its big chance in history, this is it. If it fails to deliver on investor expectations, it will be a long time before it gets a chance again.

THE PAST

The Chinese who invented 'moving metal type' printing somewhere around 970 did not find much use for it.[6] Nor did the Koreans who apparently invented it in the 14th century. The Chinese language is based on approximately 40,000 distinct ideographic characters. The Chinese found that traditional wood-block printing was easier to handle such a complicated script. The same logic applied to the Koreans, who too abandoned the movable type technology. No wonder then that history crowns Johann Gutenberg of the German town of Mainz as the inventor of printing. In 1455, with the help of a 'movable type press' based on the winepress, the *Gutenberg Bible* became the first substitute for the handwritten or manuscript book. It took two years to complete and the business of printing took off. The first big customer was the church, which wanted copies of religious publications in the form of pamphlets, books and booklets, usually in Latin.

By the time the first newspaper was launched in India, printing was a booming industry elsewhere in the world. After *Hicky's Gazette* came a succession of newspapers and periodicals, several out of Bengal and many created by English-men. There was the *India Gazette*, another weekly from B. Messink Welby and Peter Reed in 1780, and the *Calcutta Journal*, a bi-weekly from James Silk Buckingham in 1818. The first Indian-owned, Indian language paper was launched—rather appropriately—by the noted social reformer Raja Rammohun Roy in 1820.[7] *Sambad Kaumudi* was a weekly Bengali newspaper. Between 1780 until India's independence in 1947, more than 120 newspapers and periodicals were launched in almost every Indian language: some were owned by Englishmen, others by Indians, and still others by missionaries. Almost all of them began with a cause—either to speak out against British imperialism or to spread the message of Christianity among the 'natives'. None of them, it seems, had the intention of making money.

---

[6] Roughly individual letters of the alphabet are moulded out of metal and joined together in a sequence of sentences to print. A page made thus is imprinted on any variety of materials, such as bromides or rubber plates. These in turn carry the impression on to paper.
[7] There are some differences in the dates for the launch of many of these newspapers depending on the source. According to two different sources, *Sambad Kaumudi* was launched in 1820 and 1821. For the sake of consistency I will stick to only one of these. N.S. Jagannathan, 1999.

That is a big reason why the newspaper industry in India remains small. It never got out of the 'I am here to fight a battle, not to make money' mindset. While it was all right to have that approach during the time India was fighting for its independence, things continued that way for decades. Let us look at the pre-1947 days.

The pre-independence years India in those days was struggling to discover its identity and fight British rule. The need of the hour was to spread the message of independence. Newspapers sprouted all over the place—and shut down with equal speed. Many editors of defunct newspapers usually managed to get the funds to start another one. Roy started the first Indian-owned English daily, *Bengal Gazette*, in 1816. When the paper shut down, he launched *Sambad Kaumudi*, which shut shop in 1823. Before that in 1822, he started the Persian weekly, *Mirut-Ul-Akhbar* (Mirror of News). This too shut down eventually. Another of his publications was the religious *Brahminical Magazine* brought out to counter missionary propaganda.

In the south, *The Malayala Manorama*, now one of the largest selling dailies in India, began as a weekly in 1888. The first editorial, recalls Mammen Mathew, managing editor and grandson of one of the paper's founders, was about free education for untouchables. It was distributed by boats or cars borrowed from rich family members. For over nine years between 1938–1947, the Diwan of Travancore shut down the paper because of its demand for an independent Travancore. It was only because the family owned a rubber factory and a bank, among other businesses, that the paper was able to re-launch in 1947. By 1953, *Malayala Manorama* had a circulation of 35,000 copies but was still not making money. 'Till the sixties it was a hand-to-mouth existence,' says Mammen Mathew. That's when one of the family decided that it was necessary to be profitable. This essentially meant an emphasis on collection of ad revenue.[8]

The aim of these newspapers was always a cause, a revolt, a message, and a tool to counter propaganda or spread some of their own. Many of the top publications today are the ones that have lived through the freedom struggle. *The Times of India* (*TOI*); *Mumbai Samachar*; *Malayala Manorama*; *Ananda Bazar Patrika* (*ABP*); and *The Hindu*, among others, are all veterans of the Indian freedom struggle. It is ironical that these papers cropped up and played a role in bringing down the British Empire in what was then, a largely illiterate country. Many were financed by benevolent or patriotic businessmen or through donations. Even after independence most had a cause, to see to the birth of a nation and its growth. Several wealthy businessmen continued to keep running

27

[8] Malayala Manorama sold 13,73,079 copies according to ABC July–December, 2004. Mammen Mathew's grandfather's brother, Kandathil Varghese Mappillai, was the founder of *Malayala Manorama*. Mammen Mathew's father (K.C. Mammen Mappillai) followed in his footsteps.

these papers. They could afford to do it because most had other successful businesses: for example, the Goenkas who owned *Indian Express* also owned real estate.

This is the other reason which many say is Indian publishing's weakness: that it has always been a family-owned business which never looked beyond its own general reserves and the owner's limited vision for growth. Though most newspapers in the US, for example, also began as family-run businesses they soon grew, became profitable, raised money, listed on stock exchanges, expanded into other media and did all the things that Indian publishing was never able to do. 'They (the US newspaper barons) see them as commercial ventures, we are more ideological,' thinks Shobha Subramanyan, the former managing director of ABP. Indian print barons complain that they never had easy access to capital. That may be true, but they never tried hard enough to raise any either, especially through equity. For very long they did not even think of their publications as a business.

The 50s The only recorded instance—of a look at publishing as a business— that I came across was in the First Press Commission's report (1953). Appointed by the Indian government to look at press laws in the light of the country's freedom, the commission takes a detailed look at the capital invested, returns generated, revenues and costs of newspapers. However, like many other things, the report is a product of its times. The heavy influence of socialism—and the notion of protecting anything small against anything big—is in evidence throughout the report. It talks about trying to limit the growth of large metro- politan newspapers. There is a proposal to make it mandatory for large news- papers to increase their price when they increase their pages. This proposal later morphed into the Newspapers [Price and Page] Act.[9] For some sense of what the thinking was in those days, sample one comment from the report: 'The great advantages possessed by the metropolitan press has tended to draw away from the districts the talent that might have gone into the development of a local press. We do not consider concentration of the press in metropolitan cities a desirable feature, however inevitable it was in the early stages'.[10]

The meat for this book however is in some interesting tidbits in the chapters on the economics of newspapers and capital investment. A sample of 127 dailies had total revenues of Rs 110 million. The split between circulation and advertising revenues was a healthy 60:40.[11] It showed that the industry

---

[9] See portion on regulation.

[10] To be fair this kind of thinking permeated our entire economy and was in many ways the result of over two centuries of economic bondage to the English.

[11] Circulation refers to, literally, the number of copies a newspaper or magazine circulates. Usually this refers to the number of copies bought and paid for. It does not include free copies. Circulation revenues refers to the money that newspaper companies collect from the cover price after deducting trade margins.

was not completely advertising driven and that readers were paying the bulk of the cost of producing and selling a newspaper. Currently, on an average only 15–20 per cent of the revenue of an English newspaper is recovered from circulation revenue. Advertising is the biggest and only alternative source for most newspapers. This is not good for the financial health of the industry. We shall read more on that later in this chapter.

A few things remain constant. It was an owner-driven, capital-intensive, long-gestation business and it remains that way. Out of 47 companies (for which the commission had figures) only the 19 that were more than 15 years old gave a return of more than 10 per cent on capital invested. As a whole, the industry generated a profit of Rs 0.6 million or less than one per cent on a capital investment of about Rs 70 million. The calculation may look rather simplistic. However it provides a rough and ready indicator of what the industry looked like in 1951, the year for which these statistics were calculated.

Why then did proprietors continue to remain in the business? According to the Press Commission's report, there were two reasons. One, because the rest of the industry was flush with post-second-world-war profits which were parked in various businesses. Print was one of them.[12] Two, as the Commission put it, money also came in 'from persons anxious to wield influence in public affairs. The fact remains that as an investment a new newspaper undertaking does not look very tempting.'

Many of the things the Press Commission said in its 1953 report remain true today. Newspapers continue to be a capital intensive, long-gestation, low-return business. So why do people continue to be drawn to it? Owing to two reasons again.

First, if you are the leader in the newspaper business, or even No. 1 or the No. 2 or No. 3 today, you tend to get a disproportionate share of revenues and profits. BCCL, which publishes India's leading English daily *TOI* generates anywhere between 25–40 per cent in gross margins. In the financial year 2003–04 its net profit was over 20 per cent, above the average in many industries. This is true for every medium, as you will read in the chapter on television.

The second reason remains the same as that in 1951. Newspapers are still treated as tools of influence. The actual losses of the business, when weighed against the power it gives a business house or an individual in the corridors of ministries, seems to be a small price to pay. You could actually say that lobbying would have meant spending at least that much money. This is evident in the fact that while the Registrar of Newspapers for India (RNI) has more than 58,469 publications on its roster, only 990 are members of the Indian Newspaper Society (INS). The number of Audit Bureau of Circulations (ABC)

29

[12] Even the film industry during this time was flush with post war profit. For more details see chapter on Film.

members is even fewer at 411.[13] Every serious publishing house is a member of these bodies. Many companies and people just register a newspaper title. They then use it for purposes other than to make money from the newspaper.

Figure 1.1: Newspapers in India

	2001	2003–04
Registered publications	49145	58469
Total circulation	126963763	133087588

Source: Press in India highlights—2003–2004 RNI.

The 60s and the 70s There were a lot of reasons why the 'business' of publishing never got the attention it needed. One of the major ones was because it was a difficult 'business' to be in. The low returns and high capital investment in the business were combined with an acute shortage of the primary raw material, newsprint. Many major events in the business can be correlated with the rise and fall in newsprint prices. To this, add tight governmental controls on it through the Newsprint Control Order of 1962. It acted as an indirect hold over the industry. There were quotas based on the number of pages a newspaper or magazine had and its circulation. Every few months, publishers had to apply to the RNI for newsprint quota with a chartered accountant's certificate as proof of circulation. Publishers tried to get their quota increased through all sorts of means, say insiders. Even if a publisher got a big quota, under the control order, only 30 per cent of his total requirement could be imported. This had to be imported through the State Trading Corporation. The remaining 70 per cent had to be purchased from domestic, usually state-held newsprint producers. Most of these like Nepa Mills sold poor quality newsprint at the landed price of the imported material.[14]

Then there were the problems of importing printing machinery, a nightmare, with duties as high as 100–150 per cent in some years. The cost and headache involved, and the other sundry permissions required from the Reserve Bank of India (RBI) and the RNI ensured that importing the equipment never ever paid back in increased efficiencies. There were also arbitrary levies on newsprint, a wage tribunal that mandated salaries, so on and so forth. Get a publisher to recall the 60s and 70s and all he will talk about is what a nightmare it was to simply get the paper out every morning. Investing in technology, systems,

[13] The Audit Bureau of Circulations audits circulation numbers and The Indian Newspaper Society is an industry body. These numbers were taken from the ABC and INS websites at the time of writing and may have increased subsequently.

[14] A large part of this was the result of a foreign exchange shortage that was constant in those days.

people and expansion was beyond the scope of what they were occupied with in those days.[15]

The other indirect tool was the Press Council, a statutory body formed during Indira Gandhi's regime. Her father, Pandit Jawaharlal Nehru, clearly did not want to mandate the formation of a press council. As prime minister, he believed that even a bad press was acceptable as long as it was free and self-regulated. The first Press Commission had suggested a mandatory Press Council but the bill never got past the Lok Sabha, and finally lapsed before being revived during the Indira Gandhi years. Her government's time was marked by political, social and economic turmoil, much of which was blamed on the press.

All of this culminated in the Emergency declared on June 25, 1975. One of the tools to harass the press then was to cut off the power supply to Bahadur Shah Zafar Marg, New Delhi's Fleet Street, which houses some of the largest publishing companies in India. The next 18 months saw the most humiliating period in the Indian press' history. During this time, several laws were amended and others passed making it almost impossible to criticise anything the government did. The censorship meant newspapers could not report what was actually happening. This gave birth to underground magazines reporting on the realities of India.[16]

The transformation of the publishing industry into a business began post-1977, after the Emergency was lifted. There were several things that came together to force a change on the industry. The Janata government, which came to power in the post-Emergency elections, repealed most of the regressive laws. Across the country people bought more newspapers because they wanted to know what had happened in the preceding months of the clampdown. The best account of these years is recorded in a series of 11 essays on the language press and a book, both by Robin Jeffrey (2000). In the essays and the subsequent book Jeffrey traces the growth of the Indian language press from 1977–99.[17] He puts it down to three factors: the growth of literacy, the rise of capitalism and the spread of technology. The last refers to offset printing technology coupled with communications technology that allowed the use of facsimile or satellite editions. The 70s and the 80s are littered with examples of new companies and brands that hastened to tap into this growth and make money.

31

---

[15] Of course publishers too were not blameless. Most industry insiders admit that many publishing houses were guilty of under invoicing of newsprint when they had actually bought more. The surplus was sold off in the black market. In some years publishers made more money from the sale of newsprint than publishing. Others registered newspapers and got licences to import newsprint that was then sold at exorbitant rates.

[16] The Press Institute of India still houses some of the magazines brought out during the Emergency.

[17] The 11 essays appeared in the *Economic and Political Weekly* during January–March, 1997. Jeffrey's work is by far the most comprehensive and insightful piece of writing on the Indian press that I came across.

Ramoji Rao of *Eenadu* was clear from the beginning that he wanted a newspaper that would bring local news to local readers. He already had several successful businesses—Margadarsi Chitfunds, Priya Pickle as well as hotels. When he decided to launch a newspaper from Visakhapatnam in 1974, Indian Express's *Andhra Prabha* was the leader with 74,000 copies. The second newspaper, *Andhra Patrika* was losing circulation. In 1975, when *Eenadu* was launched in Hyderabad it divided the city into target areas, recruited delivery boys three months before publication and gave away the paper free for a week. In each subsequent town that the paper was launched in (Tirupati in 1982; Ananthapur in 1991; Karimnagar in 1992; and Rajamundry in 1992), *Eenadu* looked for new ways to market. By 1978, within four years of its launch, *Eenadu* had surpassed *Andhra Prabha's* circulation. In 1989, it began to produce tabloid district supplements with every copy of the paper. A copy of *Eenadu* produced in Karimnagar was sold in the neighbouring Adilabad district, not only with the 10–12 pages common with Karimnagar, but also with another 8–12 pages solely for and about Adilabad. By 1995, two rivals—*Andhra Patrika* and *Udayam*—had folded up and *Eenadu* commanded 75 per cent of the audited circulation of Telugu dailies.[18]

Meanwhile, in 1979, Mumbai saw the launch of its first successful afternoon daily, *Mid-Day*, which eventually led to the closure of *TOI's Evening News*. The 16-page tabloid was priced at 25 paise. Today, *Mid-Day* is the flag-ship brand of the eponymous company that is listed on the Bombay Stock Exchange (BSE) and did Rs 1.02 billion in revenues in March 2005. That's up from Rs 70 million in 1983. It is some measure of the little brand's tenacity that it has stood the test of time against a brand like *TOI* that dominates Mumbai. In quick succession it launched the *Sunday Mid-Day*, *Gujarati Mid-Day* and even a Delhi edition, which was sold off later.

It was successes such as *Mid-Day* and *Eenadu* that pushed other proprietors to invest in offset technology, satellite editions and distribution to push up circulation. The old set of proprietors finally began to view their publications as a business while the newer ones looked at it as nothing but that. It seems rather obvious today, but remember we are talking about a time when editorial, marketing and circulation operated on different planets. There was seemingly no connection between what people wanted to read and how the product was to be marketed or sold. There wasn't even a debate on whether there should be a meeting ground between these aspects.

Many of the new people who got into publishing did it simply because there was a business opportunity—as in magazines, for example. 'With *India Today* (launched in the mid-70s) independent magazine publishing got a boost,'

---

[18] Much of the *Eenadu* experience has been sourced from Jeffrey's essays.

says Maneck Davar, owner of Spenta Multimedia. Till then the idea was that only big publishing houses had the financial muscle to launch their own magazines. *India Today*, with *Sunday, Stardust, Savvy, Debonair* and *Society* set off a trend of sorts. In fact, Nari Hira's Lana Publishing (later called Magna) launched *Stardust, Savvy, Society, Island* and *Parade* in quick succession to become a celebrated publisher in the 80s.

These magazines took off because they offered much more than the staple political fare that newspapers did. They gave readers a mix of features on politics, films, home, women and lifestyle. A lot of this was in colour, then a new element. It also made a huge difference to how much advertisers and readers were willing to pay for the same product. *Chitralekha*, a small Gujarati magazine, was one of the first ones to take to offset printing in the late 70s and got its first computer in 1981. As a result it could take colour ads and pushed up its cover price from 60 paise to Rs 1.80. 'It paid rich dividends,' remembers former associate publisher Bharat Kapadia.[19] The quality and newsiness improved and deadlines shortened. A cover story that had to be released 10 days prior to hitting the stands could be sent in for printing five days earlier. Magazines could be more newsy. It also gave the marketing department the flexibility to accept a colour ad closer to the press deadline.

Sensing an opportunity, newspapers launched supplements in black and white and colour. 'Colour,' thinks Cyriac Mathew, former publisher of *Mid-Day*, was 'the next big revolution for newspapers.'[20] *The Saturday Times, The Sunday Review, Brand Equity* and a whole lot of other colour supplements were a response to the success of general or specialised magazines around 1990. Eventually they did help newspapers suck back ad revenues from magazines. It was an indolent time. The business had the luxury of time to deal with its own problems. That is because television had still not taken off in India. Roughly 80 per cent—may be more—of the total advertising spend in 1980, went to print. Doordarshan (DD), radio and cinema got the rest.

The Samir Jain years Tariq Ansari, managing director of Mid-Day Multimedia, joined his father's newspaper business in 1983. When asked what are the big milestones in the newspaper business in India, he immediately mentions the entry of Samir Jain. It is an opinion cutting across publishing companies that the biggest change in the 'business' of publishing came with the entry of the reclusive Jain. Most young newspapermen who took over their fathers' businesses in the early 90s use Jain and BCCL as a benchmark of what

---

[19] *Chitralekha* is a leading Gujarati and Marathi weekly. Kapadia is now the executive director for *Divya Bhaskar*, a Gujarati newspaper from the Bhaskar Group.
[20] Mathew is currently vice-president sales at Mid-Day Multimedia.

they want to achieve. The story of how he used simple marketing principles and good business sense to transform the down-in-the dumps publishing company into a profit machine is documented in a cover feature that *Businessworld* magazine did in 1995.[21] From Rs 47 million in 1987–88, BCCL's profit before tax jumped to Rs 1.3 billion on revenues of Rs 4.79 billion in the 12 months ended July 1994. Currently, BCCL is India's largest media company at Rs 23.63 billion in revenues and Rs 5.29 billion in gross profits in July 2005.[22]

When Samir Jain took over in 1986, turning it around was an imperative since the other family businesses—New Central Jute and Rohtas Industries—were in decline. Mr Jain tried to look at a newspaper as any other consumer product and played around with almost every element in the product mix. It started with hiring people from an FMCG (fast moving consumer goods) background, fixing value and not volume targets for his sales people and trying almost everything possible. From colour supplements, to different pricing on different days, to cross-brand advertising packages and price-cutting, he did everything to maximise the return from each of BCCL's brands. He tried to work around and eventually shut down a host of brands like *The Illustrated Weekly*, *Dharmayug*, *Dinman* and *Vama*: magazines that weren't great money-spinners but were well-respected editorial products. It was during this time that the first advertising encroachments into editorial space started. One of the first few brands to do it, remembers Sanjay Chakraverti of WPP Media, was Rasna. It ran an ad bang in the middle of editorial space in *The Saturday Times*, a colour supplement from *TOI*.

However, the most interesting *TOI* story is the one of Jain's triumph in New Delhi. *TOI* is now almost neck and neck on circulation and proportion of advertising share with the leader, *HT*.[23] All *TOI* did was cut prices and keep pushing up circulation, and offer a trendier newspaper for the younger post-liberalisation generation. It seems like a simple enough thing to do. But remember that *TOI* was battling its own equivalent in Delhi. *HT* has been the unquestioned market leader for more than six decades now. However, within seven years of starting to really pay attention to the Delhi market, *TOI* managed to rock the *HT* boat. It is a strategy that *TOI* has tried in Hyderabad, Bangalore, and Kolkata. Most rival publishing companies in India are roughly one-fourth the size of BCCL. With its over Rs 4 billion in reserve, it can take the losses of any price war without flinching for a long time. A smaller rival like the *Deccan*

---

[21] Most of the data for this part comes from *Businessworld* articles and BCCL's annual reports.

[22] BCCL's financial year is June–July.

[23] According to ABC figures for July–December 2004 *HT's* Delhi edition sold 10,83,263 copies. *TOI* sold 9,25,273 copies as per ABC figures for January–June 2004. These were the last available ABC audit figures for these brands at the time of writing.

Herald or even a big one like *HT* cannot bleed for long. *TOI* is now India's only truly national newspaper with a circulation of over 2.14 million[24] copies. That also makes it, claims BCCL, the world's largest selling broadsheet English daily.

Jain has long since given up day-to-day running to professional managers. *TOI* is now one of the most aggressive marketing companies with some very profitable media brands in its portfolio. Many of the things Jain tried, like differential pricing would come more naturally to the brand manager of a soft drink company than to an intellectual product like a newspaper. The difference is that Jain did these things at a time when nobody thought that the 'commercial' function in a newspaper had any importance. The notion that there should be a total divorce between a paper's editorial and its marketing was completely shattered by Jain. He has made *TOI* the best money-making machine that appeased advertisers without qualms. Today, *TOI* Mumbai brings in an estimated 60–70 per cent of BCCL's revenues. It remained unchallenged for decades. No other business house—the Singhanias with *The Indian Post* or the Ambanis with *The Business and Political Observer* have ever been able to take on *TOI* in Mumbai. Even rivals like *HT* put off a Mumbai edition for over a decade. Others like *The Indian Express* or *The Asian Age* have been reduced to mere sideshows in the city. 'The Jains were the first to look at return on investment, pricing, promotion. That's their outstanding contribution to the business,' thinks Ansari.

While many publishers criticise Jain for starting price wars and eroding circulation revenue, most followed his lead. They added more colour, pushed up circulation, added more finesse to their marketing efforts and reaped the benefits. Many Hindi dailies like *Dainik Bhaskar*, *Dainik Jagran* and *Amar Ujala*, took several leaves out of the *TOI* book. 'In the 90s we went into expansion and for the first time saw profits in millions,' says Mammen Mathew. Adds N. Murali, joint managing director of *The Hindu*, 'The business mentality started creeping in the 90s.' G. Krishnan, CEO of TV Today Network, who was formerly with *TOI*, remarks, 'Till then the market was driving media, by the late 80s media started driving the market.' 'It (price cutting) spread like a disease. But the flipside (of Jain's contribution) is that newspaper managements woke up,' adds Shobha Subramanyan, formerly of *ABP*.

Through his utter devotion to the bottomline, Jain managed to bring about a mindset change desperately needed at that point in time. His timing was impeccable. It was not only Jain's example that other newspaper proprietors were following. The post-liberalisation air was also opening up opportunities for them. By 1992, both newsprint and printing machinery were placed under

---

[24] This figure is sourced from *The Times of India*'s website. Many of these numbers are at the time of writing. They may differ from fresh data released later.

the open general licence, making their import easier.[25] Add to it one other fact. Advertising too was changing hands with multinational corporations (MNCs) taking charge of the ad industry. Says Subramanyan, 'They (the foreign agencies) had a different mindset.' It was one that matched *TOI*'s.

The interesting question this raised was about the role of newspapers. Had they changed completely from being tools for social change to mere reflectors of it? Was the purpose only to assemble readers who could then be sold to advertisers? All this talk of treating newspapers like an FMCG seems fine in theory, but there is one crucial difference—unlike soap or shampoo, a newspaper is fodder for the mind. Unless it talks to the reader in his context he cannot relate to it. If newspapers are becoming glossier, glamorous but with little intellectual food for thought, will they create a generation of socially dead minds? It is a question that only time will answer.

As an aside also notice that the industry was so busy with discovering the business of publishing that it missed the opportunity of the future—television. It was during these years that cable was taking off in India, but except for BCCL, Living Media and *Business India*, nobody saw an opportunity in broadcasting or cable. It took a CNN and a Star TV to make publishers realise the potential in broadcasting. Many then scrambled into it—Hindustan Times, Eenadu and Living Media among others.

The satellite TV years When satellite television finally took off in 1995 print was still in its domination phase.[26] It was growing—in editions, products, revenues and size. In 1995, it still had a share of 70 per cent or so of the advertising market. Rate negotiations were unheard of. However, eventually television did change the press. 'Television changed the concept of news in print and because television is good at certain things, print had to adapt,' says Vinod Mehta, editor of *Outlook* magazine. Television made newspapers less newsy. They couldn't just report the news; they had to offer analysis and informed opinion on it. Besides news, television was also eating seriously into the share of entertainment reading. With television broadcasting the news, in addition to entertainment, sports and a whole lot of things, general interest magazines suffered. And special interest ones took off. By the end of 1992, on the back of the primary issue and technology boom, specialised magazines were picking up speed. *A&M*, *Dalal Street Journal*, *Dataquest* and *Health & Nutrition*, among a host of others, sought their readers and actually managed

---

[25] While newsprint is indeed under open general licence (OGL), it is still a restricted item. A publishing company needs an authorisation letter from the RNI before it can import newsprint.

[26] While satellite TV came into India in 1991, it really took off after Zee and several other private broadcasters, like Sony, Home TV or Sun TV came into the market between 1991 and 1995. That is why I refer to 1995 as the takeoff point.

to expand the market.[27] All of them were using innovations, special features and so on to get a larger and larger share of advertising.

By 1997, however, things started going wrong. The ad industry went into a slowdown; television began eating into print's share of the audience and ad-spend. Also newsprint prices started rising again. Typically, print companies reacted by pushing up ad rates. That year saw a further the decline in print's share of national ad revenues (see Figure 0.3). It also saw another trend—of local print brands taking off across the country. While national newspapers took a share of it with city and suburban editions, local newspapers too jumped into the fray. There are standalone area-specific publications like *Annanagar Times* in Chennai or the more recently launched *Metro* (from *Mid-Day*) in Mumbai. Local newspapers are an important indicator that the print market in India has finally matured. It shows that unlike national or regional papers, those writing about local concerns can make money because local economies have become strong enough to support such ventures. Many of the local brands like *Metro* are distributed free. Their survival hinges on getting small local advertisers to buy space in the newspaper. Just like the big push of 1977 and 1986, it was time for the print industry to move on again.

These changes proved to be good for the industry. They increased competition, business innovation and forced publishers to expand. However, by 2001, print had lost substantial ground to television (see Figure 0.3). Increasing rates was no longer an option. Print brands started negotiating on rates just like television channels. 'In 2001 for the first time in 10 years, this industry has seen a dip in profits,' says Ansari. According to the numbers that Lodestar Media crunched for this book, in 2002 TV's share of the ad pie finally overtook print. In 2004 the order was reversed again.

THE WAY IT IS

Over the years, the print industry in India has morphed into something that is quite different from most newspaper markets in the world. There are several factors that set us apart.

The first is the low level of literacy. For all our pretensions of having English as a link language, the fact is that just about half of Indians can read or write. An even smaller percentage are actually capable of reading the issues that a newspaper writes about since literacy is defined as the ability to sign one's name. Unlike television or radio this one factor automatically limits the growth of print. The flipside is that the English language press commands a premium because of this reason since advertisers automatically value anyone who can

---

[27] *A&M* and some of the other magazines have since shut down.

read an English newspaper. That explains the differential in the ad rates between Indian and English language newspapers. This will change eventually because macro-economic data shows increasing semi-urban and rural prosperity. It means that increasingly the advertiser will be willing to pay the same rates to reach English and non-English language readers. It is already happening in some markets say media buyers.

The second, 'In India the sense of nation is very strong. All newspaper groups have a strong national presence,' points out Pradeep Guha, former President, BCCL.[28] India has very strong regional newspaper brands and one national brand, *TOI*, but very few local brands. That is not how the market developed elsewhere in the world. The US has just one national newspaper, *USA Today*, which is weak competition for the thousands of local papers that take away more than 80 per cent of print ad revenues. Indian advertisers, therefore, had very few options that were local or community specific. Radio was limited to AIR and television had not yet developed. This has changed in the last few years. A whole lot of print options began developing the moment television—and especially local cable channels—started taking off. By 1997, city or locality based newspapers started appearing. In 2004, print made roughly Rs 12 billion from local advertising, that is, advertising directed at any local print vehicle, either nationally or locally owned.

Third, our 'over-dependence on advertising', says Murali of *The Hindu*. 'Ad: circulation ratios used to be 50:50 even 25 years back', says Guha. That's borne out by the Press Commission numbers discussed earlier in this chapter. 'It distorts the market and makes the industry more vulnerable to a slowdown,' points out Murali. It is economically debilitating for publishers to sell for Rs 1–1.50 newspapers that cost anywhere between Rs 4–7 a copy just to print. (This does not include fixed costs.) It also puts newspapers in India at the mercy of advertisers. Unlike mature markets like the US or Europe where circulation revenues bring in 40–60 per cent of total industry revenues, in India the figure is closer to 10–20 per cent for most English language papers. (The regional newspapers do better on circulation revenues since their cover prices are higher.) While cover price cuts are common in the UK or US too, these are usually short term. In India price cuts have been used year after year by, say, *TOI* in Delhi. When dozens of brands start doing that, the value they sometimes erode could be greater than the one they create. That is what will happen if all the money coming in now goes into price cuts and circulation losses (see Figure 1.2).

What do these factors mean? An ad-driven publishing industry means that the focus of the publisher is on the advertiser and the media buyer and not on the main currency of publishing—the reader. It also means that the freedom

---

[28] Guha is currently a Director with Diligent Media Corporation a joint venture between Zee TV and the Dainik Bhaskar Group. It publishes *DNA*, an English daily from Mumbai.

that financial independence is supposed to offer is endangered if it incurs the wrath of a big advertiser. It is routine for advertisers to pull out entire campaigns if there is even mildly objective reportage on them. It happens not necessarily to critical stories, but ones that analyse the financial performance of the company and report on market perceptions of its weaknesses. This in turn has meant the gradual collapse of the Chinese wall between editorial and advertising sales departments of publications. In many newspapers and magazines it does not exist. In others, it is set to crumble. And, in several, it is strong and functioning.

Over-dependence on advertising has done more than blur the lines. It has reduced the whole debate about the mix of advertising and editorial to one of degrees of intrusion, not about the right or wrong of it. There is nothing wrong in doing a sponsored article or an advertorial, which says so clearly. If a deal with an advertiser is done behind the reader's back, the reader's trust has been violated. There is no debate on the issue that newspapers have to make money and that cannot be done on the cover price alone.

Publishers can either increase the cover price, advertising tariffs or cut costs. They cannot cheat readers to make money. Nowhere in the world do newspaper companies or others do that in the long term and survive. Unilever does not put spurious materials in its soaps in order to make money. Some of the most profitable newspapers and magazines have never had to cross the line between editorial and marketing. They do not see any conflict between creating a credible product and making money.

What then are answers to reducing this dependence on advertising?

Figure 1.2: The Shape of the Indian Publishing Business

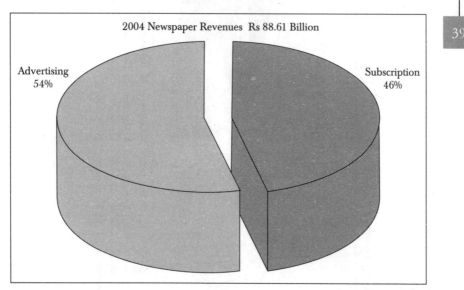

2004 Newspaper Revenues Rs 88.61 Billion

Advertising
54%

Subscription
46%

(*Figure 1.2 continued*)

40

(*Figure 1.2 continued*)

REVENUE SPLIT

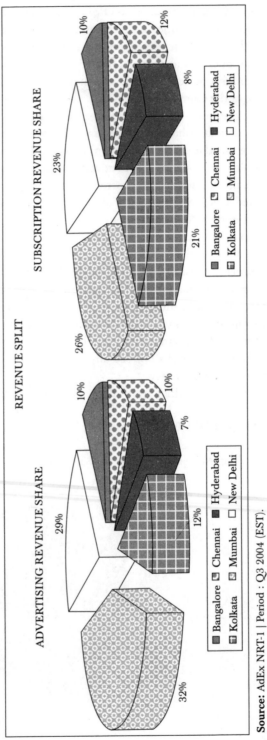

ADVERTISING REVENUE SHARE

SUBSCRIPTION REVENUE SHARE

Source: AdEx NRT-1 | Period : Q3 2004 (EST).

(*Figure 1.2 continued*)

AVERAGE ISSUE PRICE : AVERAGE WEEKDAY

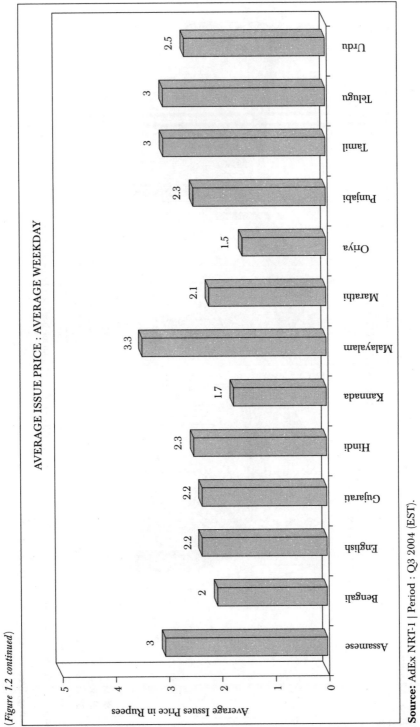

Source: AdEx NRT-1 | Period : Q3 2004 (EST).

42

(*Figure 1.2 continued*)

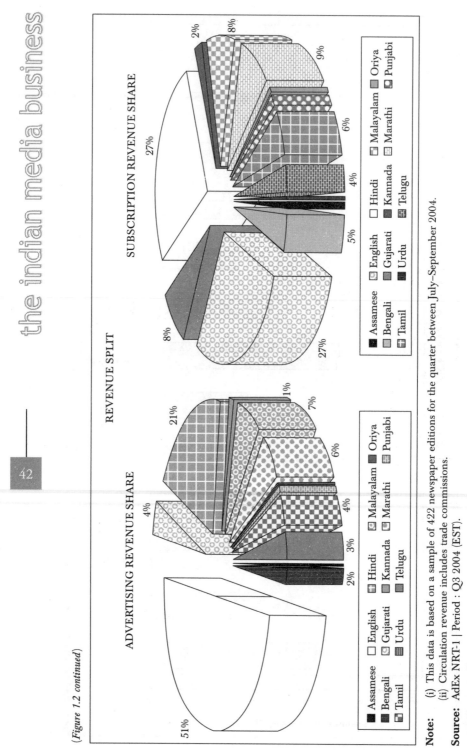

REVENUE SPLIT

ADVERTISING REVENUE SHARE

SUBSCRIPTION REVENUE SHARE

Assamese	☐ English	⊞ Hindi	▨ Malayalam	■ Oriya
Bengali	▨ Gujarati	▨ Kannada	▨ Marathi	⊞ Punjabi
Tamil	▥ Urdu	■ Telugu		

Note: (i) This data is based on a sample of 422 newspaper editions for the quarter between July–September 2004.
(ii) Circulation revenue includes trade commissions.

Source: AdEx NRT-1 | Period : Q3 2004 (EST).

A part of the answer of course, lies in de-risking the business, either by getting into other media or by increasing the revenue streams from publishing. Globally, media companies have achieved scale and depth through mergers and acquisitions. In India, proprietors' love for their stake in the company has proved to be stifling. The average size of the top publishing companies ranges between Rs 2–4 billion. Most of them are used to dominating small regional markets and have long been protected from any competition except from domestic companies. BCCL has, arguably, been the only one that has worked at creating a pan-Indian presence. Till 2002 barely a handful of Indian publishing companies had other media businesses—Living Media, *Eenadu*, *Mid-Day* and *Hathway*[29] (see Figure 1.3).

Figure 1.3: A Few Indian Publishers

Company	Revenues Rs billion	Established
Bennett, Coleman & Company	23.63	1838
HT Media	6.34	1924
Jagran Prakashan	3.77	1942
The Hindu	4.53	1878
Eenadu	4.18	1974
Living Media India	3.24	1975
Malayala Manorama	3.05	1888
Dainik Bhaskar	3.00	1948
Lokmat	2.00	1971
Mathrubhumi	1.76	1923
Deccan Chronicle	1.65	1938
Sakal Group	1.50	1932
Indian Express Publications (Bombay)	1.23	1932
Express Publications (Madurai)	1.21	1995
Mid-Day Multimedia	1.02	1938

Note: (i) The figures for Living Media and Eenadu are for the year ending March 2003. For Express Publication (Madurai) the figures are for the year ending June 2003. (ii) Figures for Living Media include Thomson Press (iii) The figures for HT Media, Deccan Chronicle, Lokmat, Jagran Prakashan and Mid-Day are for the financial year ending March 2005. (iv) The figures for Bennett, Coleman are for the financial year ending July 2005. The rest are for the financial year ending March 2004. (v) *Lokmat* started printing in 1952 but became a daily in 1971 (vi) The figures for Eenadu include TV and print.

Source: CMIE Prowess, CapitalinePlus and companies

Note that the companies which have de-risked their businesses successfully were all born well after Independence, as standalone companies. They came without the historical baggage and the love of their stake that their predecessors had.

---

[29] These companies have been chosen on the basis of the number of non-print brands they have and their dependence on print as a source of revenues. Even though BCCL has a lot of non-print brands, like Planet M, Times Music and Indiatimes.com, its core remains *TOI*, Mumbai.

Living Media spun off a television division, placed equity with financial institutions and finally took its television business public. Its rival, Hathway, too welcomed a foreign partner (Star India) into its cable business and would probably do that with print too given the opportunity. Mid-Day has taken a shot at outdoor media, radio and even a free newspaper, *Metro,* in Mumbai.

Many other publishers started making attempts to diversify. *TOI* made its first successful non-publishing foray into the Internet with indiatimes.com. It now owns radio and TV stations too. *Dainik Jagran* has launched more editions and a television channel. *Dainik Bhaskar* has launched besides several Hindi editions, a Gujarati newspaper, *Divya Bhaskar*, an English one *DNA* in a joint venture with Zee Telefilms. It plans to take the last national.

However, the biggest problem with de-risking and expansion has been access to capital and owner's love of their stake. Publishing companies have been 'axiomatically family-owned', as Murali puts it. That is, of course, part of the heritage of having newspapers that began as nationalistic vehicles. Add to it the fact that a 1955 cabinet resolution did not allow foreign investment in print. For many years most publishers did not even feel the need for capital since other businesses were bankrolling this one. It was when expansion became an imperative in the early 90s that the clamour for allowing foreign capital in went up. In 1993, when ABP wanted to tie up with the *Financial Times* it made a proposal to the government, and the debate about allowing foreign money in print started all over again. When media valuations were running high in 2000, some like Mid-Day decided to offer their shares to the public. When Mid-Day's public issue was about to hit the market in the early part of 2001, rather belatedly the government realised that FIIs too could trade in its shares or pick up at least 40 per cent equity. Overnight, the RBI changed norms to disallow FIIs from investing in publishing companies.

The FDI years Finally, under pressure from many publishers, the government announced its decision to allow 26 per cent foreign direct investment (FDI) into Indian print in June 2002. Since there were too many restrictions, which meant not too many investors came in, this was liberalised further in 2005. That is when FIIs were allowed to be a part of the 26 per cent foreign cap. These two decisions have, over three years, set in motion the process of thinking about surviving in a competitive—rather than a protected—environment. This has meant several things. One, Indian publishing companies now have other ways of raising funds rather through debt alone. Two, the problem of liquidity and exit that stopped many investors from being interested has now vanished. With FII investment banned till 2005, the shares of print companies like Mid-Day have been illiquid.

To this add the realisation that expansion and diversification are imperative if print is to survive. Print's opening up has come at a time when all other media

—TV, Internet, radio, film, mobile telephony or retail media—are booming. Competition, capital, will and business imperative have all combined to push print to grow. That is not surprising. The wonder is the speed with which print companies, now run by younger men, have reacted. Most of 2004 and 2005 have seen a breathless pace of action.

Almost every publishing company is in expansion mode. Vivek Goenka's The Indian Express Newspapers (Bombay) is launching more editions and has picked up a 10 per cent stake in Tariq Ansari's Mid-Day Multimedia in March 2005. Cyber Media, a specialty publishing company, raised money from the primary markets. HT Media has had three rounds of private equity funding, an IPO, and launched in Mumbai. It has also bagged radio licences recently. Then there are all the magazines that Worldwide Media, a BCCL-BBC World-wide joint venture will be launching. It started with *Top Gear* in 2005. Jagran Prakashan raised Rs 1.5 billion from Dublin-based Independent News and Media Plc. Kalanithi Maran's Sun Network bought out Tamil daily *Dinakaran* in 2005. Even the conservative Shapoorji Pallonji Mistry Group has got into publishing with its Forbes subsidiary, Next Gen Publishing.

And of course there is the media's favourite, the Mumbai newspaper battle that began in mid-2005. A second, strong newspaper in Mumbai has been due for some time now. *TOI* dominates the city with close to 0.60 million copies.[30] There is a huge gap between *TOI* and the second largest selling paper in Mumbai, *Mid-Day*, which does 0.15 million copies.[31] *TOI*'s Mumbai edition generates an estimated Rs 7.5–8 billion in revenues and is the company's most profitable edition. It is also used as a leverage to get advertisers for weaker editions by bundling them with Mumbai.

The media targeted at Mumbai gets about Rs 15 billion of the total advertising money spent on reaching Indians. Any publisher, especially an English one, with national ambitions needs to have a Mumbai presence. In spite of being a larger ad market, the circulation of the two leading English papers in Mumbai was less than half of the two leading English papers in Delhi: This, when Delhi is a smaller ad market at an estimated Rs 10 billion. It is against this backdrop that *Dainik Bhaskar* and Zee TV formed a joint venture, Diligent Media Corporation, to launch a national English daily. *Daily News and Analysis* (*DNA*) hit the stands in mid-2005 just after *HT*. A little before these brands got off the ground, BCCL launched *Mumbai Mirror*, a 'compact' or 'broadloid', a paper that is a cross between a broadsheet and a tabloid. Also *Deccan Chronicle*, flush with IPO funds, bought out *The Asian Age* with an eye on the Mumbai market. Each of these brands will be blowing up anywhere between Rs 1.5–4 billion each, cutting prices (and bleeding on circulation) and offering freebies to

45

---

[30] ABC July–December 2004.
[31] ABC January–June 2005.

hawkers and readers. That should lead to at least a doubling of circulation of newspapers in Mumbai to 7 million copies.

The Mumbai battle is a good example of what the coming round of capital fed growth and expansion will mean to the Indian publishing business. It will mean lots of new brands, consolidation, shutdowns, buyouts and markets that will finally get the range and variety that they deserve.

THE WAY IT WORKS

The economics of the publishing business is unusual, to say the least. It is one of those rare businesses where selling more of your product is not such a good idea.

Costs The cost of producing a newspaper or magazine depends on the number of pages, the extent of colour, the quality of paper and the total circulation. These could vary from year to year. That is because the cost of newsprint forms 50–60 per cent of the production cost, and its prices oscillate anywhere between \$400–700 per tonne, depending on demand. The more the number of copies printed, the more money is lost—unless every jump in circulation fetches an increase in advertising revenues that is more than or equal to, the rise in printing costs.

Typically, advertising revenues have always subsidised the real price of newspapers for readers. According to one calculation in 2005, just the variable cost of producing a newspaper was Rs 4–7.[32] Assume that it sells for Rs 1–2.50 like most English dailies. That would bring back roughly Rs 0.6–1.5 back to the publisher's kitty after taking out trade commission. In the years that the adspend on print was growing slowly, there was no incentive to invest in circulation for it would eat into profits. Many leading newspapers and magazine companies deliberately cap circulation. It is routine for newspapers and magazines to drop in and out of ABC in the years when newsprint costs are high. Those are the years they do not spend on circulation increase.

A distinction has to be made here between language and English newspapers. The former usually charge a higher cover price. This could range between Rs 2.5–5 depending on the language and also on whether it is a weekend edition. This is because even with higher circulation, the ad rates they can command are significantly lower than those for English newspapers (see Figure 1.2).

What remains more or less fixed are staff costs and other overheads. Roughly, people costs vary between 12–20 per cent, depending on whether it is an

---

[32] The actual cost will vary depending on number of pages and amount of colour in that particular edition.

English or an Indian language publication. That, incidentally, is lower than the cost of people in developed countries. This will go up now as the expansion has led to a shortage of people within publishing. Mumbai especially has seen salaries for both marketing and editorial people go up 2–3 times, maybe more.

Marketing costs is a new imperative in the age of multiple editions and multimedia competition. To ward off competitors within print and from television, radio or other media, it is crucial that a brand creates its own identity. A magazine like *Businessworld* doesn't compete only with *Business Today* or *Business India*, its main magazine rivals in the classical sense. It competes with the weekly supplements of financial dailies like *Business Standard*, *The Economic Times*, *The Financial Express* and *Business Line*. When it comes to the advertiser's priorities it competes with everything from business channels on television like CNBC–TV18 to the business updates on general news channels like *Aaj Tak*. Further, when it comes to the reader's attention, it fights with anything—general magazines, television channels like Star or Sony, to even a visit to the theatre. The battle is for the reader's time. To get more time, *Businessworld* has to stand out. It has to offer a compelling reason to buy and read.

A third element of cost is distribution. This includes trade margins, up to 40 per cent of the retail price of a newspaper and 45 per cent for a magazine. Plus there is the cost of returns or 'unsolds' (the copies that come back). Mumbai has an estimated 70 depots or points where newspapers are dropped. There are an estimated 10,000 stall owners and hawkers who pick up the newspapers from the depot when they are dropped there, usually around 3–3:30 in the morning. Hawkers then pass the papers on to line boys who drop the newspaper in homes usually by 6–7 am. This is called 'line sales' in industry parlance. The hawker who collects the money from readers' homes usually pays the salaries of the line boys. The hawker, in turn, makes anything between 18–25 per cent on the cover price of the newspaper. The commission could vary according to the publication, the area, the city and the norms there. It could be significantly higher if the newspaper or magazine is not an ABC member and therefore not subject to its rules. The unsolds are a regular part of the business; the average volume of these returns varies between 1–5 per cent depending on the city and its trade norms in the case of newspapers. In magazines, unsolds could be as high as 10–25 per cent moving progressively upwards as the frequency of the magazine increases.

Revenues Revenues essentially come from –

Circulation This is the money brought in from the cover or retail price of a magazine or a newspaper; the revenue that comes in after deducting trade margins and the cost of unsold copies. The ratio could change depending on a number of things—circulation, language, price, and frequency.

47

Advertising About 80 per cent of a publication's revenues come from advertising, and the rest from circulation (see Figure 1.3 and 1.4). This again could vary by language, frequency, price, market it addresses, etc. The best way to look at ad growth is to look at both advertising rates and volumes.

Figure 1.4: Where the Growth in Print Comes From

Jan–July	1999	2000	2001	2002	2003	2004
# of publications	284	299	302	300	356	371
# of categories	288	341	374	388	400	400

Source: ORG Map.

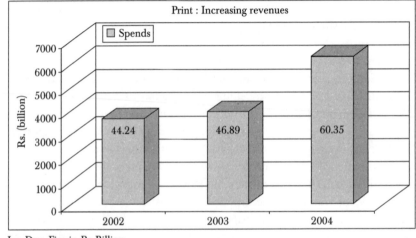

Jan-Dec, Figs in Rs Billion

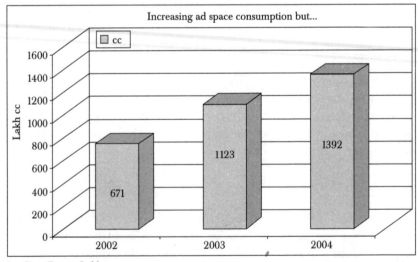

Jan-Dec, Figs in Lakh cc

(*Figure 1.4 continued*)

(*Figure 1.4 continued*)

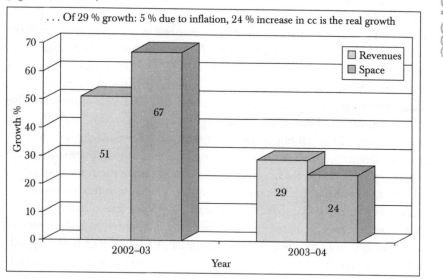

... Of 29 % growth: 5 % due to inflation, 24 % increase in cc is the real growth

Source: Lodestar Media.

Subscriptions Inspired by publications like *Reader's Digest*, magazines like *Outlook* and *A&M* launched high-profile subscription schemes. Earlier these were treated as a revenue stream. The fact is that most subscription schemes are subsidised with free gifts. While they do bring in cash they also involve a huge cost, of more copies to be printed and transported. Subscription schemes are really about buying circulation. That is, unless the magazine is actually making a profit on every copy sold and sent to subscriber, which it doesn't. Most subscription schemes are used to ramp up circulation numbers and then used to demand a higher rate from advertisers.

Brand extensions There are several ways in which a magazine or newspaper can extend the same brand to tap into different revenue streams. Events, television programmes, CDs, seminars, roundtables, syndication of content, education, among a host of other things. This is especially true for specialised magazines or papers. 'For us they started off by helping the print brand grow, now they contribute to the topline and bottomline,' admits Shyam Malhotra, director at Cybermedia, a specialist technology-publishing firm. In many specialist media companies, brand extensions could bring in anywhere between 30–50 per cent of revenues.

Online/Internet Most Indian newspapers and magazines do have a presence on the Internet, albeit a token one in most cases. Many don't even think there is much the Internet can do. 'The net is a very hyped up medium. It is not a threat to the print medium, it is a threat to TV because access time is entertainment time. Newspapers are part of a routine,' thinks Guha.

The numbers for revenues and costs, and therefore margins, vary depending on several factors:

Position: Publications that are number four or five in a market are usually the worst off. In Kolkata the market leader, *The Telegraph*, gets the lion's share of ad revenues directed at the city. *The Statesman*, *TOI* and *HT* arguably do not get a decent share of the ad pie. The same is true in virtually all the other cities.

Language: Most leading language publications like *Malayala Manorama* have a high circulation. That means extremely high printing costs. Typically, even top language brands cannot charge more than, say, one-third the ad rate of an English language publication. Many regional publishing companies have separate printing units to circumvent rules that mandate the amount of wages to be paid to journalists. This pushes costs down. They also recover money by having a cover price that gives them at least 30–35 per cent of their revenues.

Niche versus mass: Circulation revenue for niche magazines, as a percentage of total revenue, could be much higher than the usual 10–20 per cent. If *Chip* sells at Rs 100 a copy it more than covers its costs. Advertising, arguably, brings in the profits. *Chip* could sell at Rs 100 in its earlier avataar because readers are willing to pay for the content that only a scientific or trade journal can provide.[33] 'Niche publications, by design, are not price sensitive,' says Shyam Malhotra. More people won't start reading a *Dataquest* if its price goes down. On the other hand, if the cover price of a general news magazine rises, chances are that circulation will dip.

This price insensitivity also makes niche magazines less dependent on advertising revenues. That means 'more niche magazines get launched and more experiments happen', thinks Malhotra. That is what happened, especially in the later part of the nineties, when the IT boom took off. The National Readership Survey (NRS) figures show that the readership of specialised magazines has risen while that of general magazines has declined.

METRICS

Until satellite television took off in 1992, buying and selling space in newspapers was a simple affair. A media buyer had to figure out which market a brand was addressing. He would then advertise in the leading dailies and magazines in that market and decide on how best to spread the budget among them. The media, in order of importance were, dailies, magazines and DD, remembers Apurva Purohit, who entered the business in 1991. Purohit was a

---

[33] *Chip* has shut down and been re-launched in the last few years.

buyer for many years.[34] Since the magazine boom was still going strong, the real analysis took place while buying magazines. 'Should I take the cover story or the back cover, is there an editorial fit between the magazine and the brand,' are the kind of decisions Purohit remembers making. Innovations that would make an ad stand out in a magazine were just about beginning to happen. For a skin-care product, one brand attached a tissue for readers to test how clean their skin really was. 'We used to analyse magazines then the way we analyse niche channels,' remembers Purohit.

In the late 80s and early 90s, buyers did not negotiate with newspapers: they usually took whatever rate they offered. 'Print used to be the toughest to negotiate with,' remembers Gita Ram formerly with Optimum Media Solutions, a media buying company.[35] A big media buyer like Hindustan Lever (HLL) probably got a discount for signing a contract. A contract meant that it was committed to, for example, ads of 2000 cc (column centimeter) in a certain publication for a year. This meant that it could get a bulk discount. The only ones offering discounts were the magazines, which usually walked away with all the colour advertising throughout the 80s.

The big difference between then and now is the respect that language publications have gained. As late as the early 80s, Indian language magazines or newspapers did not get colour ads. This was because media planners dismissed the purchasing power of the people who read these publications.[36] English always did and still does command premium ad-rates. Bharat Kapadia, former associate publisher of the weekly magazine *Chitralekha*, a popular Gujarati publication, narrated a telling incident about how media was bought and sold in those days. In 1979 he was trying to sell advertising space to the account manager of a famous brand of shoe polish in a Kolkata-base ad agency. Even before Kapadia could say anything, the account manager dismissed the idea of advertising in *Chitralekha* saying: 'Gujaratis don't wear shoes so we cannot advertise in your magazine.' Some research had shown, strangely, that people in Ahmedabad did not wear shoes. Since most media planners and ad agency executives never did go to a market, they had no idea if this was correct. Language publications have come a long way since.

The big similarity between then and now of course remains; dailies were and still are the most powerful vehicles to advertise in. That, maintains Purohit, remains unchanged. 'If I do a four-metro plan, dailies are still more cost efficient and if I want a geography-specific impact then dailies is the best way to go,' she says. Most print buying was about scheduling and anybody with a head

---

[34] She then joined Zee TV, then Zoom and in 2005 she joined Radio City as CEO.

[35] She currently works with Synovate, a market research firm.

[36] Part of the reason was also because language newspapers did not have the best technology for colour reproduction.

for numbers would become a media planner. The important task was not deciding what brands to buy—that was evident from the ABC numbers. It was eliminating the duplication of readership. If a planner considered *TOI* and *HT* in Delhi he had to eliminate any duplication of readership before judging the plan for reach or effectiveness. Around 1989, Indian Market Research Bureau IMRB introduced the software called PEM that helped do the 'duplication tables', faster.

The biggest change in the buying and selling function in the last few years has been consolidation of media buying. It started somewhere in the mid-90s. It has changed completely how all media, including print, is bought and sold. For more details refer to a Survey of Media buying which I did for *Businessworld* in early 2005. It has been carried in this book (see Annexure 2).

One of the best things about the publishing business is its utter dependence on numbers. This has meant investment into research over many years. The main metrics used are:

Circulation is measured by the Audit Bureau of Circulations (ABC), set up in 1948 and made up of advertisers, advertising agencies and publishing companies. The ABC certifies audited NET PAID circulation figures of publications enrolled with it for continuous and definite six-monthly audit periods. It then supplies copies of the ABC Certificates issued for such publications to each member. Any free distribution and bulk sales are also shown separately on the certificates. It certifies circulation based on the publisher's records on copies shipped, newsprint purchased, machine rooms, and even surprise checks on the printing facilities at times.

The margins paid to the trade by newspapers cannot exceed 40 per cent of the selling or cover price. In the case of magazines this limit is 45 per cent if the sale is directly to the reader. In case of subscription copies, the cost of the discount, including gifts and trade commission, cannot exceed 90 per cent of the cover price of a magazine.

These were increased from their previous limits in July 2005. The ABC keeps a tight watch on trade commissions. To show increased circulation, many newspapers cut prices in the 90s. This created a situation where hawkers kept taking additional copies and selling them as *raddi* (recycled paper), even while the newspaper showed circulation increases.

ABC certificates have been the acknowledged currency to buy and sell advertising space in newspapers but have gradually been giving way to readership data. *Readership* is the number of readers—as opposed to the number of buyers for a magazine or newspaper. In 1974 the first NRS (National Readership Survey) was initiated using an urban sample size of 50,000. It was a simple report by ORG–MARG that used monthly household income to determine purchasing power and looked at cinema-going and reading habits. There was hardly any television, since DD was the only channel. In press, a handful of companies owned the brands with the largest readerships—ABP, The Express Group or BCCL. 'We never thought we would be doing it continuously,' remembers Katy Merchant. An independent consultant now, she had worked on NRS for many years, from the very beginning.

The second NRS was done jointly by IMRB and ORG. Even then, 'since the clientele was small it could not evolve into anything more than a readership-demographic study,' says Merchant. By the third NRS in 1981, the research became ambitious. Products were linked to reading habits and demographic profiles. If you read *Ananda Bazar Patrika* and earned Rs 1,200 a month, the research would also show whether or not you were a user of, say, Horlicks. That helped advertisers focus their message. By 1984, NRS covered all cities.

This was long before computers became common, so there was no software to run it all. Doing a large-scale survey like the NRS took years to collect the data, tabulate and analyse it. It was only in 1991, remembers Merchant, when NRS started using software to sift through the numbers. The fundamentals of the survey remain the same—media exposure and their linkages to product consumption. Readership is measured using the masthead method. Respondents are shown a black and white reproduction of the mastheads of newspapers and magazines. For a daily like *TOI*, the estimated number of readers is equal to the number that has looked at any issue of that daily 'yesterday'. Similarly, the time interval for a weekly publication is in the 'last seven days,' the last 15 days for a fortnightly, and so on. This is called the 'recent reading method'. In NRS 2001, the estimation of 'average issue readership' for both urban and rural India is based on this. The average issue readership also segregates readers into heavy, medium and light readers. Heavy readers are people who read for more than 10 hours a week, medium readers give it between 3.01–10 hours while readers who give it less than three hours a week are rated 'light'.

To counter the NRS, which was supported by large newspaper groups, the IRS (Indian Readership Survey) was launched in 1995.[37] Some media users got together to create the Media Research Users Council (MRUC). The idea was to offer members a readership and market study to rival the NRS. The first study was out in 1995 and then after a gap of a year, the IRS has been released every year since 1997. The IRS is a random sample survey wherein 2,20,000 respondents are selected and projected to the universe based on the last available census. It is a continuous survey, with 10 months of fieldwork every year so that the data is released twice a year and also to mitigate any seasonal biases. Many media research users and advertisers use both the IRS and NRS.

Reach is measured in circulation and readership numbers. It could also be calculated as a percentage of the population penetrated in a certain target group. It is not only the number of readers but also the proportion of readers of, say

---

[37] Data on IRS is sourced from the Media Research Users Council website www.mruc.net.

India Today, which fall within the target audience for a Maruti car. 'If I look at SEC A, the number of readers is highest for *India Today* and *Business India* and the least for *India Today Plus*. Then I look at how many, of my target group, are readers of *India Today Plus* and *India Today* and the numbers could be 5 per cent and 50 per cent. So not only is *India Today* high on the overall readership but a large proportion on my target audience is reading it,' explains Arpita Menon of Lodestar Media.

Cost per thousand is the cost of reaching thousand people through a particular newspaper or magazine. These days, planners go a step ahead and look at the average cost per issue versus the readership. Unlike television, where monitoring takes place on a day-to-day, hour-to-hour basis, numbers for print flow in every six months or one year from ABC or NRS. Therefore, 'once you know what works, it holds', says Menon. If there is a rate hike, only the cost per thousand has to be calculated again. However, with multiple editions and publishing companies offering a variety of rates for buying space in different editions, planning has got slightly complicated. Most planners find *TOI*'s basket perplexing. That's because the company offers markets where it is strong (Mumbai) with ones where it is weak (Kolkata) and it does this across brands (*TOI*, *ET*), editions and products (magazines and newspapers). That makes calculating the actual cost paid per column centimetre in a BCCL publication particularly difficult.

REGULATION

If the television broadcasting industry had almost no regulation, the press has historically been over-regulated. Till 1798 there was no law on the press except for some pre-censorship or cases under libel laws and in extreme cases, deportation. Sometimes, thugs who were hired by those people the editors had written about beat them up. Acharya Dr. Durga Das Basu (1996) documents the earliest attempt to suppress the press, which was in 1798 by the then Governor General, the Marquis of Wellesley. He was angry with *The Asiatic Mirror* for revealing the details of the strength of the East India Company and Tipu Sultan's forces. By May 1799, came a set of regulations. These required newspapers under the 'pain of penalty' to print the names of the printer, publisher and editor of the newspaper (this continues to date). All material published had to be given for pre-censorship to the Government of India. Many other ordinances and regulations followed in 1823, 1835 (Metcalfe's Act), 1857, 1860, and so on. The important ones are:

The Indian Penal Code, 1860: While it did not deal with the press specifically, portions of it laid down offences that could relate to any writer, editor or publisher: for example, with regard to obscenity.

The Press and Registration of Books Act, 1867: The idea was not so much to control as to regulate printing presses and newspapers by a process of registration and also to preserve copies of books and other matters printed in India. This Act still exists.

The Vernacular Press Act, 1878: It was aimed at punishing Indian language newspapers writing 'seditious' articles. It empowered the government for the first time to issue search warrants and enter the premises of any press without court orders. It was repealed in 1881. In a fantastic move, *The Amrita Bazaar Patrika*, a Bengali newspaper set up in 1868, converted overnight into an English daily in 1878 to escape being punished under the Vernacular Press Act.

Just like the Vernacular Press Act, 1878, various other acts that were directed against 'seditious' writing came into being at various points of time in the nineteenth and twentieth centuries. Some involved payment of a security deposit, which left most publishers too poor to print. Others involved a forfeiture of the press. After Independence, the Government of India appointed a Press Laws Enquiry Committee to review the press laws of India. It suggested various amendments and repealed several acts. The government then came up with its own way of controlling the press. There was the infamous Newspaper (Price & Page) Act of 1956, which was annulled by the Supreme Court in 1962. The Act lays down that a newspaper could not increase the number of pages it gave without increasing the price proportionately. It was an illogical piece of legislation that claimed to protect small newspapers. Similarly, laws like The Civil Defence Act of 1962 or The Defence of India Act of 1971, enacted during national emergencies and wars had clauses allowing the government to prohibit any paper printing matters prejudicial to the defence of the country.

It was during the Emergency of 1975–77 that some of the grim excesses against the print media were committed. The government introduced the Prevention of Publication of Objectionable Matter Ordinance, which was a rehash of a 1951 Act that had been repealed because of its extreme powers for censorship. The Janata Government of 1977 repealed many of the retrograde steps taken in 1975. Even without legislation the government used indirect ways like newsprint quotas to keep the press in line.

Foreign Investment In 1955, the central cabinet passed a resolution that debarred foreign companies from launching Indian editions of their print brands and from investing in Indian print companies. While it was never converted into a law, it has been treated like one for all the decades that followed. Technically, nothing stopped a foreign magazine from selling in India or launching an Indian edition or investing in a publishing company in India. However, the 1955 cabinet resolution, which never became a law or an ordinance, remained the defining word on this issue for decades. During the nineties various companies wanting to launch foreign brands in India or get in a foreign investor were prevented from doing so.

Finally, in June 2002, the cabinet passed a resolution allowing 26 per cent FDI in print. This was changed in 2005. Now the rules allow:

- FIIs to be part of the 26 per cent investment in print media in the news category.
- Publication of Indian editions of foreign scientific, technical and specialty magazines, periodicals or journals.
- Foreign investment up to 100 per cent in Indian entities publishing scientific, technical and specialty magazines, periodicals or journals.
- All registered newspapers (Indian publications) are authorised to make syndication arrangements to procure material including photographs, cartoons, crossword puzzles, articles and features from foreign publications under automatic approval. The total material so procured and actually printed in an issue of an Indian publication cannot exceed 20 per cent of the total printed areas of that issue. It should not include full copy of the editorial page or the front page or the masthead of the foreign publication.

Besides these rules, the following acts or their clauses currently govern the operations of a publishing company in India:

The Constitution of India
Indian Penal Code, 1860
Punjab Special Powers (Press) Act, 1956
The Press and Registration of Books Act, 1876
The Dramatic Performances Act, 1876
The Indian Telegraph Act, 1885
Indian Post Office Act, 1898
The Police (Incitement to Disaffection) Act, 1922
Official Secrets Act, 1923
The Emblems and Names (Prevention of Improper Use) Act, 1950
Representation of People Act, 1951
The Delivery of Books and Newspapers (Public Libraries) Act, 1954
The Drugs and Magic Remedies (Objectionable Advertisements) Act, 1954
The Working Journalists and Other Newspaper Employees (Conditions of
    Service) and Miscellaneous Provisions Act, 1955
The Prize Competitions Act, 1955 (Act No. 42 of 1955)
Hindu Marriage Act, 1955
The Young Persons (Harmful Publications) Act, 1956
The Copyright Act, 1957

Children's Act, 1960

Criminal Law Amendment Act, 1961

Atomic Energy Act, 1962

Customs Act, 1962

The Unlawful Activities (Prevention) Act, 1967

The Civil Defence Act, 1968

The Contempt of Court Act, 1971 (Act No. 70 of 1971)

Criminal Procedure Code, 1973 (Act No. 2 of 1974)

The Press Council Act, 1978

The Prize Chits and Money Circulation Schemes (Banning) Act, 1978, (Act No. 43 of 1978)

National Security Act, 1980

The Indecent Representation of Women (Prohibition) Act, 1986

Terrorist and Disruptive Activities (Prevention) Act, 1987

ACCOUNTING NORMS[38]

There are no specific standards prescribed for the publication industry. Therefore, general accounting principles would apply.

Revenues They are matched with costs as the general principle. A lot of attention is required to be paid at the point when income is to be recognised. *Circulation:* It is recognized only when the contractual obligations to the customer are fulfilled and the realisation on the sales is not in doubt, according to both Indian and international thinking, sales are recognised. Therefore, sales have to be accounted for as and when the issues are sold. However, a suitable provision has to be made for potential returns of unsold copies. It is normal to use the past historical trend of returns in projecting the future sales returns. There should be no attempt to account for returns as and when they are received. That would violate the accrual principles of accounting mandated for corporate entities. Non-corporate entities might adopt a stance that unsold copy returns are accounted on a cash basis that is as and when returned. The ultimate revenue recognition will be net of any commission paid to the selling agents. In terms of current Company Law requirement, it is necessary to show the gross sales and the commission paid to selling agents. The commission payable corresponding to the revenue recognised must be provided for even if it is not paid. Likewise, when making a provision for potential returns it is all right to

---

[38] This portion has been put together by Ramesh Lakshman & Co.

make the provision net of contracted commission likely to saved in the process. *Advertising:* This revenue cannot be taken credit for till the advertisement is published and the claim becomes due. In case a total amount is charged for a specified number of insertions, then the amount to be recognised as revenue will be proportionate to the number of insertions already completed during the accounting period.

A publisher may have publications of varying frequency such as a daily, weekly and so on. The generic rate per insertion of advertisement in each of these publications might vary based on the number of readers and the geographical spread and reach. In such cases the publisher might sell the advertisement space across publications and charge a pre-negotiated price for insertions in all these publications put together. In such a case, the negotiated amount must first be bifurcated across publications and for each publication the revenue to be recognised would depend on the actual number of insertions completed. The allocation across publications must be pro-rated on the basis of the standard charge per insertion in each of the publications.

Subscriptions: These are to be accounted for on an accrual basis. The subscription amount to be allocated over the term and the amount appropriate to the accounting period alone will be considered as revenue. It is also usual in the print media to offer subscriptions for an upfront payment and the right to cancellation within a stated period of time. Upon cancellation, the full amount is refunded. In such cases, the sales cannot be considered unless the period during which the cancellation can be exercised is over.

Royalties and other rights: The publisher might permit other publications to carry features from his products and receive royalty or fees. If the royalty or fee is agreed as a consideration payable irrespective of whether the other publication carries the article or not then the revenue will be recognised over time. Otherwise it will accrue only on the basis of what is carried in print by the other publisher.

Costs

Inventory of newsprint: The rule generally is to value inventory at the lower of cost or market value. The inventory will be charged to the income account on the basis of actual consumption. It is normal to write off the inventory value of unsold copies since publications lose value within a short period from the date of publication.

Other costs: The amount payable to contributors whether on featured columns or specific articles published will accrue once the article appears. However, if the publication buys the right of publishing the article by paying upfront, then the right to the article belongs to the company and must be accounted for as such. If the publication plans to publish the article then the cost is carried forward to offset the revenue in the period in which the article is published.

Otherwise it must be written off as expenditure once the article is bought and a decision is taken not to publish it.

Taxation Print media companies are subject to the same levels of taxation as other businesses. Currently, the net profit earned by a company or a partnership firm would be taxed at a rate of 33–35 per cent. In addition, a surcharge at the applicable rate is levied. While manufacturing companies established in select backward areas would be entitled to some tax holiday, no such concessions are granted to the publishing media companies. There is a 4 per cent customs duty on newsprint. There is also an education cess at the rate of 2 per cent of the tax and surcharge.

VALUATION

Till about 2003 not too many publishers had raised money from the market. In addition to it is the fact that the industry is extremely closed about numbers. So any analysis on how valuations work is extremely difficult. There were just a few listed print companies—Sandesh, Tata Infomedia (now Infomedia) and Mid-Day Multimedia. It was after foreign investment was allowed in 2002, that some private equity deals and later initial public offers of print companies took place. The value that the stockmarkets and private investors have attached to these companies, seem interesting. *Deccan Chronicle* had a target of Rs 1.3–1.5 billion. The 2004 issue collected Rs 1.49 billion and was oversubscribed 9.5 times. At one time in 2004 there was talk of a benchmark average multiple at 2 times revenues and 8–10 times profits. There doesn't seem to be any benchmark emerging now. Both investors and publishing companies are just about discovering each other.

Take HT Media for instance. The Rs 6.34 billion company is one of the largest publishing companies in India, with a dominating presence in Delhi, a major advertising market. In August 2005, HT Media raised Rs 4 billion, putting it among the top ten media IPOs in Asia over 2004 and 2005. This was on top of two rounds of private equity funding. It gave Henderson Asia Pacific Equity partners, one of the first foreign investors in an Indian publishing company, a partial exit. Henderson had bought 19.23 per cent in HT Media in 2003. During the HT Media IPO it sold 5 per cent at an estimated three times the price it had paid per share. Henderson has already realised its original investment. Any sales of its remaining 10 per cent share will be pure profit.

HT Media's market capitalization, at the time of listing, was higher than *The Washington Post* or *The New York Times*. That seems a bit much, for the Rs 6.34 billion company that made only Rs 0.27 billion in net profit in March 2005. However most investors point out that India and China are only markets in the world where newspaper circulation and readership is growing in the Asia-Pacific region. That is what is reflected in HT's or Deccan Chronicle's valuation. What investors are betting on is the growth potential of a stable paper like *HT*, given capital. Most think that they will see profits grow disproportionately in publishing because circulation remains stable.

The measures used to value print companies are the same as for any other. Satish Shenoy, former managing director, IL&FS Bank, worked on the Mid-Day public issue. His analysis on how IL&FS Bank analysed the Mid-Day issue provides some perspective. According to Shenoy, in April 2001, Mid-Day Multimedia raised money from the public in order to finance its expansion into radio, the Internet, and a free newspaper, among other things. *Mid-Day* is the daily that dominates the afternoon newspaper market in Mumbai.

'Tariq's (Ansari, the managing director of Mid-Day Multimedia) business model was moving on the back of print to other media—radio, hoardings, mobile. Essentially he is using his content generating abilities in a market like Mumbai and slicing and dicing it in different ways. He has in place a good network for information gathering and is using any medium to monetise the content,' says Shenoy. IL&FS then looked at international models. Companies abroad that resembled Mid-Day also had television businesses. They were usually valued at a price-earning multiple of 25–30. 'Valuations are contextual to what's happening in the market, using a P/E multiple makes sense if it is a mature industry,' analyses Shenoy. 'In the newspaper business as long as distribution is good, circulation cannot come down overnight. So the multiple for that stability is higher than say for films which is a riskier business and has more piracy,' he reasons. According to estimates, eventually Mid-Day got a price to earnings multiple of 14. What worked in Mid-Day's favour was the fact that it was operating in Mumbai, India's largest advertising market, plus the possibility of its replicating that model across cities.

Bala Deshpande of ICICI Venture would however take Earnings Before Interest, Taxes, Depreciation and Amortisation (EBITDA), as a measure for valuation. 'After the initial investment in print, it is all money for jam,' she thinks. EBITDA is a good measure to use when there is an M&A (merger and acquisition) opportunity,' says Shenoy. Or when the company is highly leveraged and the outgoings on interest are therefore high. EBITDA is the preferred base for valuing companies in industries like television, where recurring capital expenditure is a norm, especially in a developing market like India.

Several investors, especially during an M&A deal, prefer return on capital employed (ROCE). Good companies operating at optimum efficiencies can get as much as 30–40 per cent says Cyriac Mathew of Mid-Day. ROCE is an important indicator because print is a capital-intensive, long gestation business. Most companies in the business have long since depreciated plants and assets. Therefore ROCE is a good indicator of how much they have managed to get out of the capital they had put in the business.

2 television

There will be very little 'broadcasting' of television signals in the future

IT WAS AN innocuous beginning. The first experiment with television broad-casting in India involved a makeshift studio at Akashvani Bhavan in New Delhi, a low-power transmitter and 21 television sets. These were installed in the homes of various bureaucrats and ministers. Some of the equipment was a gift from a west European government. Bhaskar Ghose, who went on to become Information and Broadcasting secretary, was just a child then. He recalls with amusement that his early memories included listening to music on television. The accompanying video: that of the gramophone playing it!

Sounds primitive but that is what television looked like in India in September 1959. An entire generation, which grew up on black and white television, *Krishi Darshan* and Films Division cartoons, can recall the utter lack of imagination in the programming. From those beginnings, it is hard to believe the scale that the television broadcasting business in India has achieved today—and more incredible, that it is neither government-owned[1] nor controlled. For too long in India, all the media other than print was in the grip of government. Even the most optimistic predictions could not have envisaged the market, as we are seeing it now. There are about 160 satellite channels broadcasting into India (see Figure 2.1) and they earn revenues of more than Rs 79 billion from advertising alone.[2] Add all the other revenues, from cable advertising, DTH

---

[1] Wherever not specified, government refers to the Indian government.

[2] According to Dinyar Contractor, editor, *Satellite & Cable TV* magazine, Indian TV homes can receive up to 425 channels. Many however may be of no interest to Indians. Many of the others have little relevance to Indians. Some are in languages which may be of no interest, say Malay. They can be received because they are being broadcast from a satellite that may have a footprint in India. Of these 425, about 160 are India specific channels. Even the high end TV sets in India can receive only between 96–106 channels.

Figure 2.1: The Growth of TV

Year	Total TV Homes million	C&S Homes million	DTH Homes million	Revenues (Rs million)	
				Ad/Telecast	Subscription
1959	0.000021	none	–	na	none
1969	0.012303	none	–	na	none
1979	1.1	none	–	61.6	none
1989	22.5	none	–	1612.6	none
1992	34.9	1.2	–	3950	1008
1993	40.3	3	–	4960	2520
1994	45.7	11.8	–	8480	9912
1995	52.3	15	–	13450	18000
1996	57.7	18	–	19750	21600
1997	63.2	na	–	25840	na
1998	69.1	29	–	33670	34800
2000	na	33	–	44390	39600
2001	79	40	–	47940	48000
2002	81.57	40.49	–	47170	48588
2003	na	49	na	61480	88200
2004	00	55	na	68820	99000
2005	108	60.82	3.75	74170.5	111276

Note: (i) The figures for 1979 and 1989 are commercial revenues according to Doordarshan's annual report for the year ending March 1979 and March 1989. These are the revenues for DD only. For the remaining years Doordarshan's revenues are for the financial year ending March. (ii) The revenues from cable in the initial years are impossible to determine since there are no estimates of how many households were connected. From 1992–94 cable revenues are calculated at Rs 70 per connected household per month. From 1995–2002, they are calculated at Rs 100 per home per month and from thereon till 2005 at Rs 150. (iii) To the advertising revenues I have added, from 2003 onwards, cable advertising revenues of Rs 50 million assuming a 10 per cent increase every year. (iv) The figure for advertising revenues also includes the money that Doordarshan earned. (v) DTH revenues are only for Dish TV's 750,000 homes taking an average of Rs 200 per subscriber per month. They form part of subscription revenues for 2005. (vi) There is little individual company or industry data available so these numbers are based on available statistics.
na: Not available.

Source: Doordarshan annual reports, Ministry of Information and Broadcasting releases, NRS, *Satellite & Cable TV* magazine, Lodestar Media, TAM Media Research, TRAI and industry estimates.

(direct-to-home), subscription and so on and the industry stands at close to Rs 185 billion.[3] Indian TV broadcasting has certainly made up in size what it lacked in pomp at the outset.

---

[3] If one takes an extremely conservative average of Rs 150 collected per household per month for India's 60.82 million cable and satellite (C&S) homes over 12 months, the total is Rs 109 billion. The figure is probably much higher since in most metros where penetration is 80–90 per cent and average rates are closer to Rs 200–250 a month. Even in smaller towns and rural areas, where penetration is growing very fast, rates range between Rs 50–150 per household per month. At the time of writing Dish was the only commercial DTH operator. DD's DTH service is free. Dish TV claimed to have 750,000 subscribers who could be paying Rs 150–300 per month depending on the package it has on offer. Taking Rs 200 per month per subscriber as an average for 12 months for 750,000 subscribers, the figure is

At over 108 million TV homes, more than half of them cable-enabled, we are one of the largest cable-connected countries in the world, after China (110 million) and the US (about 70 million) .[4] That makes India an attractive market, in terms of both value and volume. In the last two years, several broadcasting companies in India have listed on the stock exchange, raised money through private equity and delivered on investor expectations. That is a rare feat for media companies in India. NDTV and TV Today Network, among others, have done the broadcasting industry proud in the way their value and their market capitalisation—that is the total worth that private equity investors or the stock markets attach to the company—has risen. There is, within international private equity investors, finally a buzz about the Indian television business.

India is yet to achieve the shine of a China or excite the interest that Brazil does. There are three reasons for this. First: size; it is still a small market. At an estimated $7 billion, China's TV broadcasting business is just under twice the size of India's. Second: bureaucracy and regulation. Ad-hocism is the hallmark of our policy on broadcasting. It slows the pace at which the industry can grow. Third is the fragmented nature of the industry across its three main segments—software, distribution and broadcasting. Software has an estimated 6,000 one-man outfits. In cable distribution, over 35,000 operators[5] control the approximately 60 million cable homes. TV broadcasting is yet to see a pan-Indian behemoth—the equivalent of a creature with the size and spread of a Star India plus Sun Group or perhaps a Sony plus Sun Group (see Figure 2.2).

Figure 2.2:   India's Top TV Broadcasters

Company	Revenues Rs billion 2004–05	Other Businesses in India	Parent Company
Zee Telefilms	13.6	Cable, newspapers, DTH	None
Star India	13	FM Radio, cable, DTH	News Corporation
SET India	10	Films, music	Columbia Tristar
Doordarshan	6.65	Radio, DTH	Prasar Bharati Corporation
Sun Network	3	Cable, FM Radio, print	None

Note: (i) The financial year for Star India is June–July (ii) The revenues for Star do not include its share of revenues from its joint venture ESPN–Star Sports.
Source: Annual reports, company websites and industry estimates.

Rs 1800 million. The actual figure may be higher or lower, but just like cable revenues, this is a good enough approximation.

[4] Some data on TV homes and revenues are estimates from PricewaterhouseCooper's Entertainment and Media Outlook 2004–08. The other is from Media Partners Asia, a Hong Kong-based consulting and research firm.

[5] These numbers are rough approximations derived from the total figure for cable homes—60 million. For example, if you take an average of 1000 subscribers per operator, that total number of operators would be 60,000. However, Contractor of *Satellite & Cable TV* magazine thinks the number is closer to 30,000–35,000.

These three factors are now seriously slowing growth. For example, we have been stuck with unorganised cable for too long and it is showing. The cable TV pipes in India are choking. Most are capable, at best, of carrying 106 channels. Yet, about 160 channels jostle to get on to your TV screens every day. Hardly any investors are willing to put money into digitising and upgrading cable because it is fragmented, unorganised and opaque.

The next round of growth that will give Indian broadcasting some heft will come from pay television. It is the natural state of things for pay to dominate the TV market anywhere in the world. In the US, for example, it brings in over 60 per cent of industry revenues. In India pay television in its truest form[6] can become a reality only when there is a set-top-box (STB) in every home with a TV. Anyone could put it there—the cable operator, MSO,[7] DTH operator, or a telecom company. Once an STB—ideally digital—is in place in a large number of TV homes, the market will take off. At a rough estimate, it could add more than Rs 50 billion to the industry's revenues. More than that it will bring variety—in operators, programming and prices. The creation of good pay TV systems could do what multiplexes have done to films— bring more variety in genres of programming, in the pricing of TV signals and in the way those signals reach homes.

By all accounts that is what is happening even as I write. A large amount of the investment flowing into television is going to cable alternatives. There are already two DTH operators, Zee's Dish TV and Doordarshan's DD Direct+. Between them, they claim to have 3.75 million subscribers: three million of them with DD, the rest with Dish TV. There is (at the time of writing) the imminent launch of three other such services: by Space TV (a Tata-Star Group joint venture), Reliance and Sun TV. Now add what broadband and telecom players like BSNL, Bharti and Reliance plan to do with Internet Protocol TV (IPTV) and there are already four distinct platforms that could offer you TV programming—terrestrial, cable and satellite, DTH and IPTV on broadband.

There is a fifth that is emerging—mobile phones. There is a lot of work happening in European markets on TV over the mobile phone or any other hand-held device. But currently all it can offer is streaming video, not live broadcasts. These are clips of news, sports or songs. The bandwidth, that is the ability of

---

[6] We do pay for our cable TV, so pay television does exist in India. However most of the Rs 109 billion collected is eaten up either by the cable operators or channelled in all kinds of other things, like local elections. According to rough estimates hardly 15–20 per cent of the money comes back into the industry as revenues. That is why it is fair to say that pay TV in truest form, where every subscriber is accounted for, and the money comes back into the industry doesn't yet exist in India.

[7] Multi-system operator, a wholesaler of TV signals. DTH is direct-to-home, another broadcasting technology.

mobile phone networks to carry large amounts of data, is as yet limited. A subscriber cannot watch a live cricket match or a complete film. That is however not so far into the future. Many of these new ways of selling TV signals, like DTH and IPTV, eliminate the word 'broadcast' from television. A lot of the channels on some of the world's best digital systems are server-based, time-lagged, packaged and not exactly live; but more on that later.

As these 'platforms' or ways of selling TV signals multiply, the market will acquire a depth and width that will finally propel the Indian TV market to a revenue size that befits our economy. It will also give consumers choice in the real sense of the word.

To accelerate this growth and ensure this choice, regulation has to 'incentivise' investment in broadcasting infrastructure instead of focusing on what Indians should or shouldn't watch. There are three steps that need political will. If taken, it will give rise to a broadcasting industry that is three to four times its current size and employ millions of more people. The communications minister has to allow the last mile copper loop that state-owned telephone companies like BSNL sit on, to be used by anyone who wants to sell television, data or voice. The government has to allow 100 per cent investment in alternate ways of broadcasting, such as digital, terrestrial and DTH TV services without equity and cross-media restrictions. Both of them must allow cable operators to offer 'voice' or telephony on their pipes. The market is bound to boom as everyone scrambles to offer everything.

The evidence that this works is already available. Every major market—from Japan to the UK to Hong Kong—has opened up cable to voice and telecom to video ensuring that everybody gains in the ensuing competition. In the US, for example, it is competition between cable, satellite and telecom companies offering TV that is giving broadcasting a fresh lease of life. Ever since the regulatory body in the US, the Federal Communications Commission, made it easier for cable companies to offer telephony and vice versa, competition between the two has meant that cable operators have spent over $85 billion in digitising and offering more goodies to subscribers. From almost nothing, DTH services—called satellite TV in the US—had an estimated 25 million subscribers by March 2005. (These may or may not be part of the cable homes in that market.) It has meant more choice and channels too. From about 106 in 1994, the total number of channels on offer to American subscribers across different broadcasting 'platforms' has gone to 400 in 2004.

Indian broadcasting already has the range in programming. Now it needs to achieve that in distribution technology and infrastructure. The available programming options make India a varied and rich TV market, compared to China, where content is regulated. That is why India has a surplus of television programming while the Chinese market has a demand-supply gap of 10:1.

Hence, the ability of investors and companies to populate all broadcasting infrastructure with programming and make money is greater in India than in China.

Indian television 'broadcasting' has certainly come a very long way.

THE PAST

The Doordarshan years Of course the government, in all its wisdom and folly, did control television for more than three decades after India saw its first television broadcast. The first school television service was commissioned in New Delhi two years after the first few experiments. This was for the institutions run by the Delhi Municipal Corporation. By 1965, television broadcasting matured to a one-hour service, which included a news bulletin. In 1972, television went to Bombay (now Mumbai), India's commercial capital and by 1975 five more cities each had a television station called Doordarshan Kendra. All this time, television broadcasting was largely a terrestrial phenomenon available in cities where the government had set up transmitters of varying ranges. Currently, there are 1,090 transmitters spread across India. According to NRS 2005, there are 108 million television homes that can receive the signals that DD[8] sends out. Several milestones mark the journey from 21 sets to 108 million: regional *kendras*, the first commercials, national network, DD metro, and colour television, among others.

Today, many of us dismiss DD and what it dishes out. All the same, it was DD that shaped the television broadcasting industry in India—not by design, but by its very existence. In most parts of the world, except in the US, it is the public service broadcasters (PSBs) who have done the pioneering work. From the British Broadcasting Corporation (BBC) to the Canadian Broadcasting Corporation, PSBs have set higher and higher benchmarks for private broadcasters to follow. The BBC, for all the bad press it gets in the UK, keeps its head above water (just about) and yet fulfils its role of being a PSB admirably well. It could be argued that it is the licence fees from British taxpayers that ensure BBC's survival. A closer look at its accounts shows that BBC gets an increasing share of its income from syndicating its content. In India, too, DD showed great promise in the early days.

The first satellite television experiments were undertaken by DD as early as 1975–76. It was under the Satellite Instructional Television Experiment (SITE) that the Indian government used the US-based National Aeronautics and Space

---

[8] Wherever it is not specified DD means Doordarshan, the state-owned broadcaster.

Administration' (NASA) Satellite ATS-6 for educational programme broadcasts in Indian villages. It was trying to solve the problem of weak transmission to distant villages through the terrestrial network. SITE was an attempt to see if bouncing the signal off a satellite would increase its coverage. It did. By 1978, the government was encouraged enough to implement its own satellite system. This was contracted out to Ford Aerospace and Communication Corporation. Then came the Indian National Satellite (INSAT) programmes, a joint effort by the Indian space Research Organisation (ISRO), the Indian Posts and Tele-graph Department, the Ministry of Civil Aviation and the Ministry of Information and Broadcasting. The INSAT series of satellites helped fulfill the objectives of getting DD into the maximum number of community television sets.

Colour transmission began in 1982, thanks to the Asian Games, hosted in New Delhi. It was around this time, in the early 80s, that the commercial contours of the industry started taking shape. During these years DD had been serialising novels and other works of literature. However, these did not make money; not that they were supposed to. In 1983 came India's first[9] sponsored programme, *Show Theme*, produced by TV personality Manju Singh. Then, in 1984, a US-based non-government organisation (NGO) approached the Ministry of Information and Broadcasting to do a serial. This would actually be a family planning message couched as entertainment. It was an experiment that had worked successfully in Catholic Mexico, where overt family planning messages could not be used. So, soap operas conveyed the message and helped push down the birth rate. The idea appealed immensely to the Indian govern-ment. That is how India's first soap opera, *Hum Log*, was first aired in July 1984.

The idea was to show a family beset with all the problems typical to a large lower-middle class Indian family: poverty, alcoholism, and illiteracy. These have also been the hallmarks of India's problems with population, then as well as now. At the end of the show, veteran actor Ashok Kumar would come on screen to say, in subtle ways, that a large family was at the root of all trouble. Unfortunately for family planning and fortunately for commercial television, the message was lost in the mad popularity of the serial. More than 80 per cent of the 3.6 million Indian television sets at that time tuned in to *Hum Log* every week. Eventually, as former bureaucrat Ghose puts it, the serial developed a life of its own. Maggi Noodles, a brand owned by Nestlé India, sponsored the first soap on Indian television. The multinational paid for the telecast fee and production cost of *Hum Log* and got about five minutes of commercial time in exchange. It used this to advertise its brands.

The success of *Hum Log* egged DD on to create more entertainment pro-gramming. *Buniyaad, Katha Sagar, Khandaan, Nukkad* and a host of other

67

---

[9] Whether *Show Theme* or *Hum Log* was the first sponsored programme on Doordarshan is a disputed fact.

popular serials and sitcoms followed in the mid- to the late 80s. Telecast fees and commercial airtime rates on DD began rising. From Rs 170 million in 1983–84, DD's revenues rose to Rs 2.1 billion in 1989–90. By the early 90s, DD began charging anywhere between Rs 100,000–500,000 as minimum guarantee or telecast fees. In exchange it gave a certain portion of the programme's airtime to the producer.

The cable years If the beginning of commercial television in India seems like a cute accident, the origins of cable broadcasting that began around the same time appears even more amusing. While the precise date of cable television's appearance is difficult to arrive at, it is clear that it began in the early 80s in Mumbai. Dinyar Contractor, editor of *Satellite & Cable TV* magazine, reckons that cable took off with the introduction of colour television and the hosting of the Asian Games in New Delhi in 1982. On the other hand, Yogesh Radhakrishnan, one of the earlier entrants, believes that cable took off when the Los Angeles Olympics in 1984 kicked off a second spurt in the sale of colour TV sets. It is likely that both these events contributed towards the phenomenon.

Regardless of the year, it began with viewers' desire for a sharper reception, especially in Mumbai where tall buildings hampered the quality of terrestrial transmission. That is how entrepreneurs like Siddharth Srivastava (ATN), Radhakrishnan, Jagjit Kohli, Yogesh Shah, Ronnie Screwvala[10] and companies like Nelco stepped in. Men like Shah and Kohli offered to set up one master antenna for entire buildings with one cable running from the antenna. This eliminated the problems of multiple antennae for different flats with their multiple wires criss-crossing the building and cluttering the terrace. Anyone who lives in Mumbai will know that the terrace is a precious space. The cooperative societies that run these buildings were glad to have anyone clear them up. In exchange for doing this, these one-man outfits were paid installation charges of Rs 500 and Rs 40 or so per household per month for service.[11]

In evolutionary terms, therefore, India is no different from the US. In the US too, cable television evolved because homes in hilly regions could not get a clear reception of terrestrial broadcasts. The difference is that it happened in the US in the 60s and 70s whereas in India the beginning was in the mid-80s.

---

[10] Shah, Radhakrishnan and Kohli later set up a broadcasting company ETC Networks and a cable outfit called Win Cable. Zee Telefilms bought a 51 per cent stake in ETC Networks in 2002.

Screwvala is the founder and CEO of UTV. He and Srivastava were among the first two entrepreneurs to wire up South Mumbai. Screwvala operated under a company called Nemula which was part of the Western Outdoor Group.

[11] A huge part of the numbers and facts here relies on the memory of the entrepreneurs and business writers of that time. The figures might not be precise but are approximately correct.

The other big difference is that local authorities quickly took over in the US and territories were sold to the highest bidder, so that only one cable operator or company controlled cable operations in one area. In India, that did not happen. Since there were no official guidelines, operators mushroomed, propelled first by the video boom and then the coming of satellite television.

Around the same time that cable began to snake its way around Mumbai, the video boom hit India. Since each building was wired up through a common cable, it could be easily plugged into a video cassette recorder (VCR) at one end to show a movie and therefore earn extra money. Thus began the true growth of cable television in India. The local cable operator in most areas would show a couple of Hindi movies daily. The tapes were of poor quality and there were too many ads, but it was manna from heaven for an entertainment-starved country. There are many stories about how cable originated and expanded in India, one of the more interesting ones is narrated by Contractor.

Contractor was working with the beleaguered colour television set manu-facturer, Nelco (a Tata Group company) at that time. The senior management saw cable as a means of pushing the sales of its TV sets. It began selling the idea of a cable hook-up to five-star hotels. If a hotel bought its television sets, it would throw in an additional three VCR channels plus two of DD at Rs 20 per day per television per occupied room. The three VCR channels were essen-tially re-runs of programmes and movies taped overseas. Just like hot water or telephone, the hotel could offer cable television to its patrons. Nelco managers toured towns like Jaipur and Udaipur selling the concept and almost all the Tata Group hotels, like The Taj and President, bought into it. Ronnie Screwvala, one of the many entrepreneurs who emerged at that time, did the programming tapes and maintenance. He was paid Rs 1.25 per room per day. 'In two years our business peaked,' recalls Contractor.

There are other equally interesting stories on how cable operators emerged. For example, as a young man, Yogesh Shah had a lot of time to spare after work-ing at the family business of trading in textile chemicals and dyes. When he saw some people checking out his uncle's television at Shanti Nagar in South Mumbai for a common antennae system, he offered, on impulse, to do it. Within a few days he had the contract, had wired up the building with 120 connections and was charging Rs 60 per home for showing two movies a day. Similarly, Jagjit Kohli, a textile engineer, saw a cable system in operation in South Mumbai in 1986–and was hooked. He decided to wire up one building in Andheri, a northern suburb of Mumbai, for a lark. A year later, in 1987, he wound up the small textile business he was running to concentrate on the cable operation. By this time he had 700 cable connections in the suburbs paying him Rs 70 each per month. 'Those days a size of 500 (subscribers or connections) was very good,' remembers Kohli.

The lure of cable for all these young men was very clear—money. It did not need too much investment, just the chutzpah to decide that it was perfectly safe to invest in running cables across trees and roads. This, when no one was sure whether it was legal (as it turns out, it was illegal). All it needed was a VCR and the money to rent a few videotapes a day plus a man to go and collect the money from people's homes. That roughly meant an investment of Rs 15,000 and approximately another Rs 3,000–5,000 in running expenses, taking the total to roughly Rs 20,000 a month. This could yield anywhere between Rs 50 and Rs 80 per home. Multiply that by an average of 100–150 subscribers that a typical operator had. Many of the youngsters who set up these businesses were making anything between Rs 50,000–75,000 a month, a lot of money then. Not surprisingly, thousands of people jumped into the business, over-crowding it, undercutting each other and stealing customers. By 1990, there were 3,500 cable operators in Mumbai, though how many homes they covered in that year is not known. Incidentally, till this time cable television had not seriously spread beyond Mumbai. The convenience of wiring up a building and getting a dozen or more households at one go was possible only there. It was somewhere around the late 80s, early 90s, that cable television moved to Delhi and other parts of India.

Also, till the early 90s, cable was limited to small-time entrepreneurs showing movies. There was the odd video magazine like *Newstrack* from the Living Media Group. However, except for Bennett, Coleman & Company (BCCL) and Living Media, no major media house showed the slightest bit of interest in this new opportunity. The other players who entered the business were either film pro-ducers or small-time entrepreneurs, or even creative people like Amit Khanna.[12]

The other bit of important history, from the same time, is that of the skir-mishes between film producer, cable operator and video right owner. Typically, video rights were given away with all other rights. However, most producers or video right owners never thought that one tape would be shown to hundreds of homes at the same time. This robbed them of revenues they would have earned if the tape had been rented by each home that was viewing it on cable. There are many examples of legal cases, consortiums and infighting, which marked the industry throughout this period. In 1989, in a landmark judge-ment, Justice Sujata Manohar of the Mumbai High Court maintained that broadcast via cable was public viewing and that cable operators needed a copyright to show films.

The satellite years Thus, in its own disorganised, albeit entrepreneurial, fashion cable continued to grow and prosper. Strangely, a government that loved regulating just about anything, seemed not to have noticed this phe-nomenon. The first piece of legislation came only in 1995. Industry observers

---

[12] Khanna is a creative person who set up his own company, Plus Channel. He is currently chairman of Reliance Entertainment.

quip that it is precisely because there was no regulation that television has achieved the growth that it has.

What propelled cable, however, was satellite broadcasting of a popular cable news channel from America! To repeat a piece of popular history, when the Gulf War broke out in early 1991, five-star hotels bought dish antennae that allowed guests to watch the war live. These hotels were already networked with cables and all they needed was an antenna that could catch the Cable News Network (CNN) signal. Cable operators too took to satellite broadcasting immediately. For them it meant an investment of Rs 200,000 (which soon fell to Rs 25,000) in the dish antenna. All they had to do was catch the signal and transmit it over the wires already connecting subscriber homes to their control rooms. They also needed a few thousand rupees more for amplifiers to boost the signal. Soon satellite dishes became a common sight throughout the country. Thus it was that CNN, the first cable news channel in the US, brought satellite television to India.

According to the news reports from that time, there was talk of CNN charging $1 per hotel room that it was being screened in. CatVision, one of the few companies selling dish antennae, was the exclusive licensee for CNN. In effect, CatVision franchisees were the only people allowed to bundle CNN along with the dish antennae they sold. The report also details the problems that arose because CatVision claimed to be authorised to collect pay revenues on behalf of CNN.

The next logical step for anyone in the business was to launch a satellite channel. Unfortunately, there weren't too many satellites that could beam onto the Indian subcontinent. Most were beat up Russian satellites like Gorizont and these were not geo-stationary: operators had to keep twisting their dish every now and then to receive clear signals as the satellite moved across the sky. Siddharth Srivastava, a cable network owner, attempted to launch ATN on one such satellite only to shut it down. A little earlier, in 1990, Hong Kong-based billionaire Li Ka Shing's Hutchison Whampoa Group, had bought ASIASAT 1, the only geo-stationary satellite over the Indian Ocean. It was a scrapped Chinese satellite that had its own parking space. Shing repaired it and gave it to his son, Richard Li. He then launched Star (Satellite Television Asian Region), the only channel beaming into China and India, in August 1991. Star began by beaming Prime Sports; it later added MTV (Music Television), BBC (British Broadcasting Corporation) and Star TV to its bouquet.

Around the same time, Li Ka Shing was also looking for companies that could buy space on his satellite. Almost every major Indian cable network owner approached him. So did BCCL's Times TV and a then little-known entrepreneur, Subhash Chandra. Finally, Chandra won the much-coveted slot on the satellite and started broadcasting Zee TV. Asia Today Limited was formed as a 50:50 joint venture between Star and Zee. Subhash Chandra's *Zee TV*,

71

launched in October 1992, became India's first privately-owned, Hindi satellite channel. It began with three-hour, largely film-based programming broadcasts before graduating to a 24-hour broadcast of sitcoms and soaps.

Zee was what Indian television audiences had been waiting for. As they rushed to get this exciting new channel on their television sets, cable operators thrived and penetration increased. By the end of 1992, India had 1.2 million cabled homes; by 1993, the number had more than doubled to 3 million. In 1994 even that figure had quadrupled to 11.8 million homes.

India went through a gut-wrenching foreign exchange crisis in 1991. The effect of this was felt in 1993 when an RBI (Reserve Bank of India) circular said that only companies with more than Rs 1 million in exports over each of the two previous years could buy the dollars needed to advertise on a Star or a Zee. There are some who believe that the foreign exchange crisis was used as an excuse to hurt potential competitors to DD. It created a piquant situation where even multinationals that wanted to advertise on these channels could not unless they had RBI clearance. Some advertisers got a case-by-case clearance from the RBI while others used the State Trading Corporation, which was allowed to use dollars for this purpose.[13]

Around this time, Li Ka Shing had sold off a controlling 63.6 per cent of his stake in Star to Rupert Murdoch's News Corporation for $525 million. By March in the same year, Star had broken up with MTV and BBC. By 1994, there was talk of pay and encryption, again rather accidentally. Star Movies claims it was the first to encrypt its analogue signals. That was because it had the right to show movies only in certain countries but the satellite footprint went beyond them. That brought up the thorny issue of paying right holders for beaming a movie in, say, Afghanistan, when it had rights to show it only in India. So it had to encrypt its signal.

This period also saw the entry of what are now India's largest regional television players. Sun TV began broadcasting with one Tamil channel, which has now gone up to 13. Currently Sun dominates completely the viewership in all the four Southern states and is one of the country's largest broadcasters. It was also marked by the rapid expansion of cable into regional markets—led by broadcasters themselves, most of the time, such as Sun TV's Sumangali Cable. In others, it was a natural corollary of the popularity of cable television. For example, in Andhra Pradesh, the launch of Eenadu TV saw cable penetration take off.

The MSO years By 1995, India had begun to resemble a respectable broadcasting market, prompting research agencies to offer electronic rating systems (explained later in this chapter). It also created a scramble in the media buying

---

[13] This circular was revoked in 2004, see section on regulation.

and selling world, as options other than print and outdoor exploded. Soon, larger Indian players jumped into the market. Home TV from the Hindustan Times' stable, Sony Entertainment Television promoted by Sony Corp subsidiary Columbia Tristar (along with a bunch of Indian investors), Eenadu TV from Andhra Pradesh's largest publishing company and a whole lot of serious players started entering the market. What was so far a cottage industry of types, run by cable operators offering channels from Star, Zee or local cable channels, was becoming bigger and bigger. This year also saw the passing of the Cable Act (see section on regulation).

As the number of channels kept increasing, so did the problem of small cable operators who did not have the space and the money to continue investing in dish antennae, cables and amplifiers. Plus, when broadcasters started charging operators for showing their channel, it meant two things. First, the operator had to start paying anywhere between Rs 2–30 for a bouquet of channels and second, he had to invest in decoders. That is because a pay channel is broadcast in an encrypted signal, which cannot be received if there is no decoder. Star Movies, one of the first to encrypt, offered operators a package of Rs 40,000— of which Rs 23,750 was the cost of the decoder. All in all, for a small cable operator with 200–300 subscribers, the whole operation was becoming unwieldy.

This is when multi-system operators (MSOs) made their first appearance. Essentially, major broadcasters or cable companies backed by serious corporations or consortiums of cable operators began setting up large control rooms or 'headends'. These had the dishes and equipment capable of receiving many more channels than a small cable operator could afford. They offered the signal to the small cable operator on the basis of a fee per subscriber. In turn the small cable operator could give this signal to the subscriber, over whom only he had control/access. For example, in 1994, United Cable Network (UCN), a consortium of five South Mumbai operators, was one of the first few companies to set up a headend or master control room. Broadcasters like Zee set up Siti Cable. Other large players like Hathway Cable from the Rajan Raheja Group, RPG Cable[14] and InCable from Hinduja, all started offering signals or the 'feed' as it is called in industry lingo, to smaller operators for a fee. As small operators started aligning with MSOs; their numbers reduced from about 60,000 nationwide, to the current 35,000.

If it sounds a little confusing, think of cable television distribution in India as a chain that starts from the signal that broadcasters send to the cable operator. Cable operators then relay this signal into our homes. By mid 1995–96, this chain had a new player, the MSO. Think then of the MSO as a wholesaler of

73

---

[14] RPG Netcom, which later became Indian Cable Net was sold to Siti Cable Network a Zee Telefilms subsidiary in 2005.

the signal while the small operator remains the retailer. Of this chain, the small operator was and still is the most powerful link. That is because he controls the last mile to your home. He is the person who collects the money from you every month. He therefore controls a significant portion of the revenues in the TV broadcasting business. If we take an extremely conservative average of Rs 150 per household/subscriber per month, for India's 60.82 million cable and satellite (C&S) households over 12 months, the total is Rs 109 billion.

According to estimates just about 15–20 per cent of this ends up with MSOs and broadcasters.[15] This happens because small operators routinely under-declare their subscriber base. Just touch upon the issue to see broadcasters, MSOs and cable operators all go on the defensive, each for a different reason.

Cable operators love to point to developed country markets. In the US, a cable company charges a certain amount for a basic package of channels. The rest is then bundled and sold in different packages at different prices. Households then buy the package they want and pay for that alone. This is made possible through a set-top-box (STB) called a Conditional Access System or CATV system, installed in subscriber homes. This is referred to as 'addressability'. Think of the STB as an electric meter. It makes it easier for the operator to supply only those 15–20 channels that you actually watch and for you to receive them and pay for them based on usage. In most markets across the world pay TV, whether digital or not, is possible only with an STB. How else can a household be billed? When cable operators point this out, they have a valid argument.

Most TV channels in India have encrypted themselves without providing addressability. As a result, if an operator covers 1,000 homes of which only 600 watch Discovery Channel, he is charged for all the 1,000 homes. Therefore if he has 1,000 subscribers, he may say he has 250. Then the next year's negotiation will yield another 100 and so on. The yearly negotiation on declarations is usually full of fights and switch-offs. ESPN–Star Sport has possibly had the maximum number of stand-offs with operators. The Maharashtra Cable Sena banned it in, as early as, 1996. A few years back the Mumbai High Court ruled that cable operators could not cut off signals when they fought with broadcasters since that would affect a third party which is not at fault—the consumer.

Now for the broadcaster/MSO point of view. Most of them have no arguments against addressability. However, it involves an investment of roughly Rs 3,000–5,000 per box per household. Even if you take a lower end

---

[15] As a result of so much cash sloshing around unaccounted in the system the cable industry has become a bit like what the film industry was earlier. The underworld is called in at times to sort out territorial disputes. According to some estimates currently about 60 per cent of the cable systems in India are owned by politicians or their relatives. This unaccounted money, say industry sources, has become a huge cash source for fighting local elections.

box of Rs 3,000, it could cost roughly Rs 126 billion. Then there is the
Rs 50,000–100,000 per channel per cable system for hardware, and Rs 1 million for subscriber management software at the cable operator level. Unless
MSOs or broadcasters are sure that they control the last mile or access to
revenues, they are not willing to make this kind of investment.

The broadcaster years The joint venture agreement between Star and
Zee created interesting accidents in broadcast history. For example, one clause
stated that not more than 50 per cent of Star's programming could be Hindi.
Similarly, Zee could not launch sports channels because Star already had Prime
Sports.

However, by 1999, Star and Zee had broken up: very loudly and very publicly. Zee paid Star $322 million for its stake in the joint venture and both
Chandra and Murdoch heaved a sigh of relief—and the battle for eyeballs reached
a different level. Once it was free of the no-Hindi clause, Star re-launched itself
as a full-fledged Hindi channel. Around this time, regional channels too were
appearing on the scene at regular intervals. There are now several channels in
every major Indian language. For example, Sun TV has 13 channels in Tamil,
Telugu, Kannada and Malayalam, spanning general entertainment, films, music
and news. It had plans for a Bangla (Bengali) channel.

The reasons for this rush were easy to understand. Transponder costs had
crashed from about $3 million at the beginning of the decade to $200,000–
300,000 by 2003. The other is the manner in which the ad market has expanded to absorb more channels. As a percentage of the total ad market, TV
has been steadily increasing its share (see Figures 0.2, 0.3, and 0.4).

There are several genres that gained as a result—news and children for
example. News broadcasting rarely makes money elsewhere in the world. Yet,
it is very popular—and profitable—in India. This is because India is a vibrant,
argumentative democracy and so diverse at that.

DD, the struggling state-broadcaster, never recovered from the body blow
of audiences fleeing to cable and satellite channels. It attempted to flank its
revenues through DD-Metro, a full-fledged entertainment channel; and to its
credit it did succeed to some extent. Then in July 2000, it leased a three-hour
slot on DD-Metro for Rs 1.21 billion to HFCL–Nine Broadcasting for a year.
As a result, for the first time in more than five years, DD began to make in-roads
into the lucrative cable and satellite homes with ratings for some programmes
touching six. However, DD refused to renew HFCL-Nine's contract in 2001 and
put the same slot up for re-bidding. HFCL-Nine, a joint venture between Kerry
Packer's Publishing and Broadcasting Limited and Indian-owned Himachal
Futuristic Communications Ltd, has already shut its Indian operations.

Today the only captive audience DD has is the 57 million homes that have
no other option. Even they won't last long. According to IRS 2005, cable and

satellite penetration, especially in rural India—DD's stronghold—has grown by twice the rate at which it has grown in urban India. In May 2000, current Nasscom head Kiran Karnik, Infosys founder Narayana Murthy and consultant Shunu Sen[16] submitted a report on Prasar Bharati. The report contained an analysis of its main problems—overstaffing and a lack of direction. It made some sensible recommendations on how the corporation could work better. So far, not much of what was suggested in the report has been converted to action. The government keeps deciding how one of India's largest broadcasting companies will be run. That's sad because DD happens to have some of the best assets in the broadcasting business. If its 1,000-odd tower network is put to good use, as the Shunu Sen Committee report suggested, it could do both—public service broadcasting and generate revenues. DD relies on a budgetary support that keeps rising every year. In 2004–05 it stood at Rs 11 billion against an expense of Rs 20 billion. There is talk of cutting it down. Till DD is financially independent, it cannot be administratively or otherwise be free of government control; and because it depends on the government financially, it can never be free to make money.

THE WAY IT IS

In the absence of seriously competitive terrestrial broadcasters, cable has had a free hand in India. It was during 2000–02, when blackouts, court cases and consumer complaints kept erupting that the government tried to usher in addressability. An amendment to the Cable Television Networks (Regulation) Act, 1995 in mid-2002 made it mandatory to watch pay channels only with an STB. This had two inherent problems. First, the law and the notifications that followed it expected all the 6.7 million homes in the Metros at the time to start becoming CAS-enabled by mid-July 2003, within six months of the act being amended. Anywhere else in the world, a CAS rollout is staggered over several years, with maybe 100,000–200,000 homes being covered at a time. Considering that India is an opaque market where conditional access technology had not been tested it seemed logical to attempt this one city/area at a time. Second, the amendment was silent on who would foot the bill. Since MSOs and broadcasters have no control over the last mile, they are reluctant to put up the money. By default, it had to be the consumer. Globally, industry reaps the maximum benefits of addressability. That is why it subsidises part of the cost of installing set top boxes. In fact, in most markets the demand and the initiative for addressability have come from within the industry—not been mandated.

---

[16] Sen passed away in 2003.

On the ground too cable operators and broadcasters lobbied hard to have the amendment changed, revamped or dropped. Neither wanted the transparency: operators because their 'real' coverage would come to light, and broadcasters because their 'real' viewership would be apparent. Only MSOs like Hathway and InCable, among others, invested money in buying CAS boxes and systems. However, the amendment was eventually whittled down and then ignored altogether. It was during this mess that the Telecom Regulatory Authority of India (TRAI) was appointed as the broadcast regulator for carriage (not content).

By 2003 it was evident that something was seriously wrong with the way TV signals were being sold in India. There was and is, even currently, a logjam on cable. There are about 160 TV channels aimed at India whereas a TV set can take in only 96–106 of them (see Figure 2.3). (In fact, the total number of channels that can be received in India is over 400, though most would hold no interest for an Indian.) This is besides the hundreds of local cable channels, the ones that show pirated films. Both MSOs and operators started charging a carriage fee to put a new channel on their system. Many now demand a placement fee. That means they charge extra money to place, say, a Channel 7 just before NDTV India or to shove Star News on to a hard-to-catch frequency and Aaj Tak on a better one.

This started putting tremendous pressure on stand-alone broadcasters. In 2005, after three years of trying to distribute on its own, Ten Sports joined OneAlliance, a distribution joint venture between Sony and Discovery. So too did MTV in 2004 after tackling the Indian market alone for years. Almost every new channel launch, and there are at least half a dozen every month, brings more money for cable operators and MSOs since they control the pipes. As long as there were 50–60 channels, it did not matter. But, as the numbers have grown, the structural problems that cable delivery has—of a fragmented, unorganised, opaque business—are beginning to impact both advertising and pay revenues.

The industry's advertising revenues are hit when cable operators keep shifting channels and viewership falls. At about Rs 67 billion, advertising growth on TV is beginning to slow down. For the two years starting 2003, yield per 10 seconds of ad time on TV actually fell for a majority of broadcasters. Second, pay revenues are hit because even popular channels now have to pay a placement fee, cutting into their subscription revenues. Since there is a mandated 7 per cent increase in cable rates, by TRAI, the scope for broadcasters to keep increasing rates to make up on this is limited.[17]

The problem is accentuated by the limitations on TV sets. Like elsewhere in the world, TV sets in India can only receive analog signals. And, as with TV transmission systems across the world, the last mile in India is analog. That explains the limit of 56–106 channels in spite of the quantity of spectrum this

Figure 2.3: The Increasing Variety in Indian Television

Total No. of Channels

2002	2003	2004	2005
158	171	212	241

Source: TAM Peoplemeter System.
Markets: All India.
TG: All 4+ yrs.

Their share by genre

2002		2003	
General Entertainment	Share (%)	General Entertainment	Share (%)
DD1	16.2	DD1	15.3
DD2	7.9	Star Plus	8.8
Star Plus	7.0	DD2	8.3
Sun TV	5.1	Sun TV	4.9
Gemini TV	4.9	Gemini TV	3.6
DD10 Sahyadri (Marathi)	2.9	Sony Entertainment TV	2.5
Sony Entertainment TV	2.7	MAX	2.2
Eenadu TV	2.3	Zee Cinema	2.2
DD7 Bangla	1.9	DD7 Bangla	2.1
Zee TV	1.9	Eenadu TV	2.1

News Channel	Share (%)	News Channel	Share (%)
Aaj Tak	0.8	Aaj Tak	0.8
Zee News	0.4	DD News	0.5
Star News	0.2	Zee News	0.4
SUN News	0.2	Star News	0.3
Udaya News	0.0	NDTV India	0.2
BBC World	0.0	Sahara Samay National	0.1
		SUN News	0.1
		BBC World	0.1
		Asianet News	0.0
		NDTV 24x7	0.0

2004		2005	
General Entertainment	Share (%)	General Entertainment	Share (%)
DD1	19.98	DD1	19.58
Star Plus	8.27	Star Plus	7.32
Sun TV	4.78	Sun TV	4.91
Gemini TV	3.21	Gemini TV	2.85
Sony Entertainment TV	2.53	Zee Cinema	2.42
MAX	2.28	Sony Entertainment TV	2.30
Zee Cinema	2.08	MAX	2.01
Eenadu TV	1.83	Zee TV	1.96
DD7 Bangla	1.82	DD10 Sahyadri (Marathi)	1.65
Zee TV	1.79	Eenadu TV	1.6

(Figure 2.3 continued)

(Figure 2.3 continued)

2004		2005	
News Channel	**Share (%)**	**News Channel**	**Share (%)**
DD News	2.18	DD News	1.67
Aaj Tak	0.71	Aaj Tak	0.67
NDTV India	0.48	NDTV India	0.5
Star News	0.38	Star News	0.46
Zee News	0.35	Zee News	0.42
ETV2 Telugu News	0.21	ETV2 Telugu News	0.23
TV9 Telugu News	0.21	TV9 Telugu News	0.18
Sahara Samay National	0.18	India TV	0.15
SUN News	0.14	NDTV 24x7	0.14
NDTV 24x7	0.11	Sahara Samay National	0.14

Note: (i) These are all India channel shares, measured as a percentage of total viewership for different genres. (ii) The target group for this is all 4 plus individuals in cable and satellite homes.

Source: Adex India and TAM Peoplemeter System.

Major Advertisers on Television

2002		2003	
Categories	**Share (%)**	**Categories**	**Share (%)**
Toilet Soaps	5	Toilet Soaps	4
Washing Powders/liquids	4	Corporate/brand Image	4
Soft Drink Aerated	4	Shampoos	3
Corporate/brand Image	3	Washing Powders/liquids	3
Tooth Pastes	3	Toothpastes	3
Shampoos	3	Two Wheelers	3
Hair Oils	2	Cars/jeeps	3
Two Wheelers	2	Cellular Phone Service	3
Fairness Creams	2	Soft Drink Aerated	2
Mosq Repellents	2	Biscuits	2
Other	69	Other	69
Grand Total	**100**	**Grand Total**	**100**

2004		(Jan–Aug) 2005	
Categories	**Share (%)**	**Categories**	**Share (%)**
Shampoos	5	Toilet Soaps	5
Toilet Soaps	4	Shampoos	5
Corporate/brand Image	4	Washing Powders/liquids	3
Washing Powders/liquids	3	Toothpastes	3
Cellular Phone Service	3	Cars/jeeps	3
Two Wheelers	3	Cellular Phone Service	3
Cars/jeeps	3	Soft Drink Aerated	3
Toothpastes	3	Biscuits	2
Cellular Phones	2	Cellular Phones	2
Soft Drink Aerated	2	Fairness Creams	2
Other	67	Other	68
Grand Total	**100**	**Grand Total**	**100**

Source: Adex India.

uses—between 550–750 Mhz. Currently all channels are transmitted in the digital mode. Most of the MSOs in metros pick them, convert them to analog and then send them to operators. There are three solutions to this logjam: digitise cable and/or push for alternate modes of broadcasting like DTH or IPTV or even digital terrestrial television.

Option one: Digitising will achieve two things. One, any digital delivery into consumer homes can only happen with an STB. This is irrespective of who sells the TV signals—whether it is a terrestrial, cable, broadband (IPTV) or DTH operator. Since STBs will be installed in every home that buys digital TV signals, addressability and 100 per cent transparency is automatic. A digitised cable system can easily be made two-way. That means it will become capable of offering voice or access to the Internet, or other services that require interactivity. But more importantly, it simply expands capacity by anywhere between 10–14 times. That is because the space that one analog channel uses can accommodate between 10–14 digital ones. Just digitising the current network could increase capacity to 560–1,000 channels on the existing network. There are, however, two issues involved.

The capital cost of digitisation is anywhere between Rs 700–3,000 per subscriber on a good urban network depending on how many subscribers there are according to a TRAI paper. That means the total cost could be anywhere between Rs 42–180 billion on just the headend.[18] Then there are the STB costs. The more the people, the lower the capital cost according to TRAI's paper on digitisation. This would require price deregulation during the transition to digital, tax sops on the equipment, licensing the cable business, increasing the foreign investment levels for cable (currently 49 per cent) and allowing operators to offer voice. All of that will add up to a substantial incentive to invest. Look at the way multiplexes took off after they were given a tax holiday in some markets.

Then there is the time and the patience digitisation demands. That just might be beyond a chaotic market like India. It took (and takes in the countries still digitising) 7–15 years going by the standards of developed countries. Remember they are smaller, less complicated markets than India. The UK, which began mandatory digitisation in 1998, will complete the process only by 2012. While the pipelines are being upgraded, signals are being simul-

---

[17] However when new pay channels are launched, rates do go over 7 per cent. Cable operators and broadcasters circumvent this by creating a separate bouquet, for which consumers are charged without informing them what it is for. So across metro cities most homes have seen cable rates go upto Rs 400 per home per month.

[18] If we take the cost at Rs 700–Rs 3,000 per subscriber, for 60 million homes.

taneously broadcast in digital and analog mode. Additional bandwidth would be needed to cope with the transition. After over 20 years of unregulated growth it would be too much to assume that this will happen smoothly.

Option two ...And this is my favourite option; a broadcaster or MSO can decide to seed the market with STBs and spend money, time and pain on digitising, say at least 10 million homes. Assuming he has that many homes signed on, his ARPUs will automatically rise since his ability to offer Internet access, gaming or even voice telephony increases and he can charge more. That in turn encourages other companies to jump in as happened in digital cinema.[19] Mukta-Adlabs just decided that there was potential and seeded 70 theatres with Rs 1 million worth of equipment in each. When theatre owners began earning more money, others came in to make India one of the world's largest digital-theatre countries in the world. If seeding of the market takes place in cable, it will result in the maximum utilisation of the investments that have already been made.

Option three ...And arguably the most practical one is to incentivise cable alternatives. The progress on this front has been pretty slow till 2004. When the DTH policy was announced in 2001 it came with several restrictions that put off investors. Then in October 2003 the Essel Group, that owns Zee Tele-films, launched Dish TV. Essel is the group that also owns Zee Telefilms. However there were no other DTH players either because their applications were not cleared or because nobody wanted to invest. At the time of writing, there were only two DTH players. One is Zee's Dish TV that claims to have 750,000 subscribers. The other is Doordarshan's DD Direct+, launched in 2004. It is a popular alternative to cable in large parts of South India. By the end of 2006 more DTH operators, such as Space TV, Reliance and Sun TV are expected to come in. That is when cable service and quality should improve. It may also force consolidation and some investment perhaps into cable digitisation.

DTH operates like regular broadcasting. The only difference being the frequency at which the signal travels (DTH operates in the KU-Band) and how it is received. The viewer has to buy a dish and an STB and can then receive the signals that a DTH operator sends directly. Therefore, there is no intermediary, cable operator or MSO. As a result the broadcaster deals directly with the viewer. Currently there are half a dozen successful DTH platforms across the world, many owned by News Corporation, 25 per cent owner of Foxtel Digital and also Star India's parent. At the invitation of Tata-Sky, I had a look at the Foxtel Digital system in Australia. For a sense of what it means, Foxtel is a good enough example.

81

---

[19] See Chapter on films.

Foxtel started as a pay TV company selling television over cable in 1995. In 1999 it launched a satellite service and in March 2004 it launched Foxtel Digital, a digital TV service that we, in India, call DTH. Till November 2005, the digital service had signed up over a million subscribers. Foxtel Digital sells over 100 channels that are packaged in bundles priced at anywhere between (Australian) $49.95–97.95 a month depending on the package. The one-time installation fee could range from (Australian) $36–395, again depending on the package.

Every DTH service has an electronic programme guide (EPG). Think of an EPG as a website's homepage on the Internet. The EPG is an on-screen guide that details all programmes according to genre, time, and channel. It can be navigated with a common remote control both for the TV and the DTH. If there is an interesting film, the EPG could give a quick synopsis that can help subscribers make up their mind on whether they want to watch it. You could choose to see what's on various channels in small pictures or text. For example, Sky News Active, the news service, allows the subscriber to choose between only weather or only sports or only political news among eight options. What it does is package the news by genre so that the subscriber can read the political news while watching a live sports broadcast. Ditto for films. Sky Box Office, a near video-on-demand service, allows viewers to choose a film every 30 minutes. They could choose certain camera angles while watching a cricket match, summon the statistics of a player, his record and any other match-related data. They can opt to watch a single film for (Australian) $5.95 on a channel that they may not subscribe to otherwise. They could also play games.

Then there is a high-end service that Foxtel offers. It includes a PDR or personal digital recorder, what is branded as TiVo in the US. This allows a viewer to 'time-shift': he can pause live programming and come back to it after attending a phone call.[20] It can be programmed to record even while the viewer is not home. It can record up to 100 hours of programming. The equipment is installed and maintained by Foxtel, which operates a complicated call centre from Melbourne to serve its DTH subscribers. It involves wiring, an STB and a dish antenna. A smart card, which is usually topped with credit beforehand, is inserted into the STB and a subscriber can only watch what he has paid for. In case he wants to watch a film on a channel he does not subscribe to, he calls in for the amount to be debited from his account.

Most of these are facilities that IPTV too can offer. In 2004, when TRAI recommended unbundling the last mile that telecom companies owned, there was some hope of IPTV taking off. But it never became policy. If anybody—cable operators or ISPs or other telecom companies—had been allowed to use

---

[20] What actually happens is that the PDR keeps recording the programme. When you play the TV again what you are watching is what was recorded when you went to take the call. While you are watching the show from the point where you left it, it continues to record the live broadcast and show it to you in the right sequence.

MTNL (Mahanagar Telephone Nigam Limited) or BSNL (Bharat Sanchar Nigam Limited)'s last mile copper to offer television to the 42 million homes they reach, there can be immediate competition for cable. Of course, it might not work quite like that. In the UK where even after the regulator mandated unbundling, British Telecom blocked others from using its last mile by keeping prices very high. Finally others started using wireless services to offer broadband, net access and TV, BSkyB being the best example. The demand for BT's last mile collapsed. Now it has a wholesale division to sell its last mile.

Even the best regulation cannot overcome the internecine wars that mark an industry. However, with broadband finally taking off in 2005, IPTV might see the light of day sooner than we think. Once consumers are used to good quality, cheap broadband, they will need more from the same pipes. That is when IPTV will really take off. Combine it with more DTH alternatives and life for television viewers should get better by 2007. Reliance, Bharti and BSNL look like the three main companies, which will eventually offer IPTV since they have the biggest wireline network in the country.

Think of pay TV technology—whether it comes from a terrestrial, cable, DTH or an IPTV operator—as a multiplex on television. The ability to track will mean a mix of options in shows, timings and prices. The low-end consumer wanting mass entertainment can see the free-to-air channels. The high-end viewer might buy a DTH system and watch only four to eight channels offering really high-end programming akin to the 100-seater in large multiplexes which screen only art films. A broadcaster can be on a portfolio of delivery platforms with different programming to fit each platform. Maybe the margins on the mass-market platform, like old-fashioned cable television, might be low but those on DTH could be high. The more platforms that are available to a viewer, the more the variety, the better the quality that he will get. As that happens, people should be willing to pay more for TV and this should lead to an increase of pay revenues as a percentage of total industry revenues. That reduces the dependence on advertising. It is already happening in mature markets (see Figure 2.4). In 2004, for the first time, paid for media revenues were more than advertising-subsidised media in the US.

Figure 2.4: The Global Pay TV Picture

Pay TV Channel Economics

	Advertising	Subscription/Other
		Revenue share (%)
US	49	51
UK	48	52
Taiwan	65	35
India	80	20
Korea	70	30

(*Figure 2.4 continued*)

(*Figure 2.4 continued*)

Who Owns the Distribution Pie?

Figures in share (%)

	Operator	Broadcaster
US	60	40
Japan	65	35
S.E. Asia Avg	70	30
Taiwan	76	24
Korea	79	21

Cable Revenue Composition (2004)

Figures in share (%)

	US	Japan	Hong Kong	Singapore
Cable TV	57	50	55	58
Digital Cable TV	8	2	19	3
VOD/DVR/HDTV	1	1	na	na
Internet	17	27	19	35
Telephony	5	18	1	1
Advertising	6	2	6	3
Others	6	0	0	0

Digital DTH Revenue Composition (2004)

Figures in (%)

	US	UK	Malaysia	Korea
Basic Tier	56	42	59	78
Exp. Basic/Premium Tier	25	28	29	16
PPV	6	4	1	2
Multiple STBs	6	3	3	1
Interactive TV	5	10	1	2
Advertising/other	5	9	7	3
PVR/HDTV/Other	2	4	0	1

Source: Media Partners Asia.

In the process, television broadcasting will become a bigger business. It is really not as much in the future as it seems. Remember, just 15 years ago you were waiting for that Sunday evening movie on DD.

THE WAY IT WORKS

The product of what started in 1959, moved forward in 1984 and took off in 1992 is what we call the Indian television broadcasting industry. Its structure is rather haphazard, unlike the US market, the world's favourite benchmark for any media industry. Investment bankers and analysts tend to do that.

The fact is that the Indian broadcast industry has a DNA, a genetic code that is its own, that has little or nothing to do with how the US market, guided by the Federal Communications Commission, evolved. There are several cross-media restrictions based on readership and viewership in the US. In contrast, the Indian industry has had no regulation whatsoever, except for some acts from 1885 and 1933 that determined the state's hegemony over broadcasting. Its imperatives for growth, adopting technology or business are home-grown to a great extent. For example, television software is still a separate industry unlike in the US, where most broadcast companies buy out software producers or integrate backwards by setting up their own production arms.

The Indian television broadcast industry can thus be regarded as a chain with three links: broadcasters, distributors and television software makers. Each is an important component in ensuring that the final product—viewer experience—is good. The television software industry is the first link in the chain. It is the point at which all the value in the business—the programming—is created. This is then sold to broadcasters who package channels around this programming; throw the signals at a TV tower or a satellite. These can be downlinked and distributed in several ways.

Broadcast There are two different business models that the television broadcast industry uses:

Buy and Telecast: Broadcasters buy programming outright from television software companies. The price could range from Rs 0.5–1 million, or more per episode. It depends on several things, the genre and the production house among them. Sitcoms and talk shows are less expensive to make since they are studio-based. Soaps are more expensive. Similarly, game shows may seem cheaper to make since they are studio-based but if the anchor is a big name— *Kaun Banega Crorepati* would be an extreme example—the cost could be high. Broadcasters then package the software with promos. Promos are advertisements for the channel or network's own programmes. Star News could carry promos for Star Plus' soaps or Star Gold's films and vice versa. This packaged software is then used to generate revenue from three main streams:

Advertising revenue is generated through airtime sold to advertisers. This is done through advertising agencies or through media houses such as Group M or Starcom. While the international norm is five minutes of advertising time per 30 minutes of programming, it is normal for Indian channels to stretch their ad seconds into the programme if they find buyers for an exceptionally popular show. India is probably one of the few markets in the world where, while the volume of advertising sold on television has risen dramatically in the last few years, rates have actually fallen in real terms, because there is so much discounting and bonusing. This refers to the practice of giving bonus seconds on sister channels or programmes as an add-on to clients buying on prime time. Bonus seconds are also offered for not delivering on TVR or television rating targets. Typically, bonus seconds drag down average realisation per ten seconds.

To capture more of the advertising rupee going to other genres, broadcasters started putting together 'bouquets'. Zee TV has a general entertainment channel, Zee Cinema (a movie channel); Zee News; Zee Cafe, regional channels and so on, taking the total to over 20. In this way, Zee has more advertising seconds to cross-sell. If an advertiser is taking a package of, for example, Zee and ETV Marathi, Zee could offer him Zee Marathi and Zee TV as a package to ensure that all the money comes into the Zee kitty.

Pay revenue is the money that comes from subscriptions. Internationally, advertising to pay as a proportion of revenues hovers around 55:45. In India it is 40:60, though a bulk of it doesn't come back to the MSO or the broadcaster, unlike global markets.

The overseas market has in the past few years emerged as a substantial revenue stream. Indian channels like Zee TV or Sun TV have discovered sizeable audiences in the UK and US. There are more than 20 million Indians living overseas. At a rough estimate, their combined income is roughly half of India's GDP. Now factor in the fact that this market is dominated by pay. That means that a subscriber wanting to see Zee TV has to pay his cable company anything between, £9.99–18.99 a month, depending on the package. This revenue is shared with the cable companies. The distribution of channels overseas is lucrative for broadcasters because programming costs are negligible. Most broadcasters re-run the soaps that are made for the Indian market with fresh promotions and ads from the local market where the channel is being telecast. For example, at the time of writing, Zee TV UK was showing its latest soap, *Rabba Ishq Na Hove,* among others. The US, UK, African and South-East Asian population of Indians settled there or Non-Resident Indians (NRIs) is a market that is available only to Indian or regional language channels.

Mobile and Internet revenues are emerging streams for broadcasters. These could be in various forms. For example, when *Kaun Banega Crorepati 2* was being telecast towards the end of 2005, Star ran a contest for this show's audience. If viewers answered the question posed during this show, via SMS, then about 30–50 per cent of the money spent on sending the SMS would go to Star India. The remainder, split between the operator and the company that runs the back-end for routing all the SMS. Star Group (India) CEO Peter Mukerjea has clearly stated that eventually mobile should form at least 30 per cent of SGI's revenues. Sony, Sun TV, almost every channel has some kind of SMS services—for alerts, song downloads, cricket highlights and other things.

Sony, in fact, made a neat packet according to reports on the 55 million SMSes that it got during *Indian Idol*. However, the potential is not just in SMS and contests; it could be in live sports broadcasts and news highlights, all in streaming video. In October 2005, Star One began offering 'mobisodes'—one-minute clips of its popular show, *The Great Indian Laughter Challenge*—on mobile phones. While these services are on offer by some mobile phone operators like Hutch, wireless bandwidth, that is the ability of mobile phone networks to carry broadcast quality audio-visual, is as yet limited. We shall know more on this in the chapter on telecommunications.

Lease and Telecast: A second business model is the one used by DD and Sun TV.[21] Typically, DD gives away airtime in slots of 30–60 minutes for a telecast fee or minimum guarantee. This could range from Rs 3–4 million depending on the time slot and advertising revenues it expects the programmes to generate. It also gives the producer a fixed proportion of seconds, called free commercial time (FCT), which he sells in order to recover his money. The producer can pay extra to buy additional seconds. The seconds that he has not used can be 'banked'.

Production companies like Nimbus, Balaji Telefilms and Creative Eye that have traditionally been suppliers to DD and Sun TV, have built up their own ad-sales teams, which sell airtime. More significantly, after a one-time telecast, DD or Sun TV don't have any right over the software since they don't buy it; they just lease out airtime to telecast it. Sun TV, for example, prefers this to the 'commissioning model' where the software belongs to the channel. Sun's Chairman, Kalanithi Maran, reckons that the telecast model ensures basic cash flows since producers pay money upfront for the slot. Broadcast networks in the US too used this model for a long time before deciding that there is a lot of value in integrating vertically into making their own software or buying it outright. Cable networks, on the other hand, charge a premium for creating original programming that you could watch only on that channel, for example HBO.

Distribution The other important constituent of the broadcast industry is the distributor. This could be a cable operator/MSO combine, a DTH operator or a telecom or broadband company. There are four main revenue streams for most distributors:

Subscription currently forms the biggest chunk of distributor revenues. This is the money cable operators/MSOs or DTH operators collect from homes.

---

[21] About 50 per cent of the programming time on Sun TV is sold for a telecast fee, the rest is used by in-house programming from Sun TV.

They charge anywhere between Rs 100–500 per household per month, depending on the city, locality, the package and so on. If the operator is affiliated to an MSO, then Rs 50–100 per subscriber per month goes to the MSO (refer to the part on 'cable industry'). Anywhere from Rs 5–40 per subscriber per home goes to individual broadcasters. In the case of Dish TV, a DTH operator, it may give a commission to the dealers who hawk its dishes and STBs. It offered two packages in September 2005 at Rs 3,990 and Rs 4,990 for installation, with one-year's free subscription. The recurring fee ranges between Rs 150–300 depending on the package you take. DD Direct+ doesn't have a subscription fee since it has only free-to-air channels. However, there is an installation charge, according to last reports, of Rs 2,300–5,000 depending on what you buy.

Advertising is another major stream. Most operators and MSOs have their own channel, such as CCC from Hathway. These air advertisements from local retailers or regional brands or for local events. A retailer in Lajpat Nagar, in New Delhi, could be advertising on a cable network in South Delhi, the area where the potential buyers for his store would reside. These advertisements are broadcast along with the films shown. While exact numbers on the size of cable advertising are hazy, a safe estimate would be approximately Rs 6.5 billion.[22]

Carriage and placement revenues: Currently there is a logjam on India's cable pipes. Since bandwidth is limited, cable operators and MSOs now make money from carriage and placement. These seem like temporary revenue streams till alternate distribution platforms emerge. The carriage rate that some really large MSOs charge is about Rs 0.5–10 million per network per year. Placement, the money paid by a broadcaster to ensure that his channel is on a good frequency, may also be paid separately. It could be paid to ensure that a channel, like CNBC-TV18, is placed before its competitor, say NDTV Profit, on the viewer's television set.

The shifting typically happens in three cases. One, when there are many launches, as in 2004 and 2005. The old channel pays to retain its position on the TV set and the new one to keep it close to popular channels such as Star Plus or Sony, so that the opportunity to sample it is higher. Two, in the 73 TVR towns: that is where TAM's Peoplemeters, the ones that track viewership patterns, are installed. Many broadcasters try to ensure their presence on the cable system to ensure that their viewership numbers don't fall. If they do, advertising falls. Three, in an area, say Lokhandwala, Bandra or Versova in

---

[22] If we assume that each of the 35,000 odd operators makes a nominal Rs 100,000 a month from advertising, the total is Rs 42 billion. Assume that not everybody gets advertising and take a very conservative 10 per cent of that number—that's Rs 4.20 billion. Most analysts usually go with a flat Rs 5 billion. If we assume that this has grown by 10 per cent every year since 2003, the figure for 2005 is Rs 6.65 million.

Mumbai, where many media buyers or advertisers have their homes. This ensures that the channel is available in all the places where key decision makers on advertising might be watching.

Software Though it is probably the smallest link in size, television software is the origin of all value creation in the broadcast industry. At a time when the bulk of the investment in broadcasting is going into creating a distribution infrastructure, the importance of software cannot be overemphasised. This becomes apparent looking at China: because it lacks a democracy, it has inhibited the growth of a robust software industry (a complex set of rules means that the authorities frown on a vast variety of programmes which would be considered perfectly innocuous in India). This has created a demand-supply gap that is now seriously affecting the growth of the Chinese TV broadcasting industry. All the money put into building great TV distribution is pointless until there is programming to be carried on that network.

The Indian television software industry is largely an offshoot of the film industry. In the initial days when DD was looking for software, it was the film industry that had the people, the skills and the equipment needed to churn out entertainment software. The trend continues. Some of the best-known names in the business have their roots in the film industry. Remember that Manohar Shyam Joshi wrote *Buniyaad* and Ramesh 'Sholay' Sippy directed it. Dheeraj Kumar, a former film actor, started his own production house, Creative Eye. In DD's heyday, Creative Eye was a fixture on its network with serials like *Adalat*. It churned out some hugely popular mythologicals like *Om Namah Shivay* and *Shree Ganesh* for private broadcasters. Later Asha Parekh, a former film actress, produced the very popular *Kora Kaagaz* on Star Plus and, the more recent, *Kangan*. Aruna Irani, another actress, has had a big hit in weekly soaps, *Des Mein Nikla Hoga Chand*. Actress Radhikaa's software firm, Radaan Pictures, has produced some of the biggest hits in Tamil and Telugu languages.

Ever since the satellite TV boom hit India in 1991, the software industry has enjoyed a scorching pace of growth. The demand for entertainment software, films, shows, soaps and sitcoms has continued to rise. From a few hours for DD, there is a need for at least eight hours of original programming a day for over 50 channels. That's a mind-boggling 146,000[23] hours a year. An average cost of Rs 150,000 for every 30 minutes, pegs the industry's size at Rs 22 odd billion roughly. This growth has increased the number of software firms from a handful in the 80s to approximately 6,000 currently. These are primarily one-man outfits. This has meant extreme fragmentation and thin

89

---

[23] Assume that of the 106 channels about 50 buy original programming. Many, like say Cartoon Network or HBO don't need to do original programmes. Cartoon Network dubs some of its shows in Indian languages while HBO is a purely English movie channel. The others, like news channels, develop their own software.

profits for individual firms. There are very few firms with the scale and the staying power to generate hundreds of hours of software, consistently over several years like the Rs 1.96 billion (2004–05) Balaji Telefilms.

Balaji Telefilms started during the satellite boom in 1994 with one serial on Zee TV. Then on, it has grown to become by far the largest (listed or unlisted) television software firm. It supplies software across the country to channels in several languages. Balaji listed in 2000 and is an investor favourite for delivering on turnover and profit fairly consistently. From 1,485 hours in 2003–04, it created 1,719 hours of programming in 2004–05. That is a pretty big number by Indian industry standards considering the mom and pop nature of the business: production firms make anywhere from 5–500 hours of programming a year. Television Eighteen, Cinevistaas and UTV Software are among the others who have also achieved scale.

The second thing that has happened as supply rushed to meet demand is that costs and prices have jumped exponentially. From about Rs 30,000–50,000 per 30-minute episode, the cost of making a soap for a top-ranking channel has gone to anywhere between Rs 100,000–300,000. More importantly, the pricing rules have changed completely. If a show is successful, producers claim a higher price or a share of revenues. When *Kyunkii Saas Bhi Kabhi Bahu Thi* was telecast in July 2000, Balaji sold it to Star for Rs 180,000 per episode. After it swept the rating charts, it began commanding Rs 600,000 per episode plus incentives at one point. The converse is also true. Now, software producers are all right about shows getting pulled off-air for not delivering an audience.

Software houses typically depend on two revenue streams:

Selling or leasing:[24] Selling is the outright sale of software to broadcasters, all rights included. Alternatively, the software company could lease telecast time from a broadcaster. It could then sell the airtime. This is how it works for DD and for at least 50 per cent of the programming on Sun TV. In such a case, the software house owns the rights to the programme after a one-time telecast.

Syndication, dubbing and overseas markets are additional revenue streams that software firms owning the copyright can exploit, just as broadcasters can. This money is pure profit since the cost of the software is usually recovered from the first telecast. Firms like Creative Eye or Cinevistaas sit on a lot of software that was made for DD but to which they own the copyright. This can be used to generate revenues through syndication, dubbing or webcasting. Many shows from software houses or broadcasters are dubbed in Tamil, Telugu or other languages either for markets within India or overseas. There is a large Tamil population in Malaysia or a Malayalam-speaking group in the Middle East. There are many Indian software firms like Balaji Telefilms or UTV that sell their Indian shows to broadcasters in these markets.

---

[24] These two models are discussed in detail in the portion on broadcast.

Buying and selling ad time When DD was in its heyday, the media planning and buying assignments were not about getting maximum reach, efficiency or impact—the otherwise usual goals for a media buyer. It was about scheduling advertising seconds in the best shows. That is because reach was a given since DD was the only channel. A popular show or a Hindi film ensured an audience of 70–80 per cent of television homes. The only job for a media planner and buyer was to decide how to split his money between DD and print media. Most of them booked slots for the year. They then spent the rest of the time scheduling the right ad with the right show. Of course, some judgement had to be exercised on which serials would do well. 'Media innovation,' says Arpita Menon of Lodestar Media, an arm of FCB Ulka, 'was getting into serial production'. That's because DD gave all the commercial time on a show to a sponsor. Therefore, advertisers preferred to finance the producer and get all the commercial time on the show.

From 1992 onwards, a media planner's job became more complex. He or she had to juggle a few more channels, with DD and print vehicles. The whole science of airtime buying and selling started evolving. Media planners and advertisers began looking at target audiences, the kind of people who watched a channel or a programme. They could decide that it made more sense to advertise a woman's product during *Amaanat* on Zee. The image of a channel and that of a programme came into play. Media planners, who had been starved for options so far, were glad that there was something to choose from.

Currently, airtime is bought on the basis of ratings and the advertising rates that channels offer. The rates are usually fixed for every 10 seconds or 30 seconds of advertising time bought. These are called spots. Ad rates differ according to the time of the day for which they are bought. The ad seconds bought during prime time, usually from 9–11 pm, are the highest-priced on any channel anywhere in the world. This is the time entire households generally watch television. The rates during the other parts of the day, called non-prime time rates, are usually lower. If a particular part of the day starts registering higher viewership, then the ad rate of that slot goes up. All TV broadcasting companies have a rate card; almost nobody follows it in practice. Discounting is common and average realisation per 10 seconds could vary wildly from channel to channel.

There are various ways in which discounts can be given. One, as a straight percentage cut on the card rate. This could vary anywhere between 20–70 per cent depending on the channel, the time of day and how desperate it is. Two, discounts could be given as bonus seconds. If HLL buys, say, 20 spots on prime time on Star, it could get five bonus spots on non-prime time shows as a preferred buyer or because a show it advertised on did not deliver on the promised TVRs. The bonus then becomes a way of making good. India is not unique in this respect. In the US, some spots (ad seconds) on the four networks[25]—ABC, NBC, CBS and Fox—are auctioned in advance. These upfront buys could get quantity discounts of up to 15 per cent. The rest of prime time inventory is sold closer to the broadcast dates and if a programme is a big hit, like *Who Wants to be a Millionaire* on ABC, a network could hike rates dramatically to reap huge profits. In India too, the system of upfront buys, before a programme begins airing, exists. However, many of these are locked in rating deliveries. If Pepsi buys time on a new soap on Zee it will do so for 13 episodes on the guarantee of certain rating points. If Zee cannot deliver on those rating points, it makes up with a hefty discount or with bonus seconds. That explains the rise in the volume of ad seconds without a commensurate rise in broadcasting revenues (see Figure 2.5).

Figure 2.5: The Growth and What it Means

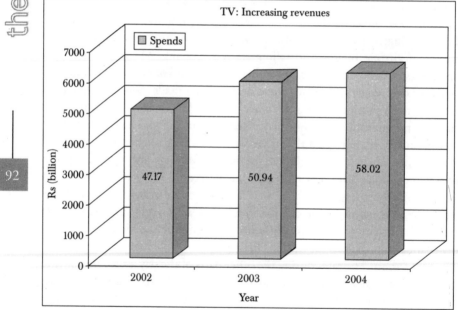

Jan–Dec, Figs in Rs billion

(*Figure 2.5 continued*)

---

[25] A network in the US refers to a terrestrial channel like CBS, being distributed via cable operators.

(*Figure 2.5 continued*)

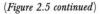

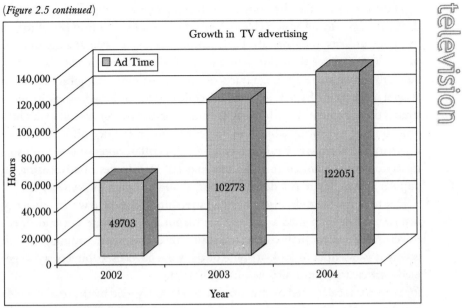

Jan–Dec, Figs in Hours

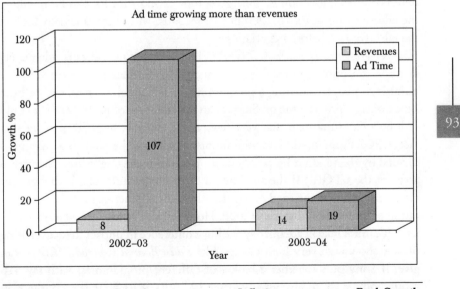

Percentage	Growth	Inflation	Real Growth
TV	14	–5	19

Source: Lodestar Media.

The economics of airtime buying and selling operate similarly anywhere in the world. For any television channel, airtime is just like the number of rooms in a hotel or seats in an aircraft. For an airline, selling a ticket at a discount or even a loss is better than not selling it at all since filling capacity is crucial. Similarly, when there are huge tracts of unsold airtime it is logical to recover at least a fraction of variable costs. Of course, a lot of broadcasters in India stretch the argument the other way around. It is normal for several to eat into programme time during a hit show, to get maximum mileage off it. While the international norm is five minutes of ad-time per 30 minutes, it is not unusual to see top rung channels in India carrying 10–15 minutes of advertising on popular shows. There is a downside to it, though: it puts the viewers off.

Due to bonus seconds, discounting or stretching, the way in which efficiency is measured or even media budgets are planned is not quite cut and dried. Advertisers do factor in discounts and shrink their budgets accordingly. Which is why it is essential to look at some of the ways advertisers/buyers try to get media efficiency out of airtime buys. These are:

Effective rate is calculated by dividing the total money paid by the total seconds bought on a channel. If the prime time rate on Sony is Rs 200,000 per ten seconds and if an advertiser buys ten spots, that is Rs 2 million. Assume that he gets two spots free or as a bonus. That gives him 12 spots for Rs 2 million, taking the effective rate to Rs 167,000 per 10 seconds. Most buyers usually look at the effective rate before negotiating.

Cost per gross rating points (*CPGRPs*): The effective rate doesn't adequately factor in the amount of reach a channel could give. Reach is measured by the number of people watching a programme on a channel. If an advertiser buys time during a programme on Sony, at an effective rate of Rs 167,000, it could well be a day time soap that very few people are watching. To get over that fact, CPGRPs are used. The total money that might be paid to a channel is divided by the total rating points on all programmes bought on a channel to arrive at the CPGRP. If the air time on three programmes can be bought for Rs 1 million and if the total rating that these three generate is 20, the cost per rating point works out to Rs 50,000. However, this method too has its weakness. It cannot take in adequately the huge difference in impact that advertising on one show with very high ratings, like *Kaun Banega Crorepati* (*KBC*), can give. If Sony puts together a basket of different programmes, with say 4–6 rating point each, to give an advertiser 20 TVRs at Rs 50,000 each: the plan looks efficient. However, the advertiser can also get the same ratings with one high-impact programme. These are the type of issues planners take into account before making a buying decision.

For more details on how media planning and buying works across media, refer to Appendix, which carries a survey of media buying from *Businessworld*.

Rating systems Many of us read and talk about ratings or TRPs/TVRs, but what precisely is it?[26] A TVR is a time weighted average of the total time that people in the sample homes spend watching a certain soap or programme. If 10 people in 10 homes spend different amounts of time watching *Kolangal* on Sun TV, the average of this, weighted by the time each has spent, becomes the rating the programme gets. Ratings can be for one minute, five minutes, 15 minutes or 24 hours. Typically, when channels share their ratings, they cherry pick the time that suits them best. If music channels are most-watched from 7–8 pm, the channel, ETC, might pick only on that time-slot that shows it at the top. In that time period ETC might have a rating of five, but on a 24-hour basis it may actually have a rating of 0.06. It is extremely crucial to understand what, why and how ratings are arrived at. This is because every decision—on whether to advertise on a channel, the products and brands to advertise for, when to air them, and which programmes to choose—is based on ratings. Ratings help in deciding what genres are working, what aren't and change the channel strategy accordingly. In 2004–05, when comedies began to do well, several channels launched sitcoms.

Indian broadcasting has had a healthy history of using tools of measuring audiences and their responses. According to Hemant Mehta of IMRB, the first measurement of television was formulated in 1983. IMRB, the research arm of ad agency Hindustan Thompson Associates (now JWT), did a viewership study on what people saw and when. The data on the actual launch of continuous ratings measurement systems is hazy, but according to Sankara Pillai, former general manager, media research at ORG–MARG, it began in 1986. Three research agencies, IMRB, MRAS-Burke and Sameer (then the research arm of Mudra Communications) introduced a system to measure the popularity of programmes on DD. It was the only broadcast channel in India then, the rest were cable channels. Pillai, who was with IMRB then, remembers that one of the projects he was part of was the launch of the diary-system of measuring ratings. IMRB distributed roughly 3,600 diaries in eight Indian cities based on the demographics of the people that advertisers wanted to talk to. There were many people who did not own a television set then. They watched it at a neighbour or friend's home. As a result, IMRB had two diaries—primary and secondary. Both the television owner and the secondary (guest) viewers filled them out.

Anyone who watched a programme for five minutes or more was considered a viewer. Along with the sex, income and age of the person writing in it, the diary was meant to record what that person saw for five minutes or more. The diary

---

[26] The term TRP though still in use, describe ratings in the diary system. When the peoplemeter service was introduced, the term was changed to TVR. Both mean the same thing.

had time slots; and all a viewer had to do was fill in what programme he or she was watching at that time. If *Ramayan* had an 80 per cent rating it meant that 80 per cent viewers (in single-television homes) had watched it for five minutes or more. These reports were then collected, the data collated and ratings arrived at. It was a fairly rudimentary method, no different from how it began in developed country markets like the US.

After 1991 it became important to also capture what cable and satellite households were watching, and that is when IMRB and (then) MARG introduced rating reports for cable and satellite homes. The method was the same, only this time viewers had to write what they were watching on say Star or CNN or MTV, instead of just DD. By 1995, the crush of satellite channels was so immense that both IMRB and (by then) ORG–MARG finally decided to invest in Peoplemeters. A meter costs several million to install and maintain. A joint industry body—comprising advertisers, agencies, channels et al was constituted. Three agencies were supposed to pitch. Just before the pitch, A.C. Nielsen and IMRB joined hands to offer the Television Audience Measurement (TAM). In July 1996, the joint industry body chose TAM. Since funds were a problem, TAM did not take off immediately.

Meanwhile ORG–MARG launched INTAM and started offering its service. A year after the joint industry body's proposal, TAM finally obtained the funds to launch its service. That is how India ended up with two television measurement systems. 'In most countries there is only one system,' says L.V. Krishnan, CEO of TAM Media Research. The takeover of A.C. Nielsen internationally by VNU (the parent of ORG–MARG) meant the merger of these two services in 2002. While TAM is currently the currency for television ratings in India, in 2004 another agency, aMap, too started a service in India.

TAM uses the frequency matching technology. Rather simply, the meter attached in viewer homes registers the frequency of the channel the viewer is watching for a minute or more. It then matches this with the map of the frequencies for each channel in its bank. If you were on the Zee frequency for more than a minute, you are a Zee viewer. The method could have one problem. Cable operators routinely change the frequencies at which they send the signal for a channel (refer to 'The way it is'). Krishnan maintains that by monitoring cable operators regularly, TAM catches any change of frequency at which a channel is broadcast and updates its system accordingly.

The data is downloaded, either in tape form or via a laptop onto the agency's servers. It is then collated and analysed. There are scores of different kinds of reports—by genre, demographics, channel, languages, cities, states, areas and so on—that are generated using the data. Most constituents in the broadcast industry—software houses, television channels, advertisers, ad agencies, media buying agencies and others pay anywhere between Rs 400,000 to about

Rs 10 million a year for the data, depending on the reports they buy. These reports are then used to devise marketing, programming, distribution or advertising strategies.

After the merger of both the systems in mid-2002, TAM covers 73 towns in India with 4,800 Peoplemeters. In June 2005, TAM announced that it will increase this to 10,300 as the number of cable homes has gone up. The larger sample will allow specialist panels—by language groups or demographics—to be created.

aMap: In mid-2004, Ahmedabad-based Audience Measurement and Analytics set up an alternative rating system called aMap. It started with 1,000 meters in Mumbai, Delhi and Ahmedabad and has plans to take these to 20,000 by 2006. While it uses the same method to record the ratings, it is different from TAM in one respect. TAM picks up the data from viewer homes every Saturday. There is a lag of at least a week before anyone knows what happened to a show or a match. However, the aMap server logs into the Peoplemeter between 2:00–4:00 am every morning and picks up the data. This is possible because it uses a GSM modem to get real time access to the data. Buyers and advertisers can actually see the ratings online and decide that they want to change their media plan. This can be especially useful for big-ticket shows like *KBC* or during elections or budget analysis when the window of opportunity to schedule advertising spots is limited. An overnight or online look at ratings helps utilise it better.

Other rating systems: Besides these two systems, DD has its own Doordarshan Audience Research Television Ratings.

REGULATION[27]

To begin with The surprising part about regulation in Indian television broadcasting, frankly, has been its complete absence for a very long time. There was nothing in the books that said foreign broadcasters could not send signals from outside Indian soil, though broadcasting was government controlled. There was nothing that said you could not hook up a VCR to a common cable for the entire building. Many portions of the television broadcast industry have been lucky (or unlucky, depending on how you view it) to escape regulation.

[27] A bulk of the information for this part has been supplied by media lawyer Ashni Parekh formerly with Nishith Desai and Associates, a firm that specialises in technology and media law. The remaining comes from the website of the Ministry of Information and Broadcasting and Kanchan Sinha of Amarchand & Mangaldas & Suresh A. Shroff and Company, a New Delhi-based law firm.

This has meant growth at a scorching pace, like in cable, without the trouble of getting licenses or permissions. The utter absence of a regulatory framework has also meant chaos, copyright violations, and the use of the underworld to settle disputes.

The Ministry of Information and Broadcasting (MIB) is the apex body for the formulation and administration of rules, regulations and laws relating to information, broadcasting, films and television. For very long, the MIB along with the Indian Telegraph Act of 1885 and The Wireless Telegraphy Act of 1933, were the two points from which any regulatory indicators came for the broadcasting industry. Government control over radio and television broadcasting is derived from the Telegraph Act where 'telegraph' is interpreted to cover the generating of signals for telecasting. The Emergency in 1975 created the demand for autonomy. As a result, a working group was formed to look into autonomy for All India Radio (AIR) and DD, the first attempt at broadcasting reform in India. The Akash Bharati Bill of 1978, which had lapsed, was re-examined and presented as the Prasar Bharati Bill in 1989. Although the Bill was passed in 1990, it was notified only in 1997. Under the Act, AIR and DD were converted into government corporations to be overseen by a statutory autonomous authority established under the Prasar Bharati (Broadcasting Corporation of India) Act, 1990. The Prasar Bharati Corporation was envisaged to be the public service broadcaster of the country, which would achieve its objectives through AIR and DD.

It was only in the early 90s, when the Prasar Bharati Bill was still collecting dust, that there was talk of regulating the cable industry since there was much litigation surrounding it. This had to do with copyright, with the right to string wires from one end of the street to another, and so on. Strangely enough, while the cable industry was technically still illegal in 1993, the government slapped it with an entertainment tax. Some media reports from the time detail the protests about the tax. However, by 1994 the market had changed from being small entrepreneur-driven to one where the big players were coming in. That's when it finally caught the regulator's eye and was declared as illegal under the Indian Telegraph Act.

Broadcasting Broadcasting regulation took a positive turn only after a landmark judgement by the Supreme Court, which finally lent legitimacy to private broadcasters. In the judgement on a suit filed by the MIB against the Cricket Association of Bengal[28] for the telecast rights of the Hero Cup 1994,

---

[28] The Cricket Association of Bengal had sold the rights of the Hero Cup to ESPN, a new private entrant into India at that time. However, being a foreign broadcaster, ESPN was not allowed to uplink from India. That made it impossible for it to broadcast the match live from Kolkata. The Supreme Court judgement was born out of the litigation that followed this controversy.

the Supreme Court ruled that the airwaves are not the monopoly of the Indian government. They are public property and have to be used to foster plurality and diversity of views, opinions and ideas. This was implicit in Article 19 (1) (a) of the Indian Constitution, granting the right of free speech to citizens, said the judgement. Therefore the supremacy of a few bodies or individuals to dominate the airwaves can cause the domination of media and would harm—not serve—the principle of plurality. It was after this forward-looking judgement that talks veered around drafting a Broadcasting Bill. After several drafts and many delays, the Broadcasting Bill mutated into the current Communications Convergence Bill. It is modelled on the Convergence Bill of Malaysia and seeks to be a master legislation for IT, telecom and media. The Bill addresses both 'carriage' or distribution and 'content' or software issues. It also provides for a super regulator, i.e., the Communications Commission of India (CCI), an FCC kind of body that would govern IT, telecom and media. The CCI would handle all licensing and regulatory functions in these three areas. The bill also provides for a spectrum management committee, essentially a body that would allocate frequency for telecom, IT or media purposes. If both the Houses of the Parliament ever passed it, the Bill would repeal:

The Indian Telegraph Act, 1885
The Indian Wireless Telegraphy Act of, 1933
The Telegraph Wires (unlawful possession) Act, 1950
The Cable Television Networks (Regulation) Act, 1995
The Telecom Regulatory Authority of India Act, 1997

The formation of a CCI could be a dramatically forward-looking step—if it works out without the bureaucracy and hassles common with most government bodies. A CCI is the ideal solution in an industry where technology changes every few months, bringing about changes in business imperatives. Therefore, having a law that locks into a certain technology would stunt the industry. The Digital Millennium Copyright Act of 1998 (DMCA) in the US was a response to a technology, MP3. While users have moved beyond MP3, the law has become largely obsolete. In a convergence scenario, locking any one part of the IT, telecom or media trio to any one technology could hamper growth.

The Convergence Bill is a long way from overcoming the hurdles that most governments around the world have with media—the need to control. The example of Prasar Bharati shows that the government still has a big role in the running of the 'autonomous body'. Prasar Bharati relies on budgetary support from the government and is therefore not really independent. At various forums and even internally, broadcast industry representatives have expressed the fear that as with Prasar Bharati, the Communications Commission wouldn't be truly independent. The Convergence Bill, tabled in Parliament in the last part of 2001, was referred to a standing committee and finally lapsed.

Distribution The regulating of the business began with The Cable Television Networks (Regulation) Act, which came into being in March 1995. Essentially, it regulates the setting up, content and equipment used by cable television operators in India. There are provisions making it mandatory for all cable television operators to register at a cost of Rs 500 with the postmaster of the local post office. It also put a foreign equity cap of 49 per cent on cable network companies.

Then came The Cable TV Networks Amendment Bill of 2000. This makes it mandatory to carry three DD channels in the prime band.[29] It also makes it the cable operator's responsibility to ensure that he does not carry any programme in respect of which copyright exists under the Indian Copyright Act without the requisite license. This implies, says media lawyer Ashni Parekh, that it is the cable operator's responsibility to first get the permission for re-transmission of any programme or film on cable TV.

To this Bill, the government added an amendment in 2002, making conditional access systems mandatory. The government's intention was good, but the amendment was flawed. It was silent on who would bear the cost of the technology and gave the government too much power to decide what channels will be watched, where and at what price. Ideally that is something that the CCI, if formed, could decide. In any case, addressability has rarely been mandated anywhere else in the world.

To deal with the litigation, protest and the mess surrounding CAS in January 2004, the MIB issued a notification expanding the scope of the expression 'telecommunication services' to include broadcasting and cable services as well. As a result, TRAI is now empowered to regulate these services. TRAI can make recommendations on issues regarding tariffs, interconnect and so on. It cannot, however, regulate content. Even TRAI couldn't do much about the CAS amendment, which collapsed under its own inconsistencies of logic. TRAI has, however, taken its role of broadcast regulator seriously. It has frozen cable rates, then allowed a 7 per cent increase, issued consultation papers and guidelines on everything from digitisation of cable TV to DTH. For whatever it is worth, it has thrown up for debate all the issues surrounding distribution of TV signals, invited everyone for its open house debates and generally played the regulator's role with some degree of common sense. In an industry where there was no regulation to one where issues of competition, pricing and technology are thrown up for discussion and where detailed consultation papers have been issued (visit *www.trai.gov.in*) is a long way to have travelled from 1991.

Direct to home broadcasting (DTH): Earlier, in 1997, the government had banned the KU-band after Star TV advertised that it was launching a DTH service. In 2001, it opened it up for broadcasting. However, the policy states

---

[29] The prime band is a frequency that all television sets in India can receive. It can however accommodate only 11 channels. Therefore having a channel on the prime band is crucial to ensuring complete reach.

that a broadcasting or cable company cannot own more than 20 per cent in a DTH venture. The total foreign equity cap in DTH is 49 per cent including FIIs, OCBs, NRIs, et al. Within this 49 per cent, not more than 20 per cent should be FDI. This is possibly the only instance of a cross-media restriction in India. Also, a DTH operator cannot create its own content or programming and therefore its own channels. It cannot enter into any exclusive contracts to distribute TV channels. The set-top-box that a DTH operator provides to its subscriber must have open architecture that meets the Bureau of Indian Standard (BIS) specifications set out in 2003. That means another DTH operator should be able to offer a service with the same box. There is no limit on the number of DTH licenses that can be issued, each for a 10-year period.

Others In addition to the above laws these are some of the guidelines and codes laid down by the Ministry of Information and Broadcasting that are applicable to the broadcasting industry:

Guidelines for uplinking from India: When satellite television came to India, foreign broadcasters were not allowed to uplink from India.[30] In June 1998, the government stated that Indian companies with Indian equity of not less than 80 per cent and effective management control in Indian hands were allowed to uplink from India through Videsh Sanchar Nigam Limited (VSNL). For this purpose, they needed clearance from the MIB. In 1999, the cabinet allowed all Indian broadcast companies to uplink without making the mandatory use of VSNL. This was further liberalised in 2000. All broadcasters, irrespective of their ownership and management, are now allowed to uplink from India. The only caveat being that they have to adhere to all the other norms, such as the advertising and broadcasting codes.

In March 2003, these norms were further changed. Any news and current affairs channel, that uplinks out of India cannot have more than 26 per cent foreign equity or foreign holding of any kind. The policy also states that any channel that has even a small component of news will be treated as a news channel and has to adhere to the guideline. There is no restriction on foreign equity in production of software, marketing of TV rights, airtime and advertisements. According to an August 2005 notification, the Government has so far permitted 58 companies to uplink 161 private TV channels from India. Seventeen companies allowed to uplink 68 TV channels have varying degrees of foreign equity. The remaining 41 companies permitted to uplink 93 TV channels have 100 per cent Indian equity. The Ministry, however, does not maintain records of channels uplinked from outside India, which are also available to viewers in India.

---

[30] Uplink and downlink—Uplink means sending a television signal from the ground to the satellite. The satellite then bounces it back to the targeted location. The process of catching the signal sent back by the satellite with a dish antennae is called downlinking. Typically cable operators or MSOs do this.

Guidelines for downlinking: In November 2005 the Ministry of Information and Broadcasting came out with guidelines for downlinking of channels that are uplinked from outside India. In essence these make it mandatory for such broadcasters to have companies registered in India. The idea is to ensure that they are tax-paying entities that do not repatriate the money they earn in India.

These state that no person/entity shall downlink a channel, which has not been registered by the Ministry of Information and Broadcasting under these guidelines:

- The entity applying for permission for downlinking a channel, uplinked from abroad, must be a company registered in India under the Indian Companies Act, 1956, irrespective of its equity structure, foreign ownership or management control
- The applicant company must have a commercial presence in India with its principal place of business in India
- The applicant company must either own the channel it wants downlinked for public viewing, or must enjoy, for the territory of India, exclusive marketing/distribution rights for the same, inclusive of the rights to the advertising and subscription revenues for the channel and must submit adequate proof at the time of application
- In case the applicant company has exclusive marketing/distribution rights, it should also have the authority to conclude contracts on behalf of the channel for advertisements, subscription and programme content

Programme code: This broadly prohibits the criticism of friendly countries, attack on religions, communities, anything obscene, defamatory or inflammatory, affecting the integrity of the nation and so on.

Advertising code: It prohibits the advertising of tobacco products including *pan masala* and liquor. Advertisements should also not project a derogatory image of women or endanger the safety of children. The products and services advertised should be in consonance with the laws enacted to protect the rights of the consumer. The Cable Act has a similar advertising and programme code.

Payment: Earlier, under exchange control regulations, advertisers buying airtime on foreign channels—whether telecasting into India or not—had to show that they have earned over Rs 1 million in exports in each of the last two years before they could advertise. This needed a banker's certificate which stated the same before paying for the airtime in rupees or dollars. Advertisers without export earnings could advertise subject to RBI clearance. This took anywhere between 2–20 days. This was because many channels broadcast into India via satellites that are foreign-owned and operated since earlier rules did not allow them to uplink from India. However, channels that were uplinked from India (or completely Indian-owned channels such as Sun TV or Eenadu) could accept any TV commercial including from non-exporters. This used to cause huge problems for advertisers on channels such as Star or Zee. This has since changed. Currently an advertiser can buy time on any channel in Indian rupees and does not need RBI clearance for the same.

Currently For some time now the government has been debating the appointment of a content regulator. This is because there have been complaints and at least one instance of a public interest litigation filed against obscene content on TV. This is with specific reference to music videos. However, nothing has yet happened on this front. There have, however, been cases of the licence for a channel being revoked. Also, it is now mandatory for private broadcasters to share feeds on events of 'national interest,' with DD. This is largely aimed at ensuring that DD can air cricket matches, even if it cannot afford to buy the rights to them.

ACCOUNTING NORMS

It is necessary to know two things about accounting issues in the Indian TV broadcasting and software industry. First, the legal standing of foreign broadcasters was till recently completely unclear. That made applying regular accounting norms to broadcasters fraught with problems. Second, unlike in the US where the accounting norms for television software, broadcast and cable companies are clearly laid out, in India none were created. That threw up problems on several fronts, primary among them:

Software costs: Under the US Generally Accepted Accounting Principles (GAAP), software (meaning programming) costs should be written off completely in the year of telecast. It is normal for Indian companies to write off only 30–50 per cent software costs in the year they are telecast. That pushes up the profit figure because expenses are suppressed.

On the other hand this also throws up the issue of revenue recognition. Since most software companies sell their wares to broadcast companies that may or may not telecast them in the financial year in which it was produced, the question of whether or not a software company should book revenues on it arises. According to chartered accountant Ajay Sekhri, if, in the contract between broadcaster and producer, there is no clause that could possibly reject the episodes already delivered in the future, a software producer is perfectly within its right to book revenues for it. This, incidentally is an issue that radio stations, film and music producers too face when dealing with revenue accounting.

Taxation: In 1996, the Central Board of Direct Taxes first prescribed a tax for foreign broadcasters in India. Under this, 10 per cent of its gross receipts meant for remittance abroad were taxable. Gross receipts are calculated net of ad agency commission or selling agent charges. It was like a presumptive or deemed profit rate of 10 per cent of the gross receipts. This created the problem of de-fining revenues and costs. The circular prescribing this did not, however, have any legal force. It was an ad hoc tool to deal with an industry that had sprung up out of the blue. After Budget 2001, any company broadcasting into India has to file a tax return like any other company and is subject to a corporate tax of 35 per cent. There is also a 12 per cent service tax.

Besides this, cable operators have to pay an entertainment tax that varies between Rs 35–50 of monthly collection per month. Cable television was brought under the service tax net in 2004. The industry is now subject to a 12 per cent service tax.

VALUATION

Value in the television business is derived from 'content or distribution assets'. That's jargon for the programmes that are made and shown on television and the ownership of networks that have last mile control over your home. In TV broadcasting parlance, these are assets, just like plant and machinery in manufacturing. This is because a show can be used to generate revenues in the future through re-telecast, syndication, dubbing, etc. Similarly, control over 10 million cable homes or five million DTH homes means steady annuity revenues. Some of the factors on which valuation of companies in the TV broadcasting industry are based are:

Software If Zee TV was to place equity with private investors or list a proportion of its shares,[31] one of the first things investment bankers would look at were its library and the equity of its channels among viewers. The valuation of the library is a fairly easy business. Take for example, *Astitva,* an extremely popular soap that ran on Zee TV. Now assume that Zee was to run it again in India, after three years. So if *Astitva* got a TVR of five, then three years later it could perhaps fetch a TVR of four. At that level of rating, what revenues could Zee generate based on future ad rates multiplied by advertising seconds that it could sell on *Astitva?* Any potential revenues that *Astitva* could get from airing on Zee TV UK or USA, or any of its other international channels or from dubbing or syndication rights, are added. The total is then discounted for inflation and the cash flows add-up over the period the serial will be aired. This discounted cash flow (DCF) uses future free cash flow projections and discounts them to

[31] Zee Telefilms is a listed company.

arrive at a present value, which is used to evaluate the potential for investment. Most often, it is discounted by the weighted average cost of capital. If the value arrived at through DCF analysis is lower then the current cost of the investment, the opportunity may be a good one.

Astitva is a soap opera. It has the potential to be re-aired. There are other genres of programming that may or may not have similar value. A talk show, like *Movers & Shakers,* or a sitcom has less value after three years because it is topical by nature. These, incidentally, are also less expensive to produce. A feature film, on the other hand, has a lot of value, especially if it has been a hit. That explains why broadcasters pay good money to get the satellite broadcast rights of films under production. On the other hand news programming has, arguably, the least value. That is because except for historical purposes or some syndication of the footage for documentaries, it has little re-run value. Therefore the total number of programming hours that a broadcaster has is of little relevance.

It is the composition of the hour by genre that is more important. Then again, within each genre, the judgement of what will click is also one that cannot be taken easily. For example, *Kyunkii Saas Bhi Kabhi Bahu Thi* may be an extremely popular soap. It has been running for five years. But what can one make of its re-run potential five or ten years later? Audience tastes may have changed by then. Alternatively, it may find a huge following with the starved-for-Indian-culture overseas audience. If Balaji Telefilms were to value its library, the exercise would be similar. The only difference is that unlike Zee, Balaji does not have its own vehicle. Also, it may not own all its popular soaps. There are some shows it makes for Sun or DD that could be re-aired on other channels.

Management Besides the library valuation, the management structure, corporate governance, brand equity and the like are also taken into account as for any other company. Investment bankers think that it is on issues like these that Indian companies lose out to their foreign counterparts. Foreign companies have a better sense of how to derive maximum value for a piece of software. Similarly both NDTV and TV Today, listed news broadcasters, command some premium for the quality of management.

Distribution Globally, distribution is valued in terms of per subscriber or per household. There are two things that are taken into consideration. First is the revenue and profit that a network is generating per subscriber. Second, its potential to increase that number. This is calculated by looking at the cost of upgrading a network, say Hathway or Siti Cable, and the improved cash flow this would generate. At its peak, Zee's Siti Cable was valued at $1.9 billion. Roughly that put a value of Rs 17,000 per subscriber that Siti Cable covered. A similar logic will be used to calculate the worth of a DTH operator or a telecom operator offering TV signals.

3 film

Welcome to the new Indian film industry

THIS BUSINESS GETS full marks, for becoming a business. The film industry, as I see it today, is not the one I have been following and writing about, for more than a decade.[1] From production to distribution to film retail, every major part of the business is either going through rapid transformation or has already transformed. One can no longer call it an industry in change mode. This is a new Indian film industry. It speaks a new language—when it is making films, when it is marketing and distributing them and when it is retailing them. There are more than a dozen major film companies that now produce a bulk of the films released in India instead of thousands of individual producers. These companies are also getting into distribution, many have a music arm and others are into film retail (see Figures 3.1 and 3.2).

In fact, it would be fair to say, that retail has led the change in the Indian film industry. Film retail, digital or non-digital, has attracted the maximum investment, and some of the best valuations in media through 2004–05. One of the biggest private equity deals in media in 2005 was when Reliance Lands bought a controlling 51 per cent stake in Adlabs Films owned by Manmohan Shetty. Shringar Cinemas, and UTV, among others, raised money on the bourses and got a good valuation.

There is an investment of over Rs 35 billion going into new cinema screens or refurbishing old ones. So, the infrastructure to bring people back to the theatres is being built rapidly. In cities and towns across India, watching a film is a much better experience thanks to multiplexes. In smaller towns and rural areas, audiences are coming back to the theatres because of digital cinemas. More than a 100 new multiplex screens, about 225 digital screens and the thousands more coming up, make retail the key element of the change.

---

[1] Unless specified the words 'industry' and 'film industry', refer to the Indian film industry.

Figure 3.1: The Growth of the Film Conglomerates

Company	Production	Distribution	Retail	Music	Home-Video
Yash Raj Films	✓	✓		✓	✓
RGV Films	✓				
Percept Picture Company	✓	✓			
UTV	✓	✓			
Pritish Nandy Communications	✓	✓			
Dharma Productions	✓				
Mukta Arts	✓	✓			
Adlabs Films	✓	✓	✓		
Real Image			✓		
Valuable Media			✓		
Pyramid Saimira			✓		
Saregama	✓			✓	✓
Time Video				✓	✓
Excel Home Video					✓
Ultra				✓	✓
Shemaroo					✓
Sony Pictures	✓	✓			✓
K. Sera Sera	✓	✓			
Shringar Cinemas	✓	✓	✓		
PVR Cinemas		✓	✓		
INOX Leisure		✓	✓		

Note: (i) ✓ represents the area of the film business these companies operate in. (ii) Distribution includes overseas distribution as well. (iii) Film retail includes multiplexes and digital theatres.

Figure 3.2: The Growth of the Film Conglomerates

Company	Revenues (Rs million) Mar–05
Yash Raj Films	5000.00
Sahara India Mass Communication	2108.1
UTV Software	1804
Adlabs Films	875.5
PVR Cinemas	862.3
INOX Leisure	614.8
Mukta Arts	480
K.C. Bokadia	408
AB Corp	398.5
Shringar Cinemas	389.9
Pritish Nandy Communications	348.8
K. Sera Sera	374.6
GV Films	28.6

Note: (i) The figures for AB Corp are for the nine months ended September 2004. (ii) The revenue for many of these companies are not only for the film business. They are inclusive of other businesses. For example UTV or Sahara are also into other businesses, like television software and broadcasting.

Source: CapitalinePlus, annual reports and industry estimates.

Digital cinemas, which open up the market in the heart of India's mass markets, make for the biggest change sweeping across the business. There are more than half a dozen companies that will be digitising over 3,000 theatres over the next three years. That makes India the digital cinema laboratory of the world. If India achieves half that number it will become the largest digital screen country in the world.

However, that milestone is less important than what it will mean for the film business. It will rejuvenate an almost dead box-office in small-town India, plug an old revenue leak, and neutralise piracy as well. Retail chains—digital and otherwise—are already changing the way thousands of Indians watch films. Eventually and irrevocably they will change the way we make and sell movies. We can fathom only a few of these changes now. For one, just the fact that a company controls 400 theatres in a sub-billion dollar badly fragmented market, gives it enough power to get a better deal from production companies. It gives film production companies the equivalent of a Wal-Mart in the film retail market. Two, it revives in-film and in-theatre advertising long given up for dead. Three, these retail chains want a steadier pipeline of films. This, in turn, is forcing changes in production and distribution of films (refer to 'The way it is').

Home video, another part of the film retail business, too shows promise. It brought in Rs 10 billion in revenue in 2004 and is expected to grow at 25–30 per cent every year, for the next few years. In marketing and distribution film companies have been quicker than music and radio companies to realise the potential of both digital distribution and digital promotion. Almost every major release has a website, a web partner and a mobile strategy that brings in a sweet sliver of revenues. In-film advertising, co-branding, on-site advertising, in-cinema advertising are all words that roll out easily from the mouths of film executives these days. By the end of 2005 the Indian film industry touched over Rs 79 odd billion in revenues—well on its way to becoming a profitable, attractive destination for investors to park their money.[2]

If there is one industry that has learnt the lesson of its bad years well, it has to be this one. It has faced the maximum derision from investors and from business analysts. How it is the world's largest yet not organised, depends on underworld money, is a den of vice and worse. For one of the most resilient, creative and prolific industries in the world, it was an ill-deserved reputation. Just like publishing, filmmaking too has been a victim of history. Making movies used to be a robust, healthy business till the star system and the lack of institutional finance led to its collapse in the late 40s. Yet, the industry survived. It continued to do so for over 100 years, without being acknowledged as an industry. It made films and kept millions of people employed while entertaining several other millions. Most people expected the industry to clean up its books,

---

[2] See Figure 3.3 for details on how that revenue figure is calculated.

make profits, 'corporatise', 'professionalise'… in short, wipe away over 50 years of business cobwebs in a couple of years. That did not happen in the immediate euphoria of getting industry status in 2000.

Now, five years later, one can say with confidence that there is an 'Indian film business.' And, it is not just 'Bollywood.' This is probably the only part of this book where this word will be used. It does not stand for or signify the Indian film industry. It stands for a pejorative term that was coined to a prolific industry that was a bit of a joke. Something that was not—quite—Hollywood. Most senior actors and film personalities in Indian cinema actually object to the use of the word. Also, the Indian film industry includes dozens of languages and all of the country's variety. It is not only the Hindi film industry. That is the other reason why making this distinction is important.

Now that the pain of transformation has passed, there is much to do. Currently the Indian film business is busy building the infrastructure in the domestic market: infrastructure to make films, to watch them and to distribute them on a large scale. This scale will also increase its risk-taking ability and therefore its ambition.

That is when it will be ready to take on the world. For some time now India has been the flavour of the times, culturally, in food, fashion and several other areas. While films generate a buzz, it has not converted into business. There has been the feeling that Indian films are only for the domestic market. And the way to crack the international markets is to make a crossover film. I believe that well-scripted, well-told, Indian stories have a market. Where Indian film companies lose, is on marketing and distribution strength. It is here that some application is needed. Dozens of Indian brands including Tanishq and VIP Luggage have tried to establish themselves in the international market. It is a long haul. Indian films have so far found success only with the diaspora. To occupy a place of pride in world cinema, it seems important, to have a mainstream release and appeal to everyone in, say, the US or UK. As they build scale in the domestic business (see Figure 3.3), as they figure out the intricacies of the international markets, with its sales agents and studios and art-house circuits and mainstream circuits, Indian film companies will eventually crack that market open too. It is a matter of time. The fun will be if they do it with an Indian story.

THE PAST

After Thomas Edison perfected the Kinetograph, a camera that was capable of photographing objects in motion, the first motion picture studio was formed to manufacture Kinetoscopes. These first few movies, essentially filmstrips

Figure 3.3: The Growth of the Indian Film Industry

Year	1978–79	1982	1998	1999	2000	2001	2002	2003	2004	2005
Number of films	612	761	693	764	855	1013	942	877	934	na
Admissions (tickets sold) (billion units)	na	na	2.8	3	3.1	3.2	2.8	2.87	2.9	3
Number of screens	na	na	12900	12900	12500	12000	na	12000	12000	12000
Box office gross (Rs billion)	2.47	3.86	16.8	17.95	21.87	24.53	28	43.05	43.5	60
Other revenues (music, TV, overseas home video, digital) (Rs Billion)	na	0.146	na	na	4	4	10	10	10	18.5
Cinema advertising (Rs billion)	na	na	0.5	0.62	0.7	0.79	0.79	0.82	0.98	1.17
Total revenues	2.47	3.86	17.3	18.01	26.57	29.32	38.79	53.87	54.48	79.67

Note: (i) The figure for box-office gross is an underestimate as money usually leaks out of the distribution system. Also the average price at which many of the consultants calculate gross is Rs 10. A higher average of Rs 15–20 might be a better indicator, since ticket prices have gone up across the country. In Figure 3.3, for 2002 the gross is calculated at an average ticket price of Rs 10, for 2003 and 2004 at Rs 15. It is calculated at Rs 20 per ticket in 2005 (ii) The box office figure for 2001 includes overseas revenues of Rs 1.46 billion (iii) In 1978/79, the box office figures are for 1978–79 but the total number of films refer only to 1978 (iv) The figures for 2003 are sourced from KPMG's report on the Indian entertainment industry, for FICCI's FRAMES conference in 2003. (v) The number of screens is taken as constant since enough data is not available. (vi) The figure for other revenues is an estimate and has been assumed constant for 2002, 2003 and 2004, since accurate data is not available. (vii) na–not available.

Source: Encyclopedia of India Cinema–Ashish Rajadhyaksha and Paul Willemen, Film Federation of India, PricewaterhouseCoopers Global Media and Entertainment Outlook 2004–08, Lodestar Media and estimates.

viewed through a peephole machine were then shown at a 'Kinetoscope parlour' on lower Broadway in New York. It was extremely popular and crowds milled around to see it.

Soon after that, films came to India. The first film was screened in India on July 7, 1896, at The Watson's Hotel, Bombay (now Mumbai). The *Arrival of a Train at Ciotat Station* and *Leaving the Factory*, the first reels ever shot of a real film had been screened just six months ago in Paris, at their 'world premiere'. The Lumiere operator Maurice Sestier was on his way to Australia. He stopped over in India to show what *The Times of India* hailed as 'The marvel of the century'. The film was presented to an audience of English and some 'western-ised' Indians. A week after the Sestier screening, Novelty Theatre started projecting short films from the Lumiere repertoire. These were accompanied by an orchestra and—of course—ran to full houses.[3]

Soon there were travelling theatre companies screening films in theatres and *maidans* across the country. There was James B. Stewart's Vitagraph shows in 1897 and the Moto-Photoscope created by Ted Hughes. By this time, the first few screenings had been made in Calcutta (now Kolkata) and Madras (now Chennai) too. The projection of short films with titles like *The Races in Poona* or *A Train Entering the Station in Bombay*, began. Many of these were shot by European cameramen or by Indian enthusiasts like Hiralal Sen. Other subjects included bazaars, religious processions, plays and monuments. A lot of the impetus for these films came from the English. By 1901, Indians became good at using the medium too. Sakharam Bhatavdekar, a Marathi photographer from Bombay, echoed nationalist sentiments in the film, *The Return of Wrangler Paranjpye to India*. Paranjpye was a mathematician who had been honoured at Cambridge. Sen and Bhatavdekar are referred to as the first Indian filmmakers.

The business of cinema started almost as soon as the medium took off in India. Whether it was setting up studios, or theatres or importing the equipment, enough people got into the act. The investments came largely from American or European companies like Pathe. It was one of the first few to open a branch in Bombay in 1907 to sell equipment. Gaumont, Éclair Vitagraph and others followed.

In 1905 came the Elphinstone Bioscope Company from Jamshedjee Framjee Madan. The films his company made were nationalistic—like Jyotish Sarkar's films on the protest rally against Partition. J.F. Madan quickly spread his wings with a chain of 'picture palaces' (cinema halls) across the country and, by 1927, owned 50 per cent of the Indian cinema distribution network. He also dominated film production in India for a long time. There were others like

---

[3] The background on the industry, names of films and dates has been sourced from three books. Thoraval, Yves (2000), Rajadhyaksha and Willemen (1994); and Vogel, Harold (1998). Each of them is outstanding in the range and depth of information they offer. The Lumiere was a brand of camera.

Abdulally Esoofally, who moved with tents, cameras and projectors to show their wares to hungry audiences across the country. Clearly, cinema had taken off. From the urban to the rural areas, people switched from theatre to cinema. In response to the growing demand, 'picture palaces' or 'permanent cinema halls' or theatres as we know them started to appear in 1906–07. By 1909, within 15 years of the first film being screened, there were more than 30 theatres in India. Audiences were watching mostly American and European (largely French art) films on these screens. Most of these were newsreels on, say, the Boer War or the funeral of Queen Victoria.

The birth of Indian cinema There is some ambiguity about the first Indian feature film. Chronologically it seems to have been *Pundalik*, a religious film released in 1912. It was directed by Nanabhai Govind Chitre, Ram Chandra Gopal Torney and P.R. Tipnis; all of them from Marathi theatre. However, Dhundiraj Govind Phalke is crowned as the father of Indian cinema. He produced, directed, processed and did everything to make the first proper Indian feature film, *Raja Harishchandra*. Unlike most film makers of those days Phalke did not have the westernised audience in mind. His vision was to use the medium to narrate an Indian story to an Indian audience. *Raja Harishchandra* was released on April 21, 1913, and needless to say became a great hit. It went on to be released in 20 versions and in eight languages.

The importance of this film is not its position in India's chronological film history, but in the three important things it signified. First, the mass of the audience was Indian and therefore making a film for Indians would get more people involved and interested. Second, Indians like to be told a story they are familiar with. At that time, mythology provided the basic fare. Everyone knew the story of *Raja Harishchandra*. In fact, for a large chunk of the illiterate audience, the explanatory texts in Hindi, Urdu and English made no sense. The live accompaniment of text and chanting did. And that is the third point, songs and dances have been an integral part of cinema's narrative form right from the beginning. The narrative form of Indian films was influenced by mythology. Earlier they were made into plays, with song and dance as an essential part of the narrative. Films followed the narrative style of drama. Indian audiences, long used to it, were completely comfortable watching it on screen. This is pertinent. Many Indians feels sheepish about the songs and dances in our movies, but there is a historical context to them. For generations, storytelling in India has been a combination of the spoken word, song and dance.

The studio years Soon Phalke set up his own studio, The Hindustan Films Cinema Company. He followed up with several mythologicals like *Bhasmasur Mohini* and *Kaliya Mardan*. There were several other studios that came up. There was Ardeshir Irani's Star Film Company; R.S. Prakash's Star of the East Film Company in Madras; Rewashankar Pancholi's Empire Film Distributors in Karachi and Lahore, among others. By the beginning of the 20s the pioneering phase was over and the business had begun in earnest. Studios vied with one another for actors, actresses, storywriters and lyricists. By 1923 an entertainment tax at 12.5 per cent was levied on films in Bombay. By 1927, a few film magazines—*Movie Mirror* (Madras); *Kinema* (Bombay); and *Photoplay* (Calcutta)—were also launched. Bombay, Madras and Calcutta were beginning to dominate the action in Indian cinema.

At this point in time only 15 per cent of the films being distributed in India were Indian. The rest were foreign, of which more than 90 per cent were American. World War I had almost killed European cinema, leaving the field wide open to Hollywood. To counter these 'American imports' with censorship, the English government appointed The Indian Cinematograph Committee. It published its report in 1927–28. The report did not recommend preferential treatment for British films. Instead it suggested a series of measures to promote Indian films. These were—financial incentives to producers, the abolition of raw stock duty and a reduction in entertainment tax. The British administration just ignored the report. As luck would have it, successive governments did the same and the film industry never did get the hearing it deserved till 1998.

Let us go back to 1931 when *Alam Ara*, the first talkies, was released. It was one among 28 films made that year. The break-up of these films gives an insight into that time: 23 of these were in Hindi, four in Bengali and one in Tamil. Bombay was already becoming the centre of the cinema business. By the 40s, films were a proper business with Bombay Talkies, Prabhat and Wadia Movietone among the top film companies. The corporatisation did not take away from the joy of cinema if one goes by the material from the period.

It was an exciting time to be in films, whether as an actor, a writer, a lyricist or even as a journalist. It was an informal world where intellectual bonding mattered more than money or connections. Many financiers and producers would actually put up writers and actors in their homes till they 'made it'. Many actors started their own companies. Ashok Kumar, for example, broke away with a few of the employees of the top rated Bombay Talkies, to form Filmistan. Bombay became very much like Hollywood, a rich cauldron of intellectual, sexual and creative bubbling that kept the dream factories going. It is clear from much of the writing of that time, or even from conversations with people from that era, that cinema was one of the few progressive/modern bastions in the country. Everybody—irrespective of religion, political leanings, nationality or social background—found a place in this world. There were courtesans and their daughters who played the female roles that 'respectable' women did not. There were leftists, right-wingers and sons of rich families who financed the films; as also directors and actors from Germany, England and Russia, among other countries.[4]

113

---

[4] The Bombay film world of the 40s is very interestingly presented by Manto, Saadat Hasan (1998). The English book is a translation of the original short pieces written by Manto in Urdu.

They enjoyed the creative process thoroughly, yet it was clear that making films was a business. The system worked like a well-oiled machine. Writers and actors and all the rest were on the payrolls of major studios. Most were based on the European or American film industry, which were organised. If someone wanted to make films, they formed a studio, hired lots of writers, lyricists, actors and actresses, and churned out films. The best studios were the best paymasters with the best staff—whether it was in acting or writing or making music. For example, the famous Hindi novelist, Munshi Premchand, was hired by Ajanta Cinetone for a salary of Rs 8,000—significantly high going by the standards of 1934.

A film was budgeted once a studio decided on it. Amrit Shah, who worked with Bimal Roy during 1955–68, remembers that he would add in 10 per cent extra for unforeseen expenses after the budgeting. The budget was then split up among the distributors of the various territories that India was divided into, by the studio. For instance, Delhi would pay 20 per cent of it. The ratio, says Shah, remains the same today. The agreements between the distributor and the studio were based either on minimum guarantees, advance or on commission or on a combination of all the three (refer to 'The Way it Works'). The usual distribution agreement was minimum guarantee (MG) plus cost of print. Once that was in place work on a film started.

By 1944, this system had started breaking up. Bloated with war profits, financiers tried to launder their money through the studio system. Star salaries and budgets became bigger and so did the egos. Breakaways became more common. Things started changing in other ways too. In 1949, post Independence, entertainment tax was raised to 50 per cent in the central provinces and 75 per cent in West Bengal. In the same year, the government appointed a committee under S.K. Patil to report on all aspects of cinema. In 1951 (and this is pertinent), the committee reported on the shift away from the studio system to independents. It noted the entry of black money and the star system into films. This may sound familiar, but it recommended major state investment in films, setting up of a film finance corporation, a film institute and film archives. The report, like others before it, was ignored for more than a decade. Some of the recommendations were finally implemented in 1960 with the setting up of the Film Finance Corporation; a film institute at Poona (now Pune); The Institute for Film Technology in Madras; and The Hindustan Photo Film Manufacturing Company. Later, in 1965, the National Film Archive of India was also set up in Poona. Many of these moves along with others—canalising imports of raw stock through the State Trading Corporation (STC) and later the Film Finance Corporation (FFC), and censorship—increased the government's hold on the film industry.

The messy years The 70s and 80s were arguably the worst years for Indian cinema. That is not necessarily a comment on the quality of films made but on the state of the business. The break up of the studio system had led to financial and systemic chaos that the film industry has to yet recover from. Studios, of that time, hired employees who would turn out about half-a-dozen films over a year or two. This spread the risk of making films, helping them cover a bad film's losses with the gains from a good one. With the break-up of the studios, many individuals became producers. There were now numerous producers bearing the individual risks of making one film each instead of a handful of studios bearing the collective risk of 5–10 films each. This fragmentation changed the economics of the game.

The first thing that changed was the colour of money coming into the industry. Since there was no industry status and, therefore, no institutional finance, most of the money flowing into the industry came from people who had a lot of black money that they wanted to park.[5] The estimates of unaccounted money range from 25–50 per cent of the total money floating around in the industry. Most producers did not question where the money came from because they were desperate. The interest rates that distributors and producers were paying on this money could range from 48–60 per cent per annum. The people making the films agreed to pay them because the risks of the business had gone up dramatically. Anybody putting their money in a film had a 2–3 per cent chance of making profits. It was like gambling with high stakes. The returns were stupendous if the film became a mega hit. It may be argued that earlier too black money could have flowed into the studio system—but the proportion must have been minuscule. In the 40s, studios operated on salaries and cheques like regular companies. It was not so easy to put black money past them. In the 60s, 70s and 80s, it seems that the only time cheques were issued was when raw stock was purchased and excise duty was paid on completion.

When a producer announced a film depending on his star cast, not the story or the director, distributors would line up to pay an advance.[6] A Raj Kapoor or a Yash Chopra had no problem getting money because they usually got the big stars; who in turn ensured a basic collection at the ticket windows. If Amitabh Bachchan starred in the film, it meant that people would flock to see the film at least for 2–3 weeks ... if not more. The chances of recovering costs and making more money were higher than when the cast was completely unknown. That is the reason he was called a 'one-man-industry'. Also, film-makers like Chopra or producers like Gulshan Rai found it easier to raise money

---

[5] One part of the reason could also be that income tax rates were terribly high. So there was less declaration and undeclared black money found its way into the industry.

[6] A producer is the man who usually puts together the entire film, from money to cast to directors. The idea may come from a writer or director, but the producer literally gives birth to the film. A distributor is like a wholesaler. He buys the film for a particular territory and then hawks it to different retailers—cinema hall owners in this case. For the purposes of distribution India is split up into 11 territories. There is usually a clutch of distributors who dominate each territory.

because they had and still have a good sense of what is popular. It was Yash Chopra's instincts that were being bet on, based on his record of course.

If a smaller producer announced a film with relatively unknown actors, he had a tough time raising money. Such producers would raise money on their own, through financiers; shoot a few reels and show the distributor. If the latter liked what he saw, he would agree to pay an advance for the film. The shooting of the film would begin, again. Some of this money was borrowed, some came from the distributor's own pocket. The glamour and the need to be associated with film-land, in spite of its endemic business problems, was so high that money kept pouring in. Unlike the men who put their money in the old studios, these new financiers wanted to dictate terms on scripts, stars, directors, music and everything else. The high risk of making a film had killed creativity to some extent, this only added to it.

The words 'formula' and 'star system' were born. 'Formula' was the safest kind of film to make. What the formula was, depended on the trend at that time. If romantic films were doing well then, then romance was the formula; if action movies were all the rage, then action it was. Nobody wanted to take a risk with an unknown subject or stars, especially the distributors who were bankrolling the film.

It was not as if experiments did not happen. These, however, were few and usually financed by the government through the National Film Development Corporation (NFDC). The 'parallel' cinema movement was the result. Even that had its caste system. Actors like Shabana Azmi, Om Puri and Naseeruddin Shah—the icons of parallel cinema—were a must if the film sought state funding. The economics of the business had therefore the disastrous effect of choking creativity.

As for the 'star system', that too was as much a result of the economics. If actors like Rajesh Khanna (at the peak of his stardom), or Amitabh Bachchan, were signed on, then it did not matter if the film was bad or delayed: it was financed. So stars became very important. This is something that happens in Hollywood too; only it is more structured. If Julia Roberts is a box-office draw, the market chases her and everybody wants her in his/her film and prices do get pushed up. However, when she signs on, she reports to a studio and is under contract to complete the film. She has to be totally professional about coming on time, completing the film and so on. Those things went out of the window from the 60s onwards in India. Delays, protracted shooting schedules that meant higher costs were and are endemic.

Over the decades, the clamour to grant industry status to films was becoming louder. It had, however, become a chicken and egg situation. Since there was no institutional finance, producers depended on stars to pull in the money from dodgy financiers. This in turn meant low creativity, a bad product and an unprofessional system. It also meant a risky, loss-making business. According to one estimate, barely 2 per cent of the 763 films released in 1982 were mega hits; 16 per cent were moderate successes and 12 per cent broke even. Of all the films released that year 70 per cent sank without a trace, along with the billions of rupees that must have gone into making them. The bottomline—films were an unattractive investment for a bank even if the business was given industry status.

The studios did not just 'put together' the film. They would aggregate the risk. When 10 films are made at the same time, their budgets, subjects and artistes would vary. A studio could make two large-budget formula-based films, three medium budget films and several smaller, more experimental films. The risk was spread across a clutch of products. Some would, others wouldn't; leaving the studio to either break-even or make a profit eventually. From the 50s onwards, individuals began bearing the risk increasingly. Depending on one's point of view, either the risk was greater or their capacity to bear it was lower. Since they could make only one product there was no portfolio and—hence—no de-risking. Plus, since there was no money to put in more than one product, they depended only on one film.

Add to this the complete lack of alternate revenue streams. Except for theatres, there were no other ways for producers, distributors and financiers to recover their money. The overseas market had a patchy record with some exceptions. Satyajit Ray's *Pather Panchali* had a successful 226-day run at Playhouse on Fifth Avenue in New York, breaking a 30-year record for foreign releases in the US. Raj Kapoor had similar success in Russia. None of this translated into huge business for the industry since marketing and distribution remained dollar-intensive. In those days of foreign-exchange shortages, the overseas markets were not something that Indian filmmakers could cultivate. Most producers sold their overseas rights for a song, to companies like Eros International. In 1982, the only year for which this figure is available, the overseas market brought in just Rs 146 million.

Music companies, another source of revenues later, hardly paid anything since HMV (now Saregama) was a virtual monopoly. As for theatres in the 80s, they were dying. Land prices were high, there were impractical rules for cinema halls, and there was an entertainment tax of anywhere between 50–80 per cent depending on the state. Theatre owners or exhibitors, charged as much as 50–60 per cent of a film's collections as rent and yet they couldn't make money. In order to do that, they had to either under-declare revenues or make do with very low returns—anywhere between 3–5 per cent—on their investment. In cities like Mumbai or Delhi, where land prices are high, most chose to morph into shopping complexes. Others ignored the need to renovate, maintain clean toilets, paint or put air conditioning systems. As a result, the number of theatres and the theatre-going habit, especially in big cities, went down over the decades. Between 1989 and 1993, the number of theatres fell from 13,355 to 13,001.

According to the National Readership Survey (NRS) data the number of cinemagoers plummeted from 12.2 million in 1986 to five million by 1992 (see Figure 3.4). It continues to do so.

New revenue streams like cable or video did come up in the 80s. Instead of adding to a film's revenues, these took away from the same. Cable television in India began on the back of video piracy. The early cable operators hooked entire buildings onto one VCR and aired the latest Hindi or English film (refer to the chapter on Television). This hit film revenues in two ways: One, it reduced the walk-ins into a theatre thereby reducing box-office revenues. Two, it did not bring in the royalties that screening old or new films on TV usually entails. This holds true even now. The latest hits are shown on local cable TV channels. Nobody pays for these; they generate advertising in multiples of tens of millions, none of which ever gets passed on to the film industry.

It is not as if the government or progressive minds within the industry were not aware of these problems. Right from the S.K. Patil Committee Report in 1951, to the Estimates Committee in 1973–74, and later, the Working Group on a National Film Policy in 1980, every committee has mentioned these. They repeatedly stressed the need to give industry status to the sector and allow for institutional financing to be made available through banks. Some of the 1980 committee's remarks are telling. 'Popular entertainment films have to be liberated from the over-dependence on standard box-office ingredients. These films should also provide an opportunity for creative expression. This can only be done if the production of popular films is freed from the clutches of financiers'. Earlier reports had pointed to the entry of black money in films. The evidence was there and so was the solution but nothing was done.

The 90s By the end of the 80s, the industry was in extremely bad shape. When satellite television hit India in 1991, the mood was despondent. Things, however, began changing around this time: partly because the industry found innovative (for that time) ways out of its conundrum, and partly because the market had altered in four ways.

One: due to cable TV, video and later satellite television, films had competition for the first time. Till the mid-80s, films had—for better or for worse—a captive audience. People had no other avenue for entertainment except films. There was one television channel and one radio station. The competition for the viewer's time had begun, and the viewer was choosing to watch a pirated film at home to going to a dirty, smelly theatre. His attention span too had reduced because he had more options. He was less likely to sit through a bad movie even if it had big stars.

Two: by this time Amitabh Bachchan, the last of the big stars, was on the decline. In fact he retired (but only for a bit) after *Khuda Gawah* (1992). There was no other major star on the horizon; at least nobody who could

Figure 3.4: Cinema Decline Across Pop Strata

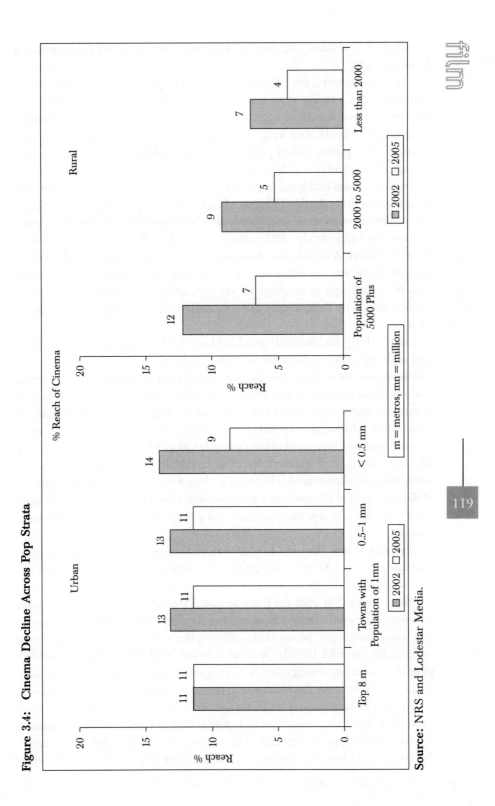

Source: NRS and Lodestar Media.

attract both financiers and audiences the way Amitabh Bachchan or Rajesh Khanna could.

Three: video and cable TV cut the time a film had to recover its money—in the theatres—to less than half. Earlier, distributors and exhibitors could wait for word-of-mouth to catch on by the second week of a film's release. If it clicked they could then keep it in the theaters for 10–12 weeks. But now, because video pirates leaked prints of the film quickly, it killed potential revenues. A film had just 2–3 weeks to recover its cost and make some money.

And four: costs had gone out of hand. In 1982 a really expensive film cost Rs 20 million to make. By 1993, this figure had gone up to Rs 30–50 million. These figures seem small compared to the budgets of some recent releases. *Lagaan* was made for Rs 250 million and *Kabhie Khushi Kabhie Gham* for Rs 450 million. A decade ago, however, these numbers were considered large because there was no other way of recovering this money except through theatres...that were in no shape to welcome audiences! Most had reverted to a rental system by then, so they did not care whether the audience was coming or not.

Clearly, things had reached some kind of nadir. The film industry did react—and with amazing chutzpah for that time. It did three things. The first was to use the music more effectively. By this time the music industry was booming. Various music companies were vying with one another to pay advances to filmmakers for music rights (refer to the chapter on Music). The rights to Subhash Ghai's film, *Khalnayak,* were sold for a reported Rs 10 million. This became a crucial source of revenue/working capital. Other filmmakers tried to get in-film advertising, and sponsors for some scenes or songs, so that some of the costs could be taken care of. The fact that these two—sponsorship and music—could cover part of the cost, was a boon to many filmmakers. They not only saved on interest but also got free promotion as a result of the tie-ins with music or a brand.

The second was the use of some very rudimentary marketing techniques that had never before been used by the film industry. Since music was the best way to draw audiences, it became common to release it a few months before the film—instead of after the film's release. The *Ek do teen* song from *Tezaab*, for instance, played a huge role in making the film a hit in 1988. Other tactics like teaser campaigns, promotions, offering free gifts, story contests and even advertising the film heavily, were also being used. From almost nothing, producers started spending roughly 10 per cent of a film's budget on promotion. Earlier, it was only the distributor who spent on radio spots, posters or trailers.

Last, on the distribution front, the industry did something that is common in the US. Since the amount of time a film had to recover its money had reduced, it made sense to release the film in a burst in a large number of theatres. By doing so, a filmmaker pulled in a major chunk of potential viewers before a film's video-copy came into circulation. It also did not allow negative word-of-mouth to catch on. Movies like *Hum* and *Khuda Gawah* were released in 450–500 theatres nationwide: against the average of 200 of that time. Releasing them simultaneously in so many theatres ensured a huge 'initial' or the first rush of viewers walking in, given that the pre-release marketing was good. This is an expensive strategy, because every additional print of the film costs more than Rs 60,000 and 450 theatres would mean 450 prints!

Many of these moves helped ease the pressure on revenues. By the late 90s, music, overseas markets and satellite television emerged as major revenue streams, bringing some more good news. The music of a really big-budget film could bring in as much as 25–30 per cent of the film's cost. *Lagaan* fetched a reported Rs 60 million from Sony Music; and *Yaadein,* Rs 85 million.

By 1998, the overseas market had emerged as a major source of revenue bringing in 30 per cent or more at times. The TV and the Internet meant a smaller world where the tastes of urban Indians matched those of Indians living overseas. Both wanted a heavy dose of culture, weddings and songs— all garnished with the right costumes and colour. Both did not want to know anything about the angst of India. The overseas market came to everyone's notice because of the 1994 family saga, *Hum Aapke Hain Kaun,* which did very well in the UK. It was followed by *Dilwale Dulhania Le Jayenge (DDLJ),* set partly in the UK and partly in India, followed by a host of other films. *DDLJ* alone did about Rs 200 million worth of business abroad, as against Rs 500 million in India.[7] Soon, films like *Taal, Pardes, Mohabbatein* and *Kuch Kuch Hota Hai* were being made with the Non-Resident Indian (NRI) audiences in mind.

Many of these films did well in semi-urban India, but really made money in the Indian metro, the UK and the US markets. It was a market that looked set to grow. The 20 million or so Indians, living overseas, earn an equivalent of roughly half of India's GDP. The difference in the currency value alone hiked what each ticket brought in. A film ticket at $10 was more profitable than the maximum of Rs 80–100 that could be charged in India then. This translated into increasingly more films with weddings and songs and dances thrown in. Note that none of the big local hits like *Satya, Sarfarosh* and *Company,* which used other themes, did significant business overseas. The only other really big overseas hits were Mani Ratnam's *Dil Se* and the Tamil, *Muthu*—both in Japan.

Cable and satellite broadcasters became big buyers of films bringing in roughly 10–15 per cent of a film's revenues. Some were sold for even more. Most broadcasters recovered that money from advertising. If a channel paid Rs 30 million to screen *Dil To Paagal Hai,* most of this money could be recovered through one or two telecasts of the film.

121

---

[7] Most of the figures for collection are as reported in the press at that time.

Finally, satiated with satellite television and the repeats of old and new movies, audiences started coming back to the theatres. The fall in NRS numbers stopped for a bit. That prompted theatre owners to begin refurbishing cinema halls. It also meant that ticket prices rose—to as much as Rs 200 in some theatres.

By 2000, music, satellite television and the overseas market were totting up roughly 70 per cent of a film's revenues. It meant a fundamental shift in the way filmmakers thought, and producers planned. It also meant filmmakers could take more risks—creatively and financially: Financially, because the business seemed to be de-risked; and creatively, because smaller, offbeat subjects or films that explored a theme that not too many people may be interested in could be made. Earlier a movie like *Astitva* would have probably run lackadaisically for a week in some seedy theatre. Instead it now ran to packed houses in smaller, 50–100-seat, theatres.

The transition years A lot of this apparent 'de-risking' and growth drew a welcome and an organised interest towards the film industry. The government, consultants, analysts, investment bankers and foreign investors all turned the spotlight on the film business.

First came the announcement giving it industry status in mid-1998.[8] Around the same time came a Federation of Indian Chambers of Commerce and Industry (FICCI) conference on the entertainment business. This was followed by the decision to allow 100 per cent foreign direct investment in films. Later tax-free multiplexes too were encouraged. The Indian Banking Association too came out with norms on film financing. This meant that banks and financial institutions could now lend to the film industry.

There was, through 2000 and 2001, a very positive air surrounding the industry. This was evident at the FICCI and CII conferences on the business.[9] All this hoopla affected filmmakers too. Budgets went up in expectation of the increased revenues and easy finance. So did the prices for music, satellite and overseas rights. A lot of this well-meaning excitement missed two things:

The first was the inherent inequity in the way films were still being made— take *Baba* as a case in point. According to reports, the Rs 100 million film sold its domestic theatrical rights to 150 theatres in the four southern states for Rs 330 million. Overseas was sold for another Rs 80 million and music

---

[8] While the announcement granting industry status to the entertainment sector, including films was made in 1998, it was notified under the IDBI Act of 1964 only in 2000, according to Siddhartha Dasgupta of The Federation of Indian Chambers of Commerce and Industry (FICCI).

[9] From 2000 onwards FICCI has held an entertainment industry event every summer. From 2001, it was branded as FRAMES. It is a 2–3 day entertainment industry event. Similarly the Confederation of Indian Industry (CII), began Entermedia, another event focusing on the media and entertainment business.

for Rs 30 million. Add in product endorsements worth Rs 60 million. The distributors, music companies and overseas buyers bought the film based on some rushes. Even before its release, *Baba* had made an estimated profit of Rs 400 million, without anybody having seen it. However—and this is very pertinent—the profit went only to a handful of people. In this case to the film's actor, Rajnikant himself, since he was also the producer. All the theatres that picked up the film, the music company and the one that bought the overseas rights, lost money. Now, multiply the *Baba* experience across five decades and thousands of films. Since distributors advanced money to producers (refer to 'The messy years'), there was an inherent inequity in the way Indian films were financed, distributed and sold. The entire risk was being borne by the distributor and/or the theatre owners. It was routine for theatre owners and distributors to under-declare revenues for good films to make up the losses for the bad ones.[10]

Second, from the late 90s onwards, sharp schisms had cropped up in film viewing habits in India. The divide between A and B class India had become wider. The urban, up-market viewer and the overseas audience, both connected with the movie *Dil Chahta Hai*. The rest of India could not. Audiences in semi-urban and rural India, which has over 50 per cent of the total theatres, prefer conservative fare. The 2002 release *Ankhiyon Se Goli Maare* (an old-fashioned formula film) did twice the business in the interiors than it did in the cities. More importantly, urban audiences were willing to pay Rs 100 or more (against the average of Rs 20) to watch something that appealed to them, and in a good theatre. The market was demanding more variety—in filmmaking, screening and pricing of tickets. Many filmmakers missed the point and continued to make one-theme-fits-all kind of films. A bulk of the new investment went into trying to reach a pan-Indian audience, at a time when there wasn't any left.

As a result, movies started flopping. Music companies, overseas buyers and domestic distributors started losing money. Each of them reacted by shunning the business.

Tips lost a reported Rs 55 million on *Yaadein*. Of the 13 albums it released in 2001, it lost money on nine. Saregama made Rs 250 million of operating losses, on a revenue of Rs 1.12 billion in 2001–02. Result: the going price for the music of big films fell to Rs 10–15 million. Smaller films were being picked up on a royalty basis.

---

[10] If one takes very conservative numbers—an average ticket price of only Rs 10 for the 3.2 billion tickets sold in 2001, Indian films should have grossed over Rs 32 billion at the box office in that year. They actually did only Rs 25 billion. Most analysts reckon that an average ticket price of Rs 15-20 would be more accurate. The fact is money leaks out of the system in large quantities and then resurfaces either as finance for films or in other industries.

Satellite channels such as Sony or Zee had paid very high prices for films, in 1995–96, when they were hungry for a spike in their ratings. As viewers started getting hooked to soaps, there was no need to spend a lot of money on films. At its best, a blockbuster such as *Kuch Kuch Hota Hai* generated television ratings (TVR) of 11 and revenues, arguably, in excess of Rs 50 million. As the reach of television increased, a hit show could do more on both counts: TVRs and revenues. Result: satellite channels began buying under-production rights or libraries. Mukta Arts sold its library—with blockbusters like *Karz, Karma* and *Ram Lakhan* among others—to Sony for Rs 160 million in 2002. Sony also bought the Indian satellite telecast rights for *Lagaan,* after seeing the film but before it was released and before it was declared a hit.

The overseas dream soured, too, because greed and over-expectation hiked the prices for all films. This, despite the fact that most filmmakers knew that the overseas market delivered only when a film had three ingredients—weddings, cultural ceremonies and (actor) Shahrukh Khan. Also, too late in the day, producers discovered that milking the overseas market needed marketing dollars. In a sub-billion-dollar, highly fragmented industry, not everybody had that. Yash Raj Films had been the only one till then to set up its own distribution offices in the UK and US. Others still depended on shady distributors. In addition there was piracy, especially on digital video discs (DVDs) that were out within the first week of the film's release. Most Indian film companies did not have the resources to fight it. So the odd *Lagaan, Kabhie Khushi Kabhie Gham, Mohabbatein, Muthu* and *Taal* remained the only overseas successes, from among the hundreds of films made every year.

However, the biggest blow was to theatres. If producers had become greedy in pushing all the new revenue sources too far, even distributors did the same. The bidding for films reached some terrific highs in 2000–01. Distributors who paid advances for *Yaadein* suffered heavy losses when the film did not do well. Add in a host of other disasters through parts of 2001 and almost all of 2002. The result—costs spiralled from an average Rs 50 million in 1999, to a whopping Rs 100–150 million. Margins were squeezed—even for successful films—from about 100 per cent to 25–30 per cent.

THE WAY IT IS

This churn in the business, combined with alterations in policy, finally forced some structural changes on the Indian film industry.

The first is that advances are out. This is the first and *most important* structural change the slowdown of 2002 brought into the film industry. Meaning, for the first time in 50 years, films are being bought after they are made, on a commission basis. All the revenues and profits they earn will be shared along the distribution chain—with exhibitors, distributors, producers—instead of just one man, the producer, making money at the expense of everybody else. New players like Sony Pictures Releasing of India too are pushing this change. The subsidiary of the US-based Sony Corp entered the market for the distribution of local films in 2001. However, it works only on a commission basis. Therefore film companies and producers have to work hard at getting organised finance. K. Sera Sera borrows money at 3–4 per cent from the overseas markets, to finance its films in India. That keeps a lid on interest costs. Stars, who account for a chunk of a film's costs are asked to take a share of its revenues. Many film 'companies' —such as iDream and K. Sera Sera—have access to bank finance to the extent of 50 per cent of the film's cost. The remaining is being brought in either through their own resources or through the involvement of a production company.

Second, this need for organised money in turn is forcing consolidation in the business. This is because banks, venture capital firms and even private equity firms, prefer not just companies but large companies. UTV, Yash Raj Films or Percept Picture Company, sign deals with creative houses like Ram Gopal Verma's or with dozens of individual directors. This commits them to say 2–3 projects with the film company. If UTV has 12 directors on board, it has in its pipeline, say, 30 movies for 3–4 years and can then get economies of scale on production. It could then ally with any other company to co-finance each film. Note the number of films that have two or more names as presenters or producers; almost every film company has one or more partners on every one of its projects. This consolidation at the production end gives these companies both distribution and retail heft. It operates like any other consumer product business; the more variety and scale a company has, the more is its clout with retailers and distributors. This consolidation also works across segments of the business. There is Yash Raj Films that forayed into music, home video, international and domestic distribution. Adlabs produces and retails films; recently it got into domestic and international distribution, and international production. These vertically and horizontally integrated conglomerates will streamline the business.

The third structural change is the discipline this consolidation is forcing on to the process of filmmaking itself. UTV or Yash Raj Films insist on a written-and-bound script before they discuss any project. This is then vetted. The Industrial Development Bank of India (IDBI), that offers financing for films, has an advisory committee of 12 people that vets scripts every quarter. After the film company has a proper script, it is translated to screenplay, shooting schedules, casting and dates; every detail about the movie has to be put down on paper. Now pre-production takes anywhere between 4–9 months, compared to a few days earlier. The idea is to have every detail down on paper and have alternate plans or shooting schedules for every scene—down to location and the things needed there—completely organized, before the spending begins.

125

The pre-production process would involve hardly a dozen people, as against the scores that actual shooting would entail. It therefore makes sense to iron out the details before the company starts spending money.

The retail revolution The fourth, most important structural change is in retailing. Multiplexes, digital theatres and home video, the three major ways in which consumers watch films have got a bulk of the investments.

Multiplexes Half a dozen multiplex chains—Fun Republic, PVR Cinemas, Adlabs, Fame Cinemas, and INOX Leisure among others—have come up across different cities in India. According to various estimates, about a 1,000 more multiplex screens will be added to the 100 or so currently, in the coming years. That makes it easier to screen and make money on all kinds of films, from *Devdas* to *Bend it Like Beckham*. This is because unlike a regular 1,200–1,700 seat theatre with one screen, a multiplex has four or five screens with 200–400 seats each.

This gives it flexibility. In the first few weeks, *Kal Ho Na Ho* could be shown in the 400-seater. Later, as collections start dipping, it can be shifted to a smaller screen. On the other hand, an offbeat film like *Jhankar Beats* can be screened in a smaller auditorium. If it works, then the number of shows could be increased. The sheer permutations and combinations that a multiplex offers—to mix films, shows, timings and prices—makes it easier to make money on it even with mediocre films. Most of the new multiplexes claim to average between 60–70 per cent occupancy. Even with an occupancy between 40–50 per cent, along with food and beverages and advertising, most end up making a healthy profit. The current entertainment-tax exemption—the duration of which varies from state to state (refer to 'Taxation')—means they make 70 per cent gross margins. Even after the tax exemption goes, estimates put margins in the range of 20 per cent. Also, since ticket booking is computerised and transparent, there is no leakage out of the system. The money comes back into the industry.

If multiplexes are changing viewing in the cities, digital theatres are changing it in smaller towns and in rural India. This adds a pan-Indian flavour to the changes sweeping across film retail. I discovered this while travelling in interior Uttar Pradesh for my first story on digital cinema in 2004. Since then, every time I have looked at digital cinema, it has surprised me with the speed with which it is spreading.

Digital theatres: The logic for digitising theatres is simple: the more copies of a film print that are released, the higher the chances of milking it in the first few weeks. Ideally a film should have 12,000 prints one for each theatre in India. At Rs 60,000–70,000 per copy, this is not viable. An average film releases with 150–200 prints nationally, and a very big one—like *Kal Ho Na No*—with 400–600. Once it exhausts all the business in the top 400–600 theatres, it moves to smaller theatres in big cities and then to smaller towns. In the interim, piracy soaks up all potential business. When the print do reach these markets, they are scratchy and impossible to watch.

Digital technology, meaning a server and a digital projector, could cost anywhere between Rs 1–10 million to install. This enables the theatre to show the film from a digital file. This could be a hard disk that is changed every week, or the film could be received via satellite and stored on the hard disk of the computer. It is then played for an agreed number of times before the file disintegrates. The first copy, from 35 mm to digital, costs about Rs 100,000–200,000. Every subsequent copy on a hard disk retains the visual quality of the original and costs about Rs 2,000–3,000. It ensures that every screen in the country can get the film on 'first day, first show'—killing piracy, pushing up attendance and getting more revenues back into the industry.

For years nobody, in Hollywood or anywhere else, wanted to take the plunge. That is because while everyone gained, nobody wanted to make the investment. In China and several other countries, governments decided on digitising theatres and the projects moved. In India in June 2003, Adlabs began seeding its Rs 1 million apiece digital system in theatres. In September 2003 it floated Mukta Adlabs Digital Exhibition in a joint venture with Subhash Ghai's Mukta Arts to seed theatres. It quickly signed on over 50 theatres, either on a revenue-share basis or through lease. In some cases, the equipment was sold outright. Then came Dhirubhai Shah's Time Cinemas followed by the Sushilkumar Agrawal's Ultra Group. While the models were different the idea was the same, getting moribund B&C class theatres up and running.

One hundred and thirty theatres later, in January 2004, the results were startling. In digitised theatres in Maharashtra, Punjab, Uttar Pradesh or West Bengal average occupancies had jumped from 8–10 per cent to 20–50 per cent. On good days it could go up to 100 per cent. In towns like Mangalvedha or Gulewadi in Maharashtra, where house-full collections barely touched Rs 6,000–10,000 a week, the average had gone up to Rs 50,000 and more. Audiences were coming back to the theatres for the quality of picture and sound, and to watch a new film in the same week as the rest of the country. This was bringing small town India, along with portions of B-grade audiences in large cities, back in the reckoning after a long time.

By May 2005, about half a dozen digital cinema projects were underway (see Figure 3.5). All put together, these companies will spend over Rs 5 billion, maybe more, to digitise over 3,000 theatres till 2008. If all these projects go as scheduled, India's dominance over the digital cinema revolution in Asia will be absolute. A network of 1,600–1,700 cinema theatres downloading films via servers offers opportunities to reach audiences for everything, from films to advertising to live telecasts of cricket matches. Most of the 225 digital theatres sign leases with, say, Mukta or Time or with the distributors who install the system there. Alternately they pay the digital cinema company, such as Valuable

Figure 3.5: The Digital Theatre Revolution

Company	Digital Theatres		Solution	Cost per Theatre Rs million
	Current	Planned (incl current)		
Mukta-Adlabs	40	100	hard disk	1–1.2
Sathyam Cinemas	1		hard disk	6.0–8.0
Pyramid Saimira	none	1500	via satellite	2–2.5
Real Image	100	450	via satellite	1.4
PVR Cinemas	none	100	hard disk	10 per screen
Valuable Media	60	2000	via satellite	1.5

Note: (i) All figures as in November 2005 (ii) The cost per theatre figure for PVR Cinemas is the total cost of retrofitting the theatre and putting digital equipment into it. Therefore it is higher than the others which is just the equipment cost.

Source: *Businessworld* magazine.

Media, based on the number of screenings. In either case everything they earn is shown on the books and recorded as collection. The software will not allow them to decrypt the film file otherwise. This means the money comes back into the industry, just like in multiplexes. Even in towns and suburbs with digital theatres, video parlours are shutting down and thus killing piracy.

What could cause problems is the choice of technology. The essential difference in the quality and cost of a digital cinema solution is the projector, since servers and satellites cost roughly the same. The globally accepted DLP Technology from Texas Instruments is licensed to several projector companies—Barco, Panasonic, Christie's. However what Hollywood approves of is are very high-end projectors. A Christie's DLP Cinema Projector, like the one Chennai-based Sathyam Cinemas has, could push the cost of the entire solution up to Rs 6–8 million.[11] On the other hand a regular DLP projector solution (along with the server and other things) costs anything between Rs 1.2–1.5 million. The cost difference is significant.

The Mukta-Adlabs projector was a simple one-chip piece that cost about Rs 0.2–0.3 million. Although the Digital Cinema Initiative (DCI) in Hollywood (a body of seven major Hollywood studios) has approved the server that it uses, the solution is called a low-end one. Time and Ultra's equipment too was not high-end. Time used a Proxima LCD projector. In fact in international trade journals India's digital theatres are called E-cinemas not D-cinemas. Mukta-Adlabs's projectors started packing up at some point in 2004. They were changing course and ordering high-end ones when I last spoke to them.

All the other companies are adhering to at least a basic DLP technology projector, of various brands. So their technology is far more robust than the first

---

[11] Sathyam is the only theatre in the country with Hollywood-approved technology for screening films. This means it can get digital prints of Hollywood films unlike other digital theatres which cannot screen them.

round by Mukta-Adlabs and others. But that brands their rollouts as E-cinema by the rest of the world. There is an industry-wide debate on, why using a projector below standards set by Hollywood, should make it E-cinema. It still is digital cinema since the technology is digital. The only reason most Asian countries follow that definition is because an E-cinema tag means that you cannot play Hollywood films on local screens. Except for Sathyam, there are no reports of any orders of high-end DLP Cinema projectors from India. The upside of installing it in multiplexes, which already offer good resolution film projection, is not clear. Moreover, Indian films cannot yet be converted to the DLP Cinema format; so all Sathyam will play on this equipment for the coming months are those Hollywood films that are released in digital format.

Also the cost differential, Rs 1–1.4 million for a basic digital cinema system, versus Rs 6–8 million for one that is Hollywood-approved is so high, that the Indian industry is sticking to the basic model for now. Rightly so, considering that the ticket price in small towns can be pushed up only to Rs 60–80, not to Rs 150 like it is in big city multiplexes. Therefore the ability to recover costs—quickly—is limited. Once the bulk of India, which stopped watching films in theatres, gets used to a better cinema-watching experience, the shift to a high-end system can happen.

Home video The other part of the retail revolution is home videos. Home video is typically defined as entertainment on any device than can be seen at home. Currently this includes, largely, video compact discs (VCDs) and DVDs. At over Rs 10 billion, home video now sells almost as much as music in its physical format. Unlike music, which is shrinking, the home video market is estimated to be growing 25–30 per cent or maybe more. It is turning out to be the biggest source of revenue for Indian films, after satellite TV and the overseas market.

The prices of home video rights range from Rs 0.5 million to Rs 10 million. That is roughly equal to the price of one territory for distributing a film in India. Reportedly the home video rights to *Baghban, Koi Mil Gaya* and *Munnabhai MBBS* were bought for over Rs 10 million each. Some of the older hits such as *Sholay* had sold over 0.2 million copies at the beginning of 2004. Though pirates still take away half the market, their share is down from about 90 per cent just two years back. There are more than half-a-dozen home video companies emerging with a strong hold on the market.

They fall in two categories. The first is the former video libraries or video companies. These include among others Shemaroo, Ultra, Excel Home Video, Time and Bombino. Their strength is a strong network with the filmmakers and an ability to deal with the hurly burly of the film distribution trade. Many, like Shemaroo, also double as suppliers of content to cable operators, and TV channels. That helps them leverage their acquisition costs better. The second is the big music companies and studios. It includes, among others,

Saregama, Sony-BMG and Columbia TriStar. These companies are strong on distribution and marketing. They use the same network to sell home videos (refer to the chapter on Music).

Globally home video is typically two to three times the size of the box-office revenues, especially in the mature markets. In the benchmark US market, it was estimated to have brought in $27.96 billion in 2005 against box office revenues of $10.49 billion in the same year. In the US, in fact, analysts are accusing studio heads of tailoring films to home video formats and release cycles. The numbers on volumes are larger too. Finding Nemo sold 15 million DVDs on the first day of its home video release in the US.

How soon can home video take over the box-office in India, ask analysts. After a long time would be the safe answer, considering other retail formats—theatres in particular—are just about finding their feet.

Advertising Besides these structural changes, there are other strong revenue streams emerging, in-film and in-theatre being the major ones among them. According to one estimate advertising raked in revenues of about Rs 2 billion, in 2004. There are specialist companies like Interactive Television that now aggregate theatres and offer them as opportunities to advertisers for promotions or in-cinema advertising. This figure also includes the money that comes from brand placements inside films.

The future Many filmmakers worry, rightly, about this change sweeping across the Indian film industry. They think it could straitjacket the creative process—especially if executives who know nothing of the creative process start butting into the actual thinking on the film. This is what happened in Hollywood and other markets. That is when independents started cropping up. A few years ago, a bunch of unknown amateurs made *The Blair Witch Project* for under $50,000. The film went on to gross a little under a quarter of a billion dollars.

Straitjacketing of creative is a situation that India is far from. There is little doubt, within industry circles, that the business needs conglomerates. The more integrated the process—from ideation to music, to production and distribution across different media—the easier it is to capture the value of what has been created. Since Yash Raj Films produces many of the movies to which it owns the rights for music, television, home video, overseas—if it does all this itself, all the value comes within the company.

What will this new morphed industry look like? Well, less fragmented, to begin with. As a few companies start dominating the business of filmmaking, the economics of the game will change. The global markets will become more important as companies start looking for larger audiences. So, while dependence on music and satellite has already gone down, that on the overseas market will start going up again—this time not only with films targeted at Indians or Asians but at a global audience, a la Hollywood.

So expect to see a lot more films that attempt to talk to a global audience in order to capture a larger market such as *Bend it like Beckham* and *Monsoon Wedding*. The latter grossed an estimated $35 million in markets across the world—a chunk of that in the US, a market where Indian films do not earn more than a couple of million dollars.

The Indian film industry has changed. Wait then, for the world to notice it.

THE WAY IT WORKS

Anyone who has an idea for a film needs money and people to put it together. The person with an idea could be a complete outsider and may not necessarily make the film. Or, it could be someone from within the industry—a director, financier, an actor or a writer. These days it is typical to approach a film company such as Yash Raj Films or UTV with the idea or a script and take it from there.

Once the idea is decided upon, the film is budgeted depending on the star cast, the time it will take to make, the locations it has to be shot in and so on. Finances, from distributors, or financiers are organised. It is common to shoot a few scenes and show them to distributors who can then buy the rights for a territory. They could pay 50–60 per cent of the money as an advance to enable the shooting to start. For the last decade or so, music and satellite too had become big contributors as discussed.

While the arrangement with music and satellite television companies is a straightforward one-time payment, the one with distributors could be varied. These arrangements have remained the same for as long as anyone associated with the industry can remember. 'What has probably changed is that the actual numbers involved have gone up with the cost of film making rising', says accountant Amrit Shah.[12] So has the number of territories. While geographically India was divided into 11 territories, the overseas market, music and satellite television give enough returns to be classified as a separate territory.

While there could be nuances to it, the different producer/distributor agreements are:

Minimum guarantee (MG) It is also referred to as Royalty MG in industry lingo. If a distributor buys the rights to screen *Lagaan* at Rs 10 million for the Mumbai territory, the price is usually based on or is a percentage of the

---

[12] A chunk of the information on different types of agreements between distributors, producers and exhibitors comes from Amrit Shah. Septuagenarian Shah has been handling the finances of producers in the Indian film industry for more than five decades now.

production cost of the film. Usually about 30–40 per cent—maybe more—is paid in advance and the remaining against the first print. In addition, the distributor will bear the cost of prints in his area. If the film is being released in 100 theatres in Mumbai and he needs to make 75 prints, then he will bear the Rs 60,000 or so each print costs, plus the cost of publicity. Assume that his total bill for screening the film is Rs 20 million, he charges the producer a 20 per cent commission after he has recovered the Rs 20 million from box office collections. If there is more money coming in after his Rs 22 million is covered, this 'overflow' (in trade parlance), is split halfway with the producer.

Advance If the distributor doesn't want to take a risk then he will just advance the money to the producer. The rest of the arrangement on prints, publicity and commission, remains the same. If the film doesn't make enough money to cover the advance, then the producer has to reimburse the money to the distributor.

Commission Basis Under this agreement the distributor doesn't take any risk. He just takes the film and releases it throughout his territory for maybe a 10 per cent commission on the takings. The entire risk is borne by the producer. This is now becoming the more popular form of distribution.

Outright The distributor pays a lump sum to the producer and picks the film up for exploiting in his territory for five years or so. After that, the rights for that territory will revert to the producer. This is usually done for a Hindi film being distributed in, say, Tamil Nadu, where it is difficult to determine of how much it will really earn. 'In the old days,' remembers Shah, '99 per cent of overseas rights were sold outright, so there are no statements, no accounts of how much the movies actually made there.'

Any of these four types of agreements depends on the film, the producer, the distributor, the territory he owns and the expectation each of them has from the film.

The agreements between distributor and exhibitor (the theatre owner) could be of three types:

Theatre hire basis This essentially works like a fixed rental. Assume that the maximum financial capacity of a theatre is Rs 1 million a week. If the thumb rule for that area is 50 per cent, then the distributor will keep 50 per cent of the full house capacity and give the remaining to the distributor. If the film collects Rs 1.2 million, then the exhibitor keeps Rs 500,000 and the remaining is given to the distributor. However, if the film collects Rs 700,000 then the exhibitor still keeps Rs 500,000 and the distributor gets only Rs 200,000 that week; and in case the film does less than 50 per cent of its full-house capacity, say, Rs 400,000, the exhibitor's share is nevertheless Rs 500,000. The distributor may not pay him immediately. The final settlement takes place only when the accounts are squared off after the film has been pulled out of the theatre. If in the end the exhibitor is not getting a full Rs 500,000 per week, the distributor pays the balance.

Note that the capacity of the theatre is measured not in number of seats but in terms of the money it can make. That is because entertainment tax and local state rules tend to create huge variations in ticket prices. Theatre hire is the most popular way of letting out theatres, especially in metros where ticket prices are very high so exhibitors can make enough money if they get a fixed percentage of peak capacity. It de-links the exhibitor's fate from that of the film completely. This is now changing. Many theatres are willing to take a smaller hire charge but want a share of revenues or overflows.

Percentage Basis This type of agreement is not used much now, according to Shah. Under this agreement the exhibitor keeps a fixed percentage of 40–50 per cent of the collections every week. If the collections are high, he makes money, if not he doesn't.

Fixed Hire Under this agreement, the exhibitor takes all the risk. He pays the distributor a fixed amount every week irrespective of the weekly collection. If the capacity is Rs 200,000 then the fixed hire could be Rs 100,000 a week. If there is a surplus, he could share it with the distributor depending on the terms of the agreement. Usually when the film is given in the interiors of the country where it is difficult to measure the capacity or estimate how popular it could be, then the distributor takes the safe way out and gives it away on fixed hire. However, according to Shah, who has handled thousands of cases of unpaid dues between distributors, producers and exhibitors, this system has inherent scope for mischief. It is common for distributors to take money in cash from the exhibitor and declare a loss on paper in order to under-pay the producer.

This is very common in Bihar, Uttar Pradesh, and Punjab where a bulk of the transactions are in cash and films rarely show a profit. The exhibitors, especially in smaller towns, have a monopoly. They probably own the only theatre in town so the film keeps making money for months after the producer thinks it is out of the theatre. However, for all practical purposes, all he sees is that collections were small, so after paying the hire to the distributor, it seems that the theatre owner has nothing left. There is little a distributor can do. Even if there are three theatres, the owners/exhibitors could get together and decide that they will pay only Rs 100,000 a week as fixed hire, so distributors too have no option but to work with either one of them.

Remember that it is the distributor who has a relationship with the exhibitor, not the producer. The exhibitor too is one of the sources of finance for the distributor who then lends the money to the producer. Usually, the exhibitor part-finances films that he really wants to show in his theatre: the high profile ones.

133

While the finance from the distributor and exhibitors could help with about 40 per cent of a film's cost, the remaining could come by, only part-paying artistes, credit from the film processing labs, advances from music, or satellite television companies. That gives a filmmaker another 20–50 per cent of his money, taking the total financed through the trade to 70–80 per cent. The remaining money is raised from financiers. Based on the producer's reputation for completion of projects, the stage of production and subject to a completion guarantee, interest rates could vary from 2.5–4 per cent a month. Many of these financiers become the world rights controller for the film. Most distributors are happy when there is a world rights controller. It means that a producer is bound to complete the film or pay penalty. They could also get, depending on the agreement with the producer, a share of the profits or overflow.

Once the film is complete, the negative is delivered to the producer who then releases it through the distributor. Satellite and home video releases now happen within months of the same in theatres.

Typically, the revenue streams (discussed in detail in the main section) are:

- Theatre release
- Cable, satellite release
- Dubbed versions for regional or foreign markets
- DVDs, VCD, Home Video

The main elements of cost (also discussed throughout the main section) are:

- Production
- Artistes
- Distribution (including Prints)
- Marketing

METRICS

The main metrics in the film business would be:

Walk-ins Just like any other retail store, walk-ins are very important in multiplexes or film theatres. They determine not only the box-office gross, but also how much food and beverages are sold and how much premium advertisers attach to putting money into a theatre or a chain of theatres. This translates into capacity utilisation. For most film retail chains about 35–40 per cent utilisation combined with a robust food and beverage sales and advertising helps to break even and make money.

Ticket prices This is by far one of the lowest in India. According to the PricewaterhouseCooper Media and Entertainment Outlook for 2004–08, the average ticket price in India is 23 cents against $6.67 in China or $8 per ticket in Taiwan. This determines to a great extent the profitability of a market. One of the reasons why investment is coming into film retail in India currently is because multiplexes charge Rs 100–150 per ticket, so the average is well over $2 in the metros.

REGULATION

While there has been plenty of regulation of the film industry, most of it has been centered on content. There has been very little on financing, distribution or exhibition, areas where it could have helped the business. In fact, whenever there was any suggestion of improving regulation to create a good business infrastructure for the film industry, it has been ignored. Some cases, laws and history is outlined below.

History A brief look at how film regulation evolved in India:[13]

1918: The Indian Cinematograph Act, modelled on the British Act, sets the terms for censorship and cinema licensing.
1927–28: The Indian Cinematograph Committee (1927–28).
1932: The Motion Picture Society of India (taken over by The Film Federation of India in 1951). Later, different states formed their own motion picture associations.
1944: The government appoints a Film Advisory Committee.
1943: State control on raw stock distribution. The Defence of India Act, 1971 is amended to force all distributors to pay for and show the Indian News Parade. Both these restrictions were removed in 1946.
1949: Films Division is set up, the Cinematograph Act, 1952, amended. More importantly, entertainment tax is raised to 50 per cent in the Central Provinces and 75 per cent in West Bengal. The S.K. Patil Committee is appointed.
1950: Jawarharlal Nehru announces a freeze on building theatres; it is finally lifted in 1956.

135

[13] The best source for regulation history was Rajadhyaksha and Willemen (1994). From the Rights and Piracy onwards, large portions have been put together by Kanchan Sinha, Amarchand & Mangaldas & Suresh A. Shroff & Company, a New Delhi-based law firm. The section on current laws and policies has been put together for Ashni Parekh, formerly with Nishith Desai and Associates.

1951: S.K. Patil Committee report, on improving film financing. Film Federation of India is set up. Film censorship centralised under a Central Board located in Mumbai.

1968: G.D. Khosla Committee Report on film censorship. It criticises censorship norms saying that if the censorship guidelines are strictly adhered to, not a single film, Indian or Western, is likely to be certified. It sparks off a debate on whether censorship violates our constitutional right to free speech.

1973–74: The Estimates Committee blames the government for ignoring earlier enquiry committee reports that suggested making institutional finance available to the industry. It points out that the result had been the large-scale entry of black money into the industry.

1980: The Film Finance Corporation (FFC) is merged with the Indian Motion Picture Export Corporation to become the National Film Development Corporation (NFDC).

1980: The working group on national film policy points out that the sector should be recognised as an industry and institutional finance be made available through banks.

1982: Andhra Pradesh and Orissa give it industry status.

1984: Infringement of copyrights in films is made a cognisable offence.

1994: The censor code is amended, following the song *Sarkailo Khatiya* from *Raja Babu*.

According to Amarchand & Mangaldas & Suresh A. Shroff & Company, a New Delhi-based law firm, the basics one needs to know about regulation in the Indian film industry are:

Rights and piracy The rights conferred by Section 2(a) of the Indian Copyright Act 1957, are in the nature of an exclusive right conferred on the producer of a film, to do the following acts:

- Make a copy of the film, including a photograph of any image in the film like a still of a movie;
- Sell, hire or offer for sale or hire a copy of the film irrespective of whether the copy has been sold or hired before; and
- Communicate the film to the public.

The rights of the producer may be violated by making unauthorized copies on video and other medium like compact discs (CDs) and by the exhibition of such copies through cable networks.

A film itself consists of several potential copyright infringing components. If the movie is based on a literary work, then the author of the work has the copyright on the making of a movie. If the movie has songs in it, the lyricists and composers have a copyright on their efforts in creating that song. Therefore, the producer must first obtain permission from all these people before the movie can be made. Earlier in the absence of formalised corporate structures, the Indian film industry had few precedents relating to formal documentation between different copyright owners (such as the script writer, and the music director) and the producer of the film.

The anti-piracy measures under the Copyright Act as described in the chapter on Music, apply to the film industry as well. With regard to the film industry, one of the anti-piracy measures adopted includes the execution of agreements between film producers and cable-network owners. Under these cable-network owners undertook to refrain from screening unauthorised copies of the movies over their cable network channels. Cable operators are governed by the Cable Television Networks (Regulation) Act, 1995. It makes it mandatory for all cable operators to secure the copyright of programmes that they telecast.

The Cinematograph Act, 1952 A Board of Film Certification for the purpose of sanctioning films for public exhibition has been set up under this Act. An application has to be made to the Board for a certificate by any person wanting to exhibit any film. The Board grants a 'U' Certificate or a 'UA' Certificate, if the film is suitable for unrestricted public exhibition. In case a film is unsuitable for unrestricted public exhibition it gets 'A' or 'S'. Any person who exhibits a film that has been restricted by the Board is punishable with three years of imprisonment or a fine of Rs 100,000, or both. In case of a continuing offence, this may extend to Rs 20,000 for each day during which the offence continues. If a film without a certificate or one with 'A' certification is exhibited to the general public, the police have the power to seize it.

Case law R.G. Anand vs Delux Films (1978) 4 SCC 118; AIR 1978 SC 1613— The relevant law relating to copyright stated as follows:

- There can be no copyright in an idea, principle, subject matter, themes, plots or historical or legendary facts, and violation of the copyright in such cases is confined to the form, manner and arrangement and expression of the idea by the author of the copyrighted work.
- Where the same idea is being developed in a different manner, it is manifest that the source being common, similarities are bound to occur. In such a case the courts should determine whether or not the similarities are on fundamental or substantial aspects of the mode of expression adopted in the copyrighted work. If the defendant's work were nothing but a literal imitation of the copyrighted work with some variations here and there, it would amount to a violation of the copyright. In other words, in order to be actionable, the copy must be a substantial and material one which at once leads to the conclusion that the defendant is guilty of an act of piracy.

- The surest and safest test to determine whether or not there has been a violation of copyright is to see if the reader, spectator or the viewer after having read or seen both the works is clearly of the opinion and gets an unmistakable impression that the subsequent work appears to be a copy of the original.
- Where the theme is the same, but is presented and treated differently so that the subsequent work becomes a completely new work, no question of violation of copyright arises.
- Where, however, apart from the similarities appearing in the two works there are also material and broad dissimilarities which negate the intention to copy the original and the coincidences appearing in the two works are clearly incidental, no infringement of the copyright comes into existence.
- Where however, the question is of the violation of the copyright of a stage play by a film producer or a director, it becomes more difficult for the plaintiff to prove piracy. It is manifest that unlike a stage play, a film has a much broader perspective, wider field and a bigger background, where the defendants can by introducing a variety of incidents give a colour and complexion different from the manner in which the copyrighted work has expressed the idea. Even so, if the viewer after seeing the film, gets a totality of impression that the film is by and large a copy of the original play, violation of the copyright may be said to be proved.

Further, an infringement of copyright can arise even though the essential features of a play correspond to only a part of the plot of a film. Such a situation can arise where changes are effected while planning the film so that certain immaterial features in the film differ from what is seen in the stage play.

Current laws and policies The film industry is subject to the:

- The Constitution of India
- Copyright Act, 1957
- Cinematograph Act, 1952
- Guidelines to Board of Film Censors, 1978
- Cine Workers and Cinema Theatre Workers (Regulation of Employment) Act, 1981
- Cine Workers Welfare Cess Act, 1981
- Cine Workers Welfare Fund Act, 1981
- Bombay Cinemas (Regulation) Act, 1953
- Guidelines for shooting of foreign films
- Guidelines for import and export of films
- Foreign Direct Investment (FDI) Regulations under the Foreign Exchange Management Act (FEMA), Annexure 4

- Indian Penal Code, 1860
- Law of Torts
- Reserve Bank of India (RBI) Guidelines for Film Financing

Financing Even before the film business got industry status, a working group was formed under the aegis of the Indian Banks Association, in 1998. It came out with a fairly detailed report urging industry status for films and also providing the broad framework within which institutions and banks could lend to the film industry. Individual institutions were left to their own devices on the specifics. The IDBI, or other institutions therefore have the IBA recommendations to fall on while framing their guidelines.

Foreign direct investment up to 100 per cent is allowed into films. This is subject to the following conditions:

- The investing company must have an established track record in films, television, music, finance or insurance.
- The investing company should have a minimum paid-up capital of $10 million if it is the single largest equity shareholder in the Indian company and at least $5 million in other cases.
- The minimum level of foreign equity investment should be $2.5 million for the single largest equity shareholder and at least $1 million in other cases.
- The Indian company's borrowing must not exceed its equity.
- Dividend balancing provisions apply. This means the Indian company must have an export income greater than the dividend paid to foreign investors under a prescribed formula.

Foreign investors in both Indian production houses and multiplex construction companies can apply under the FDI route.

ACCOUNTING NORMS[14]

Film as a media is different from others mainly because of the capital intensity. The cost ranges from anywhere between Rs 10–500 million or more. It comprises various elements—payment to artistes, directors, hire charges for equipment, studio, travel cost for shooting at locations, etc. This cost should be charged over a graded scale with larger write offs in the initial weeks of the release of the movie and smaller amounts towards the later period. There are no specific standards in India for both costs and revenues for this business.

---

[14] This part has been put together by Ramesh Lakshman of Ramesh Lakshman and Company.

Costs The entire cost of making a film is accrued as and when incurred and charged off to revenues over a certain number of weeks. It is customary to write off the expenditure over a shorter period against the revenue earned during that period. Any income earned thereafter would be pure revenue without any corresponding expenditure. If the film *Devdas* collects Rs 350 million against a cost of Rs 500 million, it is written off as a flop with losses of Rs 150 million. However, *Devdas* could continue to generate revenues for a few more years, either on television or through DVDs/VCDs. While there are no accounting prescriptions under the law or by the Institute of Chartered Accountants of India (ICAI), there are some guidelines available from the Income Tax Rules, which stipulate the basis for apportionment of income. The entire production cost is to be treated as expenditure if the film is released for distribution for more than 90 days. If not, the cost equal to the amount realised is charged off, and the balance carried forward to be charged off the following year.

It is possible that the producer of the film sells the rights to music for a capital consideration. This is because the music is recorded much ahead of the actual shooting. Since the cost of the music forms part of the cost of production, it follows that the capital amount recovered be adjusted towards the cost of production of the film.

Revenues A movie might do well at the box office and thereafter generate a brand value. For instance consider the successful film, *Lagaan*. The brand image is leveraged in various different ways to generate revenue. This will be pure revenue income and should be accounted as such.

In the US as usual, there are strict rules for revenue recognition. Only when all the stipulated conditions are met can revenue be recognised. Similarly, the capitalised cost is to be amortised according to a prescribed formula. The proportion of revenue earned to the estimated future revenue (as at the beginning of the year), is the amount to be amortised during the year. The standard would cover not only motion pictures but also television and videos.

Taxation While the power to sanction films for exhibition vests with the union government, the power to regulate places of exhibition and imposition of entertainment tax vests with the state. Most states have enacted their own legislations to levy entertainment tax. As a result the tax could vary between 10–100 per cent across different states, based on differences in the scope of the law. These differences could be based on—the nature of the place of entertainment; its location; the identity of the ultimate consumer (individuals or organisations such as hotels); the medium of entertainment (different rates for regional language films); and varied compliance and reporting requirements. In the last few years there has been intense lobbying to rationalise the tax across states to say 20–30 per cent. Since some states have an entertainment tax as low as 10 per cent, there has been some resistance to this. If the tax is increased to 25 per cent in these states it would affect box-office revenue.

In 2000, various state governments announced tax exemptions for the construction of new multiplexes or the refurbishment of old theatres. In Maharashtra there is 100 per cent exemption in the first three years, and 75 per cent in the fourth and fifth year. Also 50 per cent of the profits and gains derived from the business of building, owning and operating multiplex theatres are allowed as tax deduction. In order to avail of it, the theatre must have been constructed during the period between April 1, 2002 and March 31, 2005; and must not be situated in Mumbai, Kolkata, Chennai and Delhi. The deduction is available for five consecutive assessment years.

In 1994 the film industry was brought under the ambit of service tax. For every facility that a filmmaker uses—recording shooting, dubbing, photography or mixing—there is a 12 per cent service tax. For one film, the tax could total up to 60 per cent according to Supran Sen of the Film Federation of India. At present, the revenue department treats distribution of films as a service and imposes a tax of 12 per cent on it.

In addition to this there are various import duties on equipment such as cameras, lenses, studio lights and filters.

VALUATION

In 2000 several media companies raised money from the stock market. These included several film companies such as Pritish Nandy Communications, Mukta Arts and Adlabs. In the same year Shringar Cinemas was one of the few companies to raise money through private equity. It sold 26 per cent of its shares to GW Capital for Rs 158 million. When Shringar raised money through the primary market in 2005 it got a valuation that was just over four times what it got in 2000. That means GW Capital, which sold 14.9 per cent of the 26 per cent that it owned during the IPO has made its money and more. However such examples are few and far in between. Largely film companies have made for disappointing investments since their business performance and therefore stock market value has been lackadaisical.

As a result till 2003 there were very few examples of private equity placements in the film business. ICICI Venture picked up a stake in PVR Cinemas in 2003. Otherwise some of the biggest film deals, so far, happened in 2004 and 2005. Most of these were in the area of multiplexes and digital theatres. The Reliance-Adlabs deal is one such instance.

The valuation of a film company, irrespective of the basic multiples that will be used, would centre around three things.[15]

---

[15] See chapter on telecom for an explanation on the ways in which valuation could work.

Content The logic for valuing film content is the same as that for television software. The potential for future revenues though different revenues streams, theatres, DVDs, satellite rights, music, syndication and dubbing are calculated based on discounted cash flow to value a film.

Distribution and retail The companies in film retail are valued just like the ones in television distribution or plain retailing. Their potential to earn revenues is based on the walk-ins, ticket prices and the spread of revenues. Almost every theatre chain tries to de-risk revenues through advertising and in-theatre promotions. Typically 30–40 per cent comes from promotions and food and beverages. Much of this is dependent of course on the pipeline. Most film retail companies have some pretty sophisticated software that can predict walkins based on the genre of the film, time of the year, show timing, the last big hit and so on.

Integrated Adlabs has more than 75 screens—digital or multiplex—and is planning to expand this number to 1,000. It is into film production and film processing. It has just stepped into distribution and plans to target both the international and Indian market. As it scales up, the money it makes from every film that it makes, distributes or picks up for distribution, gets better. Therefore the valuation it would get is better. Similarly Yash Raj Films does not own a retail chain but is into production, distribution (India and overseas), home video, and music. It does this for its own films as well as others. It therefore uses, say, the distribution network it has built overseas to push through a wider portfolio than rivals. Integrated companies like Adlabs, Yash Raj or UTV command better valuations since the risk of dependence on one business is less.

music

The music industry's future is already here. All it has to do is acknowledge it

IT IS VERY easy to understand the Indian music market if you know one immutable fact—that Indians love films. For a majority of them entertainment means films and music means film music. If that is clear, it is not very difficult to understand the music business in India. The incestuous relationship between films and music in India—they routinely finance each other and the success of one usually means that of the other—makes the industry's structure completely different from anything else in the world (see Figure 4.1). Many international and Indian companies have tried to break the hold films have over the Indian music market. Some of them have been mildly successful. That is why the share of films in the total music market fell from about 95 per cent in the early 90s, to between 60–70 per cent of the Rs 15 odd billion music market in 2005.[1]

This is a small market for a country with a strong tradition of music. It is, in fact, just a fraction of the $29.57 billion that the global market was estimated to be in 2005. According to the Indian Music Industries Association (IMI) estimates the Indian market has been shrinking for the last couple of years after double-digit growth throughout the 80s and the early 90s.

This is largely due to the other immutable fact about the Indian music market—piracy. Of the Rs 15 billion, just about half comes from companies

---

[1] The IMI figures for the India market amount to a total of Rs 10 billion—legitimate and pirated. The PricewaterhouseCooper's Entertainment and Media Outlook estimates the legitimate Indian music market at Rs 7.7 odd billion. Even if I go by the IMI numbers, it doesn't include many companies, including Super Cassettes Industries, India's largest music company. If one includes about Rs 2.5–3 billion for SCI and another billion or so for digital downloads, the market is closer to Rs 13–15 billion. Volume estimates make no sense in a market like this.

Figure 4.1: Film Music Rules

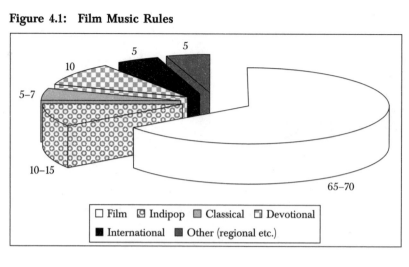

that are legitimate, tax paying enterprises. The rest comes from the factories and sheds of small-time entrepreneurs who copy old and new albums to which the legitimate companies own the rights. It is these people along with hundreds of organised players who slice up an already small market into further unprofitable parts. 'The music industry is too fragmented and dependent on Hindi (music)', thinks Bala Deshpande, of ICICI Venture. That makes it an unattractive investment. India's top 10 music companies account for about half the total music market. Compare that with the five music companies that control 75 per cent of the global music market (see Figure 4.2).

Figure 4.2: India's Leading Music Companies

Company	Revenues Rs million
Super Casettes Industries	3000
Saregama India	1008
Universal Music	600
Sony Music	580
Tips Industries	280.8
Venus Records and Tapes	200
Vatsa Music	167

Note: (i) The figures for Tips, Saregama, Super Cassettes and Vatsa Music are for March 2005. The figures for Sony-BMG are for March 2004. The rest are for March 2002 (ii) NA means not available.

Source: Annual reports and CapitalinePlus data.

It is not that there is no hope for the industry. There is, in mobile telephony (ringtones, ring-back tones and so on), in the Internet, in satellite and FM radio stations. In India these revenue streams already generate 10–30 per cent if not more for most music companies. There is also money to be made from home video sales. Most music companies now buy the video compact disc (VCD) and digital video disc (DVD) rights to a film for its domestic and at times international distribution along with the music rights. This not only offsets the cost of buying the music but also creates a neat little revenue stream through the same distribution channel. So the problem is not potential or growth.

It is that, globally, music has become an industry of whiners. The fact is piracy exists. Over four years, piracy in developing markets and illegal file sharing in developed ones, has knocked $9 billion off the topline for the music industry. The industry however has not been blameless. First by letting the Internet become a threat instead of an opportunity and now, by ignoring the good news that satellite radio or mobile telephony is bringing, the industry is wallowing in its misery instead of trying out new ways of connecting with consumers. All the innovation, on music distribution or new formats, like the iPod, has originated from outside.

The fact is that India is a young market that is seeing double-digit growth rates in almost every other media segment. The problems of mature markets where the stronghold of the music majors has suppressed innovation in formats and musicians, is hardly the case here. There has never been so much experimentation in the creative part of the business. From Rabbi to Shubha Mudgal to Indian Ocean and *Bunty Aur Babli*, in every genre musicians, singers, composers and lyricists are trying out new sounds and audiences are enjoying them.

Audiences are willing to pay Rs 30 for the download of a ringtone or ring-back tone of, say, *Kajrare, kajrare*. In fact, FM radio stations routinely complain about how much money they have to pay as royalty and how it eats into their margins. If one adds all the other bits and pieces the Indian music industry, has probably grown. But internationally the music industry has an agenda—to go after pirates—so it suits the majors to focus on the bad news. The International Federation of Phonographic Industries (IFPI) and IMI newsletters are full of news on only one thing: piracy.

The music industry's history is littered with examples of its negative attitude to almost every new technology that came up for distribution. Concert musicians protested against the phonograph; later music companies resisted cassettes, television, radio, compact discs (CDs), and so on. These cries have been the hallmark of the music industry over the decades as different technologies allowed consumers easier, faster and cheaper access to music.

Yet, currently, music companies in the US get more than 60 per cent of the royalties they earn, from all the technologies that many cried foul about. It is this attitude that the Indian music industry has to stop mimicking, if it wants to enjoy what half a dozen new ways of distribution are bringing to the business today.

THE PAST

Till Thomas Edison invented the phonograph in 1877, the music business was largely about live concerts. By 1890, a German immigrant in the US, Emile Berliner, perfected the phonograph for home use. This was later modified to the gramophone introduced by The Victor Talking Machine Company. Competing technologies like radio put huge pressure on the music business in the early part of the twentieth century. There was confusion about who would pay royalties to whom and for how long. Radio station owners insisted that once they had brought a recording it was theirs to use without any further financial obligation. There was the usual outcry against these new technologies. The record business was in limbo for a long time after World War II, because of a protracted musicians' strike. They sought compensation from record companies for income lost because more people were listening to recorded performances, which meant that the demand for live performances declined.

Back home in India, during the 1890s in Bombay and Calcutta, many traders had taken on the phonograph as an additional item of trade, along with their other merchandise. By the early 1900s they were offering 'private cylinder' recordings of eminent singers to induce potential buyers.[2] Later, one of these traders, Valabhdas Runchoddas of Bombay, became the first official wholesaler for Edison, Columbia and Pathe Products. In 1901, came the first music company in India, The Gramophone and Typewriter Company of India Limited, also called Gramco.[3] Set up as a trading company, it was the first overseas branch of the Gramophone and Typewriter Company that had been set up in London in 1898. Soon after setting up the branch office, some officials came down from London and took about 550 recordings in Calcutta in the latter half of 1902. These were then pressed into discs in Hanover, Germany, and sold in India.

During the early part of the 1900s, Gramco had competition from several European and Indian companies. There was Singer Records; The James Opera Record from The James Manufacturing Company; Beka records, Rama-Graph Disc Record; H. Bose's Records; and Royal Record and Binapani Disc Record; among others. The competition forced Gramco to start manufacturing out of Calcutta in 1907. That gave it a competitive edge as it could press discs faster than rivals who had to send them to Europe. It remained the only gramophone records manufacturing company in India till 1970. In its early years it made

---

[2] Before recorded discs there were wax cylinders that reproduced songs.

[3] Gramco, GCI and HMV are used synonymously throughout this chapter. They refer to the same company—Gramophone Company of India, was renamed Saregama India a few years back.

both gramophone records and the gramophones themselves (incidentally it also used to sell electric irons, refrigerators, etc., imported from the parent company in the UK).

By 1912, many of its competitors shut down while Gramco continued to record hundreds of titles in various parts of India. In 1925, it introduced the HMV label in India. In 1928, competition came from the Columbia Gramophone Company. However, Gramco lived long past all real and potential rivals to become bigger and stronger in India. One reason was the international merger of Columbia, Gramophone, Odeon and Pathe; all rival brands into one company—Electric and Musical Industries Limited or EMI, in 1931. It is one of the largest music companies currently at $3.68 billion in revenues.[4]

The HMV years From the 30s onwards, the 'talkies' or films with sound came into India and film music started dominating what was earlier a classical and light music market. That has remained the shape of the market to date. Various labels from the south and north tried to break Gramco's monopoly over the market by luring singers onto their side, but most folded up soon. The setting up of a recording plant and selling them was a capital-intensive business and Gramco had a head start. Not too many companies could therefore survive against it.

By the 60s, HMV had grown into a monopoly. Most other rivals were insignificant. That is because almost all of them—Hindustan and Megaphone in east India; Ace, Sangeetha, Hathi and AVM in south India; and Brijwani and Marwari in north India—used to be manufactured by Gramco. The first time Gramco faced a serious threat to its monopoly over film music was when Polydor came into the market in the late 60s. Producers and music composers finally had an alternative and were glad for it. It was a new experience for HMV to not have every piece of film music created, come to it. Old-timers remember that Gramco would boycott composers or producers who sold the rights of their film's music to Polydor (later called Music India).

Reminisces Shashi Gopal, who used to work with HMV in the seventies and later set up Magnasound; 'that was a different time. There was no information on the international market, new technologies, there was only one

---

[4] Till 1964, Gramco was managed directly by EMI representatives. By the next year, The Gramophone Company of India (Private) Limited was formed. In 1968, the company went public. In 1976, the foreign holding was further diluted to 40 per cent under the now defunct Foreign Exchange Regulation Act (FERA). During the sixties and seventies, besides gramophones and the records to play on, it manufactured record playing equipment, music systems, radio receivers, wooden cabinets, wooden flash doors, sewing machines and so on. That's because gramophones used wooden cabinets and the company had excess capacity to make wooden articles. During this time Gramco also sold calculators and tape recorders among other things as traded items made by third parties. In March 2005 EMI held 7.71 per cent in Saregama.

television channel and one radio station. We were a total monopoly. Even artistes who later became very famous had to wait outside the office of the general manager A&R for two months or more before they were given a hearing'.[5] According to one estimate 50 per cent of all the music ever recorded in India is with HMV.

The early part of the 20th century was also the richest in terms of music. Some of India's most talented music directors, lyricists, singers—Lata Mangeshkar, Mohammad Rafi, Naushad, S.D. Burman, Saigal, Suraiya, Sahir Ludhianvi, Hemant Kumar—among hundreds of others, recorded their best work on an HMV record or cassette. It was a highly profitable business. HMV, the market leader, made net margins of 20 per cent on the records business, though the consumer electronics business usually pulled the actual figure down to 5–10 per cent throughout the 70s. It was during this time that Polydor with a national repertoire, CBS in Western music and Inreco with eastern Indian music too became known names.

The T-Series years In the 70s, when cassettes were taking off internationally, HMV dismissed it as 'just a technology,' say insiders. Instead it poured money into a new record factory in Calcutta. It did set up a music cassette plant in the late 70s with a licensed capacity of 1.2 million units per year. The licence came with a 75 per cent export obligation. That meant that of the 1.2 million cassettes Gramco made, it had to export 0.9 million cassettes—only 0.3 million could be sold in India. At that time this condition did not make much of a difference to Gramco. The thinking within the company was that its main business was records. It did not do anything to popularise cassettes, since it wanted to avoid eating into the share of records. The prices of cassettes were kept deliberately high so as to discourage consumers.

It seems silly in retrospect; but consider that Gramco was the only major company selling music in India for over 70 years. It had never seen real competition and had no need to fear it. Besides, its manufacturing was in high-cost, union-led Calcutta. The incentive to keep those plants going even when the record factory in Bombay was shut down in 1981 was very high. It had a consumer electronics division that was a millstone around its neck. As a large sector player it had to pay 25–35 per cent duties as compared to the 10–15 per cent for small-scale companies. Then there were high overheads plus labour costs. Much of this made the record player unit unviable. In 1968 when it had to make a choice between shutting it down and investing more to make it viable, Gramco chose the latter. By the late 70s Gramco had lost the market to better products from Philips, Sonodyne and Cosmic.

---

[5] A&R—Artistes and Repertoire. Essentially the department/function in a music company that searches for new talent which can be recorded and sold by the company. Think of it as the department that goes through all the creative raw material and tries to find the good pieces.

The company was very taken up with what it had and therefore what it could sell. Somewhere along the way Gramco lost sight of a crucial fact. While record manufacturing involved billions worth of investment, making cassettes was a cottage industry. If a company did not pay royalty or taxes, a cassette could be produced for as little as Rs 8 per unit according to one estimate. As against this, each gramaphone record cost Rs 20 to make. Tape manufacturing involved putting together easily procurable things like cassette covers, liners, shields and screws and getting the tapes copied by the multiple cassette-duplicating systems from a master or original tape. The cheapest duplicating system was available for Rs 50,000, the most expensive was Rs 5 million. The whole operation could be put together by almost anyone with some money and a small place.

However, from HMV's perspective, since records made for a capital-intensive business and piracy was unknown, it did not expect any competition. Till 1980, the total music market worth Rs 200 million comprised only records and only organised players. By 1982 though, HMV's world turned upside down. In the early 80s, Gulshan Kumar, a former fruit juice seller, discovered a loophole in the Indian Copyright Act. As long as he used new singers, he could use the same tunes that HMV owned. Kumar started a cassette manu-facturing operation with completely unknown singers rendering popular Lata Mangeshkar, Mohammad Rafi or Kishore Kumar songs. These were called 'version recordings'. To get around licensing and taxation problems, he had a series of companies, each a small-scale operation, so that there were no capacity restraints. Unlike Gramco, which depended on just dealers, Kumar distributed through every possible retail outlet—*paan* shops, on the streets and through *kirana* (grocery) shops—at anywhere between Rs 10–15 per cassette. It is alleged that it was by evading sales, octroi and excise duties that Kumar's company, Super Cassettes Industries, could price its cassettes so low.

This changed in a very fundamental way the power equations in the music industry and made music accessible to a large chunk of Indians. In 1983 the cost of a cassette was Rs 25 against Rs 40 for a record. A cassette player cost Rs 600 while a record player cost Rs 1000. Combine the low cost of entry with the low cost of usage and it was evident that the market would grow. Initially HMV continued to use only 25–50 per cent of its cassette-making capacity. The red ink resulting from the loss on record sales, and the bleeding consumer electronics division, pushed HMV further down. In 1982–83, sales dropped to Rs 87 million and the company made a total loss of about Rs 42 million.

It then pushed up production to about a million cassettes by sourcing them from outside. That backfired. First, because the contract manufacturers got hold of the master copy and started producing illegal copies. Second, quality was a problem. The dice was further loaded against any organised sector manu-facturing of cassettes because the budget of 1982 imposed an excise duty of

26.75 per cent on pre-recorded music cassettes. Also, there was a 13 per cent royalty to be paid to artistes and 15 per cent sales tax that the pirates never paid. All of this served to widen the gap between the pirate's prices and that of HMV.

Just like T-series, a host of other players started getting into the act. There came up not one but several alternatives to both T-series and Gramco, like Venus and Tips. Many others started off just like T-series by first copying original HMV tunes and then starting their own legitimate business of buying rights and selling the music. As a result the market took off and penetration increased. From Rs 200 million in 1985, Gulshan Kumar's T-Series brand hit Rs 1.3 billion in revenues by 1989.

While the way some of these companies started could be questioned, their contribution to the business cannot be ignored. When the leader ignored a new, cheaper technology that could give consumers a better option, others grabbed the opportunity. By 1983, estimates put all the pirates' share of the recorded music industry at 95 per cent.

Kumar's entry is important not only because it expanded the market but also because what he did symbolises the larger truth about music—or for that matter any media product. *New technologies always offer the promise of faster, easier access. It is up to existing companies to make something of these opportunities. In the 80s it was the cassette, in the 90s the CD and now it is the Internet and mobile telephony.*

Back in the 80s, HMV reacted in many ways. It shunned film music completely, lobbied for a clampdown on piracy. The Indian Copyright Act was amended to make piracy a cognisable offence and an excise duty was slapped on blank cassettes, the main raw material for the pirates. It also got the industry to rally around and form the Indian Phonographic Industries Association (IPIA) in order to fight piracy. HMV, CBS, Polygram, Master Records and InReco were the founding members. IPI later became IMI—Indian Music Industries Association, the current industry body.[6] Finally, it also got the excise duty on pre-recorded cassettes abolished in 1984. As a result, the price of a cassette dropped to a minimum of Rs 18 and a maximum of Rs 34, in the organised sector.

By the time Gramco managed to do all this, it had become a sick company thanks to its non-performing consumer electronics division and the almost defunct record business (see Figure 4.3). In 1984–85 it shut the year with a loss of Rs 59 million on a turnover of Rs 141 million: this, at a time when the market was booming. It needed money to expand its cassette-making capacity, to pay off its debts and to run its operations. Finally, EMI found a saviour in RPG Enterprises, which took over the Gramaphone Company of India (GCI). The RPG Group has interests in other businesses such as tyres, carbon black, tea and chemicals.

---

[6] As far as I can make out Super Cassettes is still not a member of the IMI.

Figure 4.3: Gramco's (now Saregama) History

Year	Sales revenue Rs million
1965	24
1970	43
1981–82	204
1983–84	137
1986–87	124
1990–91	312
2000–01	1650
2001–02	1120
2002–03	989
2003–04	691
2004–05	1008

Note: The revenues for 2003–04 are for the nine months ending March 2004.

Source: Case study on Gramco by the Management Development Institute, Gurgaon and annual reports of Saregama Limited.

The good years In September 1985, Pradeep Chanda took over as chief executive officer (CEO) of HMV.[7] He started out with a voluntary retirement scheme (VRS) to cut costs. But it was the changes he made in the music business that reaped returns for HMV.

The first was a fundamental change in its marketing—a function that never got much attention earlier. Till it could earn enough money to buy film music, HMV decided to use its rich repertoire to generate revenues. HMV had been the only major label for over seven decades. Every piece of Hindi music ever recorded in India, from K.L Saigal to Kishore Kumar, was (and is) in its library. All it had to do was repackage them in as many forms as possible. The Collector's Series of Indian Greats was retailed to institutions like Citibank, which used them for promotions. The Golden Collection was promoted for more than seven months and is still paying off. It was a good idea in media business terms. Any sale from the repertoire adds straight to the bottomline, since the costs of creating the music (or any other content) are zero.

Second, and crucially, it went back to film music albeit in a different way. HMV started offering an advance (royalty) to producers against the music rights. Till then the whole system operated only on payment of royalties after the music was released and sales tabulated for each year. By paying an advance Gramco took the risk of the music being good or bad, but it also meant getting the music cheaper than it would be if it proved to be successful. This practice became very popular. It became a means of getting working capital for perpetually cash-strapped film producers. HMV would then promote the

---

[7] A large part of Gramco's background and what happened in those days has come from an interview with Chanda who finally managed to turn Gramco around.

music of these films heavily, something it had never done earlier. Sunil Lulla who was with HMV in the early 90s remembers, 'with (the film) *Darr* we did everything you could do with a soap. There were even *Darr* matchboxes.'[8] It had a good run with hits like *Chandni*, *Ram Lakhan* and *Saudagar* but the film that turned it around, according to Chanda, was *Maine Pyar Kiya*. A totally unknown film from a down-in-the-dumps production house Rajshri, became a runaway hit and sold over eight million cassettes.

By the early 90s, many music companies like Tips and Venus also started financing films completely, instead of just offering advances. The music industry was beginning to look very robust compared to the piracy, falling-cinema attendance plagued film industry. At one point there was talk of the music industry overtaking films in size. That of course never happened, but the link between the success of a film's music and the film became stronger. If people liked the music of *Taal*, for instance, it inevitably meant higher box office collection for the film and vice versa.

Third, just like Super Cassettes, HMV began investing in new, non-film artistes. Among others, it 'discovered' Alisha Chinai and Malkiat Singh. Super Cassettes had used this route of betting on absolutely unknown music composers, lyricists and singers quite successfully. Young unknown singers and musicians are happy to work for small sums of money. The only cost that a recording company incurs is of mass manufacturing the tapes and distributing it. If the singer is a hit then the returns are disproportionately high compared to the investment. In the process T-Series discovered some popular singers like Sonu Nigam. In a way this is something that all music companies' A&R division is supposed to do; though, in reality, most prefer to bet on safe and established voices.

Finally, HMV also expanded its dealer network from 2,500 in 1985 to 35,000 retailers whom wholesalers sold to by 1991. While earlier it threatened withdrawal of dealership rights, this was a different market and HMV had learnt the rules.

All of this worked. By 1989–90, HMV was in the black again with a small profit of Rs 1.6 million on revenues of Rs 284 odd million. Meanwhile, Kumar too had been very active. He had forayed into a variety of businesses—tape decks, film magazines, CD players, video cassettes, television sets, and even washing powder! His most important diversification however was into films. As Kumar said, in a *Businessworld* story chronicling his success, 'A hit film means increased turnover and profit for many of my divisions'.

For the second time Kumar had recognised an essential truth about the music business (of that time) that his old respectable rival HMV missed. Since films

---

[8] Lulla is currently CEO of Times Global Broadcasting, a Bennett, Coleman & Company group company.

brought in 90 per cent or more of a music company's revenues and since (by now) music companies paid huge advances to acquire film music, it made business sense to integrate forward into making the film itself. That way a music company could have a greater sense of the risks involved and would be better placed to reap the benefits of a hit. Venus, Tips and a whole lot of other music companies followed in Kumar's footsteps. Earlier in the decade, CBS had tried the strategy with the moderately successful *Sadma, Agar Tum Na Hote,* and a few other films. The first few products from Vishesh Films, Kumar's film company, were—*Aashiqui* (a hit) and *Lal Dupatta Malmal Ka* (a moderately successful video film).

The satellite TV years By the early 90s, music was operating like an industry, thinks Chanda. Around this time two important events gave another cassette-like fillip to the market.

The first was the birth of music channels—like MTV and Channel V—and of music videos. The second was the entry of big multinational and Indian companies into music software and retailing. These changed the size, scope and expectations of returns from this business. The third change, the coming of CDs, did not have any immediate impact on the market.

Take a look at the first trend. The coming of channels like MTV, Channel V, Zee Music, ATN and, later, ETC, gave music an audio-visual feel that, so far, watching the song on film, in a theatre or watching *Chhayageet,* a show based on film songs, could give. Till that time no singer had ever had a music video. Nor was there a Billboard type of listing or ranking of popular music. Soon music videos became very popular with audiences and with music companies. They exposed listeners to different types of voices and music and gave the industry several 24-hour platforms for promoting their products.

153

Making a video alone could cost anywhere between Rs 0.5–1 million; then there was the airtime bought on a music channel. Therefore costs doubled. The good part was that new artistes started getting breaks since television made it easier to promote them. If Gulshan Kumar had taught the industry a lesson in distribution and pricing, music channels took it a step further and taught them the importance of promotion and brand tie-ins. As a result of music channels airing music videos, non-film music, especially segments like Indipop, *ghazals* and devotional music, grew significantly from about 10 per cent of the market to about 30 per cent.[9]

---

[9] Almost all the numbers in this chapter are estimates based on IMI figures, industry estimates and the background reports available on the industry. The global numbers are from IFPI or the International Federation of Phonographic Industries.

The second trend was of investments coming in from large companies. Sony Corp set up Sony Music (now Sony-BMG) in India in the late 90s. At one point in 1999, the total investment coming into the industry was pegged at Rs 1.5 billion. A chunk of this was in the area of retailing. Bennett, Coleman & Company (BCCL) started investing in Planet M, its chain of music retail stores across India. The south-based LMW Group was investing in 12 stores across the region; and there were also stand-alone stores that came up—like The Groove in Mumbai, and RPG Enterprise's own chain, Music World. This was the most crucial investment in the business so far. After Kumar's attempt at expanding distribution through *paan* and *kirana* shops, nothing had really happened on that front. Except for Rhythm House, Mumbai did not have a single large music retail store till Planet M or The Groove came up. Music companies needed larger retail stores to display their latest releases and catalogue albums (a collection of archival music). Typically catalogues generate 50–60 per cent of the sales for large companies. Without the depth and space that a large store can offer, it was impossible to tap into this market.

The third trend of the early 90s—compact discs (CDs)—did not take the market to a digital world immediately as it did in other countries. India remained a cassette-driven market. Both the price of CDs (about Rs 300–600 as against Rs 25–100 for a cassette) and CD players were a deterrent to its growth initially. In 2001, only six million of India's 50 million or so middle-class households owned a CD player, since it is a high cost hardware. Also, for some reason CDs were associated with international music. Just two per cent of film music volumes came from CDs whereas 10 per cent of international music volumes come from CDs, the highest in any genre. However, in 2002, most music companies dropped CD prices to Rs 99. The impact has been a doubling of CD volumes to about 15 per cent of the total music volumes sold in 2005.

The music industry had a particularly bad time between 2001–04. This was due to piracy, mediocre music and the rising cost of buying rights. Tips paid Rs 85 million for *Yaadein* only to make a loss of Rs 55 million on it. Of the 13 albums Tips released in 2001, it reportedly made a loss on nine. HMV lost Rs 160 million in fiscal 2002, thanks to film music.

Also, piracy struck again. At some point in the mid-90s, when it hovered between 25–40 per cent of the market, it looked like piracy had been controlled. That was because of the raids and seizures made by ex-super-cop Julio Rebiero and his band of former police officers across the country. Incidentally, piracy is endemic to most of Asia. Pakistan doesn't have a music industry because piracy eats away more than 90 per cent of the market. In 2003, after two years of stagnation and one of de-growth, the IMI has got increasingly active on both raids and public awareness campaigns. But the level of piracy had already jumped to 50 per cent.

Piracy combined with high fragmentation explains why a lot of international companies do not see any merit in investing in India. Universal did so, somewhere in the late 90s, as did Sony-BMG. Both haven't achieved any critical size so far. The others have a peripheral presence in India.[10] If international companies haven't achieved much, none of the top 10 companies in India like Super Cassettes or Saregama, have any size to boast of, considering that they have been around for decades. Super Cassettes, the largest company, is an estimated Rs 3 billion.[11] Saregama, the oldest company is still a little over Rs 1 billion.

The hope of growth comes from several new avenues of distribution emerging.

Internet The IMI was one of the first bodies in the world, probably, to give out experimental licences to Internet radio stations and portals that offered streaming music or downloads in 2000. Several companies like *Hungama.com* bought these licences. Most have become retail stores that aggregate all kind of music, digitise it and sell it either to mobile phone companies or to subscribers directly.

Mobile phones This has the potential to become a large chunk of music industry revenues in the next two years. Many mobile phone users pay anywhere between Rs 5–30 to have the tunes of songs, of say *Dil Chahta Hai*, as ringtones on their mobiles. As both mobile penetration and usage goes up, music and mobile companies both stand to gain.

Over 15 per cent of the 80 million mobile phones in India are MP3 enabled. That means they can download music from the Internet. Nearly 40 per cent of all new phones sold have the ability and bandwidth to plug into the Internet and download songs.[12] Almost every mobile phone company is investing in offering users song downloads—for ringtones, ring-back tones or for plain listening. Many reckon that after short text messaging (SMS), music will be the next big non-voice revenue generator.

According to one report, Indians were downloading 25 million ringtones and ring-back tones every month. Another estimate put the money that could come from mobile downloads, at 10 per cent of the music industry's revenues by the end of 2006. Saregama, for instance expects digital downloads to touch 50 per cent of its revenues by 2007–08.

---

[10] With the recent buyout of BMG by Sony internationally, Sony-BMG now operates in India as one company.
[11] Estimates are only pertaining to its music business.
[12] These phones are GPRS or general packet radio service enabled.

None of this is unusual. In the US, digital distribution went up by five times in one year between 2002–03. By 2008 it is expected to touch $2.2 billion or about 19 per cent of the total market then. Globally it is expected to touch just under $4 billion by 2008.[13] In several markets where mobile and broadband penetration is high, the growth rates will be faster. South Korea is the first market in the world where the digital music is equal to the physical format business. Both stand at $100 million each. Of the digital business 80 per cent comes from mobile and 20 per cent from the Internet.

As a result of this move towards digitisation, all kinds of aggregators, such as *Soundbuzz.com* or *CrimsonBay.com*, are coming up. They help open up the overseas market too. For instance, *CrimsonBay.com* is an online store that offers user downloads from 40,000 odd songs from Indian films at 69 cents or 99 cents, depending on how the song is bought. These include, among others, songs from Saregama, the company that has the largest repertoire of Indian music. *CrimsonBay.com* shares the revenues with Saregama and others keeping a small margin as the retailer of the music.

The overseas market was a promising revenue stream coming up in the mid-90s. At one point it brought in as much as 30 per cent of a music album's revenues. Piracy and the lack of distribution and marketing money, however, limited Indian music companies from exploring it fully. But the fact is that it exists. There are more than 20 million Indians overseas who are potential buyers. Digital music, whether on the Internet or satellite ratio, can help unlock this potential.

FM stations As private FM stations go live all across India, they are creating another revenue stream for music companies. Currently there are just over a dozen. As the phase two licensing takes off and there are at least over 350 stations, the money that companies make from FM royalties too should go to 20–30 per cent of revenues.

Satellite radio stations WorldSpace or XM are also becoming big buyers of music rights for their subscription-based services. WorldSpace already has over 60,000 subscribers in India. While this may or may not become a big revenue source, it is a great way to market a repertoire that cannot sell big numbers in the physical format. WorldSpace has stations dedicated to specialist genres like classical music, jazz, and so on.

Home video A music company is usually among the first ports of call for most film companies launching a new project. That is because the sale of music rights brings in working capital. Now many music companies have started leveraging this to pick up home video rights too. It is one of the fastest growing

---

[13] PricewaterhouseCooper's Global Entertainment and Media Outlook 2004–08.

film retail formats (refer to the chapter on Film). The distribution channels are largely the same—Planet M or MusicWorld or any of the mainline music stores also stock DVDs and VCDs.

If Sony-BMG buys the home video rights of *Lagaan* along with the film's music, it can design posters, publicity material in bulk, can pump up the trade in advance for the release of the home video. The music and home video is sold as a package across the same distribution network of 300 wholesalers and 10,000 retailers. It helps promote the film better if Sony-BMG also owns the home video rights. It is a revenue stream that almost every major music company is tapping into. About 10 per cent of Saregama's revenues in March 2004 came from retailing Warner, BBC and Universal videos.

Sony-BMG is an example of what a music company could be doing in this new scenario. Its revenues in March 2004 jumped to Rs 580 million compared to about Rs 320 million in March 2003. This happened in what has been a bad year for the industry. What worked for Sony-BMG was diversification. It has been licensing music for ringtones, commercials, FM stations and websites. That brought in over Rs 100 million in contribution. That means the money went straight to the bottomline. Home videos in the form of VCDs and DVDs brought in over 13 per cent or Rs 80 million of its revenues. It has also signed on the sales and distribution of EMI-Virgin's products. It is therefore making use of every distribution format available, as well as every other line of business across which it can extend its strengths.

THE WAY IT WORKS

There are three different ways in which business is done in the music industry:

Film music When Aamir Khan Productions made *Lagaan* it sold the rights to the film's music and songs to Sony-BMG (then Sony Music) for a reported Rs 60 million. For Aamir Khan Productions, the money was a part of the working capital for the film. Sony-BMG then packages the music in tapes and CDs and pushes it through music and other retail outlets. This is an outright sale. Sony-BMG retains the rights to the music completely and bears the cost of promoting it and the risk of its failure, and the rewards of its success as well.[14] After paying the cost of promotion Sony-BMG needed to sell 3.5 million tapes of *Lagaan* to break even: it sold 3.2 million to start with. In all probability it will more than make up on its shortfall over the next few years.

---

[14] A lot of this depends on the agreement between the music company and the production company. It is possible for a music company to pay a smaller amount upfront and tie the producer in for a share of revenues.

So the costs are those of acquisition, promotion, marketing and distribution. Margins could be as high as 30–50 per cent. After the album has achieved breakeven, all the money is added directly to the profits. It is a high-cost high-risk strategy, especially since the cost of acquiring films had peaked to unrealistic levels recently. This is completely different from the way it works anywhere in the world. However, in the non-film market, the Indian music business operates like the rest of the world.

Non-film music There are some music companies that do not buy film music since the cost of acquisitions is high. They try to discover new talent. The cost of producing an album differs according to the artiste. To record and market a small time unknown artiste costs between Rs 1 million—Rs 3.5 million. If he becomes successful, like Adnan Sami some years back, the company can promote him aggressively to get higher sales. Initially Magnasound did a low-key release for Sami's album. When he proved to be a hit, it released a music video and then a remix version. That helped push sales from 18 million to a record 25 million copies. This album probably mitigated the losses for all the non-performing Magnasound albums!

This is called the *portfolio approach* and most music and film companies use it regularly, not only for new talent but for their entire portfolio. Saregama nurtures new talent and acquires film music. Not all the films that it acquires might produce successful music. It could buy high-cost rights to two big-banner, expensive films, three medium budget ones, a couple of small films and maybe introduce a couple of new singers. The idea is that at least one of them will deliver a blockbuster. In 1999–2000 Rakesh Roshan's *Kaho Na Pyar Hai*, a medium budget film with an unknown star cast proved to be the big seller for Saregama, instead of its own home production *Godmother*. The idea is very similar to how a mutual fund would manage a portfolio of stocks; some high-risk, high return, and some low-risk low-cost on which it could potentially get higher returns.

Catalogue There are some years when nothing works. In 2001, none of the big albums broke even or made money. Except for Adnan Sami, nobody saw a single hit that year. What do music companies do in years like that? They depend on the steady sales from their libraries. Saregama has the best catalog in the Indian music industry with about 300,000 tracks, a chunk of this from films. From April–September 2004, in a particularly bad phase for music, it got 40 per cent of its revenues from its catalogue, essentially of old Hindi film songs. This money goes directly to profits since there are hardly any costs involved in putting these on shop shelves, except promotion and trade margins. Internationally most music companies get about 60 per cent of their revenues from catalogue sales.

METRICS

There are no major metrics that are used in the industry. Most would revolve around the quality of music. The others are generic, like copies sold.

REGULATION[15]

Till liberalisation in 1991, there was no specific regulation impacting the music industry. Just like other sectors, it couldn't get foreign labels or money into India easily. Shashi Gopal remembers that when he quit HMV in 1985, he wanted to get Warner into India. He claims that it took him about four years to get the proposal cleared.

The IMI represents the recording industry of India and is affiliated to IFPI the World Industry body having 1,450 members in 75 countries. The IMI, a consortium of over 50 music companies strives to protect the rights of phonogram producers and in the process promote the development of musical culture. It also acts as the face of the industry for lobbying and other purposes.

Some pieces of legislation and issues that impact the industry:

The Copyright Act, 1957 It contains the most important legal provisions affecting the music industry. It defines some of the basics that shape the industry. These are:

Musical Work means a work consisting of music and includes any graphical notation of such work, but does not include any words or any action intended to be sung, spoken or performed with the music.

Sound Recording means a recording of sounds from which such sounds may be produced regardless of the medium on which such recording is made or the method by which the sounds are reproduced.

The Copyright (Amendment) Act, 1994 provides certain exclusive rights called 'performer's rights' for the benefit of various kinds of performers like singers and other performers. Such rights subsist for 25 years from the year of performance. The performer has the exclusive right to do the following:

- To make a sound recording or visual recording of the performance
- To reproduce a sound recording or visual recording of the performance

---

[15] The information on regulation has been put together by law firms Amarchand & Mangaldas & Suresh A. Shroff and Company (New Delhi) and Nishith Desai and Associates (Mumbai).
[16] The Act defines Broadcast to mean communication to the public:

a) By any means of wireless diffusions, whether in any one or more of the forms of signs, sounds or visual images; or
b) By wire and includes a re-broadcast.

159

- To broadcast the performance
- To communicate the performance to the public otherwise than by broadcast[16]

A musical work must be original in order to qualify for copyright protection. There is no copyright in a song as such because a song is not one of the types of work in which copyright exists. A song has its words written by one person, while someone else composes its music. Therefore the words have a literary copyright and so has its music. In a musical work, copyright is in the melody or harmony reduced to printing, writing or graphic form. Though registration is not compulsory to enjoy the rights conferred by the Act, it acts as a supportive measure, since registration is considered to be 'prima facie' evidence that the person registered is the owner of the copyright.

The Copyright Act prescribes various remedies and penalties for impinging the diverse forms of protection under the Act. These include:

- Civil Remedies—the copyright owner is able to recover damages suffered on account of piracy. The copyright owner may also seek an injunction against the infringers, to prevent them from carrying on with piracy.
- Penalties and Punishments—not only for those who directly indulge in piracy related activities, but also for these who aid and abet such activities. The Copyright Act provides for imprisonment up to three years and a maximum fine of Rs 200,000. An enhanced penalty has been prescribed if the same offence is repeated.

Piracy: This is a big issue in the music industry, it is what most laws focus on. In India some of the most common forms of piracy faced by the music industry are:

- Counterfeiting—refers to the unauthorized copying of the original sound recording.
- Bootlegging—affects the recording rights of the performance by various artistes. Very often, the performances of the artistes are recorded without the permission of the copyright holders and sold in the market.
- Pirate recording—is the process of duplication made from legitimate recording, compiled together and distributed in the market for commercial gain.

Remixes: There was for some time a debate raging on whether the remix of a song amounts to a violation of the copyrights in the original song. The Act currently has no provisions specifically for remixes. The Act does provide for cover versions. The now notorious section 52 (1) (j) states that cover versions can be made two calendar years after the end of the year in which the first sound recording was made, and after obtaining a licence from the owner of the sound recording. Further, no alterations should be made to the original sound recording without obtaining the consent of the owner. A remix of a song could violate the copyright in the original song, if in the remix, a substantial part of the original song has been copied and the people listening to the remix can associate it with the original song. However, if the remix maker has taken the licence from the owner of the original song to use the song or alter the song, he may be protected under the law. Most don't do that and remixes have flourished. There has been strong lobbying by the music industry to have the section either scrapped or amended.

IPRS and PPL The Indian Performing Rights Society Limited (IPRS) is a non-profit-making body set up on August 23, 1969. It is the registered copyright society (by the central government) under the Copyright Act, 1957, and is permitted to carry on the copyright business in musical works and any words or any action—intended to be sung, spoken or performed with the music. IPRS administers and controls the performing rights, mechanical rights and synchronisation rights in musical works. It does so on behalf of its members and those of its sister societies with which it has reciprocal agreements. Its membership includes virtually all the Indian composers, authors and music publishers whose works are publicly performed. The members assign their past, present and future rights to the IPRS and amongst themselves, control nearly 97 per cent of the total Indian music. The IPRS represents more than 500,000 foreign composers, authors and publishers through its affiliation agreements with similar societies in countries all over the world.

Phonographic Performance Limited (PPL) is the exclusive Copyright Society engaged in the business of music licensing of the recording industry, with affiliates in 45 countries of the World. For instance India and UK, have signed an agreement that allows both these bodies to act as licensees on behalf of the other. That means if Sunrise station in the UK wants to play a track from Times Music, all it needs is a licence from PPL UK, a local body instead of sending someone to India or dealing with PPL India. All the 50 plus IMI members automatically make their repertoires available for airplay in Britain with this agreement and vice versa for English music companies that are PPL members there. UK, the third largest music market in the world, is also one of the bigger markets for India's predominantly film music. It has over two million Asians who are big buyers of Indian entertainment.

This agreement however is the exception. Typically the IPRS and PPL are an area where international and national companies wanting to license music from the industry face a problem. Producers, music composers and lyricists who are members of the IPRS assign all the rights in their musical and literary works to it. Similarly, music companies assign all their rights in sound recordings to PPL. When a company wants to broadcast or webcast a song from a Hindi film there are three works in the song, lyrics (literary works), music (musical works), and the recording of the literary and musical works (the sound recording). As of today, such a person has to obtain two licences for the same: from IPRS for the lyrics and the musical works, and PPL for the sound recording. If the sound recording, which includes the musical and literary works, has already been assigned to PPL, the person should be able to obtain the licence from PPL directly to broadcast the sound recording, without approaching IPRS. PPL can internally have a mechanism to distribute the royalties to IPRS, if so required. A vice versa approach, wherein the person approaches only IPRS for the rights in the musical and literary works may also hold good. The practice of obtaining two separate licences to broadcast only one song is a burden on the broadcaster and needs to be amended reckons media lawyer Ashni Parekh.

Others Recently the IMI has got increasingly active in fighting piracy and taking up the cause of the industry with the government.

- In November 2004, it joined hands with the UK Trade and Investment, a British government body to promote Indian music in the UK and vice versa.
- Recently it also joined hands with the Gramophone Workers Welfare Association, to demand a reclassification of music cassettes and CDs as Intellectual Property Software under the value added tax (VAT) regime. They argue the current classification will drive the VAT rate on music cassettes/CDs up to as much as 17–22 per cent. This will push up piracy since the prices of the legitimate products will go up. IMI is attempting to seek a parity of music content with other Intellectual Property Rates under proposed VAT of 4 per cent.

Accounting Norms[17]

The primary accounting issues are revenue recognition and cost allocation.

Costs Music depends entirely on the purchase of music rights from producers of movies or by paying royalties to artistes. The company might have its

---

[17] The accounting norms have been put together by Ramesh Lakshman of Ramesh Lakshman and Company.

in-house musicians to compose and create the targeted music, but the general trend is for them to sign exclusive or other rights for recording music. The company might compensate the musicians in diverse ways for the music recorded. These might include:

- An upfront, lump-sum fee with all rights to the music resting with the company
- A fixed fee plus agreed royalty on actual sales
- Only royalty from actual sales
- The musician sharing part of the recording costs and sharing in the profit from the sale of the recorded music contributed by him.

In the absence of any specific standard in India, it is left to the discretion of the company to deal with this. It is imperative that any method adopted be followed consistently.

Music rights: The cost of an album or a piece of music can be allocated to the number of copies of the album produced in the first instance and charged to the revenue account in proportion to the units sold. Alternately a company could decide to write off the entire amount paid upfront in the year in which it is paid, on the argument that there is no guarantee about whether it will be recovered or not. Such an accounting will necessarily result in volatility in earnings. For example, if Sony-BMG writes off the entire Rs 60 million it paid for the rights of *Lagaan* in 2001 then the profits for 2001 will naturally be lower than they actually are. The assets side of the balance sheet is bound to include the value of publishing rights bought and would be categorised as intangibles.[18]

Advances: These could be paid to artistes and others against future royalty. Such advances are usually guaranteed minimum payable and hence non-refundable. These are treated as assets and amortised over the period of the contract. They could be amortised in proportion to sales as well.

Production expenses: They can be written off in the year in which they are incurred. However, the cost of production should be factored in the value of the cassettes and CDs held in inventory. Consequently the production cost proportionate to the units sold would be charged to revenue.

Royalties: The publisher of the music may enter into contracts to pay royalty and the royalty may accrue from different sources on the basis of use. The liability needs to be accounted as and when it accrues and income should be recognised only when it is earned beyond doubt. Accounting would depend upon the terms of each contract. In some cases, the income to be accounted

163

---

[18] In copyright law parlance music has to be written out or published before it can be eligible for copyright protection.

may be net of the royalties payable. An artiste might create a brand-value by selling all future performance rights to a company. Such capital payment should be written off over the life of the contract or over the estimated sales realization from the same.

Revenues The stage at which the revenue is recognised follows from the terms of contract with the distributors, retailers and customers. If the tradition is that defective products will not be taken back since the defect could have originated while using, then the sales revenue is recognised once the goods are shipped. If a right of return exists, then appropriate provision has to be made for potential returns. If the distributors are entitled to return all unsold items then also an appropriate provision has to be made for the anticipated or estimated returns. If the distributor is acting as an agent then sales is recognised only when the distributor has sold the goods.

Taxation Music companies are taxed like normal companies at the applicable rate of tax. Corporate entities and partnerships pay income tax at 33–35 per cent. However, if music software is exported, the export income enjoys a tax rebate on a gradually reducing scale. The sale of music may be liable to sales tax according to the norms in different states.

Comparatively, the US Generally Accepted Accounting Principles (GAAP) is more specific in the accounting treatment for music industry. Some of the issues raised above are specifically dealt with by the standard with the appropriate prescription of the accounting treatment. Recently the President of the Institute of Chartered Accountants of India in his communiqué to members has indicated that the Institute is contemplating coming out with industry specific standards.

VALUATION

After breaking away from Magnasound, Suresh Thomas set up Crescendo Music in 1992. Four years later, in 1996, he sold 51 per cent of the company to BMG Music, an arm of the German Media conglomerate Bertelsmann. At that time, the Rs 20 million Crescendo was valued at Rs 8 million. Assuming that profit after tax was Rs 2 million, Crescendo got a valuation of four times its earnings.[19] In those days there was only one listed company, HMV, and very little history of either private placement or primary issues in the music industry.

---

[19] Crescendo is now an Indian company since BMG sold its stake. Also, as mentioned in footnote 10, BMG got bought out by Sony recently, internationally. The new company is called Sony-BMG.

That is true even today. The only recent entry to the listed club has been Tips Industries in the latter part of 2000. Usually, the valuation game in music works on libraries and their potential to generate cash flow, which is then discounted for the future just like in other media businesses (refer to the chapter on Television). The big difference is that a library or catalogue is more valuable in music than other media. Films or television serials wear off or go out of fashion after a couple of viewings. An S.D. Burman album or an Asha Bhonsle hit, from the 50s or the 60s, is being sold even today. It holds appeal to a new set of consumers and the older one keeps replacing their worn out software because they want to continue listening to it. Notice how many singularly untalented people make money from re-mixing popular old songs. However, a re-release of *Buniyaad*, the biggest hit on DD in 1987, did not generate the same excitement (or revenues) 10–12 years later. While the re-release of *Lagaan* four years later may generate excitement, the music of *Lagaan* is more likely to generate steady revenues year after year.

A music library's ability to generate money also depends on how many distribution formats it is used across. Earlier there were only retail stores. Now there are radio stations, music channels, the Internet and broadband. The better the music company is at mastering these technologies, the more are its chances of getting a good valuation with a good library.

The game of valuing music companies is not very developed in India because many investors see very little value in investing in small companies with small catalogues. Many investors, like Deshpande of ICICI, argue that the pricing of music products should be freed, to unlock the value in the business. She points out that there is no maximum retail price (MRP) in the US. That means a company is free to hike prices for a hit album like the *Titanic*. 'Why do you need an MRP? It is like telling a television channel don't charge more for your highest rated programme', says Deshpande. Others like banker Satish Shenoy think that the industry has to fix its piracy problem and get a clearer picture of its revenue before valuations can start making sense.

 **radio**

The best years of radio are yet to come

IF THIS CHAPTER had been written in 1999, all it would have contained is the history of All India Radio (AIR). In 2003 it talked about the hopes of new private Frequency Modulation (FM) stations that had begun broadcasting. Now, in 2006, there is truly some hope.

It is true that private operators have made losses.[1] But it is also true that the market has expanded. Penetration, listenership, and revenues everything has increased. From about Rs 1 billion in 2001, when privatisation took off, radio advertising revenues have grown to over Rs 3.6 billion in 2004[2] (see Figure 0.3). AIR alone saw a doubling of revenues within the first year of privatisation, proving that it is good for everybody. There are more than 215 AIR stations and about a dozen private ones. Also, there is one major satellite radio service, WorldSpace, with about 40 stations of different genres bringing in a slice of subscription revenues.

In July 2005 the government announced a new radio policy. It was, in large measure, well thought-out. The second phase of radio privatisation has begun well. The closed bidding was completed in January 2006 and almost every company that took part agrees that it was transparent and fair. With any luck, the end of this year or the beginning of 2007 should see 337 stations in 91 cities: a bounty by any standards. It means a bigger market, and a larger share of ad spends.

---

[1] According to TRAI data in 2003–04, 20 licensees had total revenues of Rs 1.15 billion and expenses of Rs 2.37 billion. So they were all making huge losses. Of the expenses licence fees alone was 1.08 billion.

[2] The figure for radio advertising revenues is from the numbers Lodestar Media has put together for this book. Even if we factor in discounts, the total ad-spend on radio was at least Rs 2.7 billion. AIR alone had revenue of Rs 1.58 billion in 2004–05 according to a press release by the Ministry of Information and Broadcasting.

There are at least five large national players emerging. There is Kalanithi Maran's South Asia FM and Kal Radio (Suryan) with 71 stations, Anil Ambani's Adlabs Films with 56, the Bennett, Coleman & Company owned ENIL (Radio Mirchi) with 28 stations and India Value Fund-Music Broadcast owned (Radio City) with 20 stations. Some such as Sun will probably have to give up a few stations since it cannot have more than 15 per cent of all the stations allocated under the new policy.

Even if Sun and Adlabs give up a few stations, what are emerging for the first time is national players in private radio and an alternative to AIR in these markets. Both Sun TV and BCCL also own newspapers and TV stations. Wait then for more variety in what you hear on radio as hundreds of stations jostle for your time. Add in a few other major players joining in. The Kuala Lumpur-based Astro All Asia Networks has joined hands with NDTV and Value Labs to buy out Living Media's Red FM brand in 3 cities in 2005. Then there is BBC Worldwide that along with investor Rakesh Jhunjhunwala picked up an undisclosed stake in Radio Mid-Day West.

Why then is there an air of, let-us-see-what-happens about the radio business?

Well, because going by the record so far, how many of those 337 stations will see the light of day is an open question. The world's largest democracy is still struggling to get rid of the vestiges of government control over a medium that, unlike TV or print, covers over 99 per cent of India. It is a medium that is not dependent on literacy or electricity. All it needs is a receiver and batteries. Yet, radio remains an insignificant part of the Indian media scene. Its potential was first suppressed under AIR and, after privatisation, by policies that did not allow it to make full use of liberalisation. The new licensing requirements still do not allow a radio company to own more than 15 per cent of all the stations in the country, making consolidation almost impossible. They still do not allow private stations to broadcast news or to use programming across their own stations freely. Radio broadcasting in India is stuck somewhere between the government's desire to protect AIR and to free the medium.

That's a shame, because radio can do so much. In a market with over 160 television channels, thousands of newspapers and magazines, the Internet, mobile phones, multiplexes and what have you, radio still stands a chance. That is evident in its growth since privatisation. Its utility as a high-frequency medium to hammer home a message, has only begun to be used in markets like Mumbai, Delhi, Ahmedabad, Bangalore, Indore and Chennai. The growth of local cable channels, language news and entertainment channels and small local newspapers proves that radio too can use local advertising to get bigger.

It is on the back of local advertising, its ability to connect with the music business and with new media that radio has grown in the rest of the world. Globally, radio was estimated to have got $31.8 billion in advertising and

$11.3 billion in subscription revenues in 2005. In the US alone, more than 14,000 stations were estimated to generate over $22 billion through the two streams of revenue. Radio manages to get 12–13 per cent of the total American ad spend, going by the trend of the last few years. Those numbers converted into an average margin of more than 17 per cent for the radio broadcast industry in the US through the 90s.

Except for a few odd years in the past there is no such record of profits at AIR. 'Radio in India is underused,' points out Harish Bhimani, one the most popular voices on radio. After 78 years, AIR generates just about Rs 1.58 billion in revenues. The 27,000 people on its rolls wipe out that—and much more. The result: AIR lives off a government handout every year (see Figure 5.1).

Figure 5.1: AIR's Revenues

	AIR revenues
Year	Rs million
1967–68	1.9
1975–76	62.6
1980–81	125.1
1990–91	393
2000–01	739
2001–02	624
2002–03	1322
2003–04	1410
2004–05	1583

Source: Annual Reports of AIR and the Ministry of Information & Broadcasting.

There was some hope that private channels would create an alternative for all kinds of music and all kinds of listeners. But the dozen or so stations that survive do so by playing film music interspersed with pointless comments by inexperienced radio jockeys. Most can't pronounce in any of the languages they speak; almost all of them know nothing about music. It is not that the music is bad, but the variety is missing. There are no talk shows, no dramas, no classical music concerts, no short plays, no genre-wise splicing on programming that makes radio listening an 'appointment' activity. More than 70 per cent of radio listening happens at home and forms the background sound to other activities. That means advertisers discount the medium heavily.

Radio operators blame it on high costs and licence fees and the government blames the operators for overbidding. Both have a point of view (refer to 'The FM years'). Now with the second phase beginning with, largely, a clean slate and lots of goodwill, there is fresh hope that so many more stations will change the face of the radio business. They should. It is time radio re-wrote its history.

In February 1920, the Marconi Company made the first successful attempts at radio broadcasting in England. By November 1922, the British Broadcasting Corporation (BBC) was on air with regular programmes. In the US too, radio had become a popular medium by the mid-20s, on the heels of recorded music taking off (see the chapter on Music). AM (amplitude modulation) radio was the first to take off. FM, which is now the more popular form of radio, did not become commercially viable till the late 60s and early 70s.

The English years In India, it was in August 1921 that *Times of India (TOI)*, in collaboration with the Post and Telegraph department, broadcast from its Bombay (now Mumbai) office a special programme of music at the request of the governor of the province, Sir George Lloyd. He listened to it in Poona (now Pune). Thereafter, as H.R. Luthra documents in great detail in his book *Indian Broadcasting* (1986), the development of radio took place in fits and starts. In 1923, after a meeting with manufacturers and the press, the government set about preparing licences for radio broadcasting. Meanwhile, temporary permission was given to the Radio Club of Bengal in November 1923 and later to the Radio Club of Bombay and the Madras Presidency Radio Club. Most of these stations were operated by enthusiasts and were put together with small budgets. They broadcast European music, stories, music lessons and church services. To reach out to people, who had not even heard of radio, six loudspeakers were installed at public places in cities like Madras (now Chennai).

After a lot of public debate, it was decided that radio broadcasting in India should be a private enterprise since it was a capital-intensive business. In 1925, the government issued a 10-year licence offering a five-year monopoly to the Indian Broadcasting Company (IBC). The biggest shareholders in the IBC were Raja Saheb Dhanrajgirji Narsinghirji and The Indian Telegraph Company. Numerous individual shareholders held the balance. Most of the employees were English.

On July 27, 1927, the Bombay station went on air, and was soon followed by Calcutta (now Kolkata). About a fortnight before the launch of these stations the IBC also launched a magazine, *Indian Radio Times*. It carried details in advance of programmes. These were classified as European and Indian. European music was sourced under an agreement with the Performing Rights Society, London, by paying a royalty of 150 pounds a year. Indian music was sourced from the largest music company at that time, The Gramophone Company of India (GCI, now Saregama). The GCI was content with the publicity generated from its songs being played on the radio. The initial hype and

169

speeches around radio broadcasting were full of the hope that it would be a good 'public service'. Since the feeling of Indian nationalism ran strong then, radio was a much-censored medium. The (British) government banned the broadcast of any political or industrial statement.

Unfortunately for the IBC, people did not take to radio. From about 3,000 radio sets in December 1927, the number barely crawled up to 6,000 in one year and to a little over 7,500 by the end of 1929. The IBC had two revenue streams: advertising and licence fees. While the first was minuscule, the second had the problem of unlicensed sets estimated at 50 per cent of the total. As a result half the listeners were not paying the licence fee of Rs 10 per set that IBC was banking on for its operating costs. By the end of 1928, it was clearly in trouble, having spent a chunk of its subscribed capital on setting up the Bombay and Calcutta stations.

In March 1930, when the company went into liquidation, the government finally took over IBC. For some time it was called The Indian Government Broadcasting Service, Bombay (and similarly for Calcutta). By October 1931, even the government found it difficult to run the service and it was shut down. When there were protests from members of legislatures and the press, the service was resumed in May 1932. To increase revenues the custom duty on radio and wireless equipment was increased. The Indian Wireless Telegraphy Act was amended to make stricter the provision about evasion of licence fees. At the same time, in 1932, the BBC had started its empire service with strong short wave transmitters. This gave a fillip to radio. By the end of 1934, there were over 16,000 licensees and 6,000 subscribers to the *Indian Radio Times*. As a result, in the four years from 1930 to 1934, the government actually made a profit on radio.[3] This encouraged it to invest more money in the medium. It was during this expansion phase that the name All India Radio came into existence (see Figure 5.2).

None of the dates or milestones can ever capture the joy that AIR brought or the many struggles that went behind the scenes to get good programmes on air. 'Before independence, the whole of the 40s and maybe a little into the early 50s, AIR was one of the finest radio broadcasting organisations in the world,' remembers Ameen Sayani, one of the oldest and most familiar radio voices in India. Some of the best speakers, presenters, newsreaders and well-known people from the world of literature would work for AIR, he remembers. It used to be a matter of pride to do that. Old-timers remember Durga Khote, Ravi Shankar, Naushad, Ustad Bismillah Khan and Hari Prasad Chaurasia, among other big names.

Working for AIR also presented piquant cultural problems. Some of the singers and musicians invited to AIR's north Indian studios came from what

---

[3] According to Luthra, radio made a profit of Rs 0.22 million on revenues of Rs 1.28 million.

Figure 5.2: The Growth of Radio

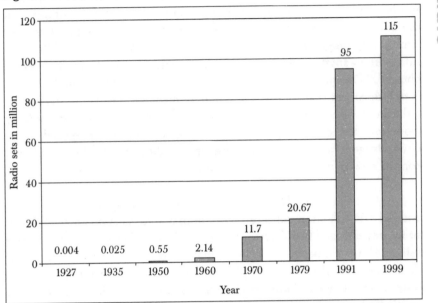

Note: (i) Since 1985 there has been no licensing on radio sets making accurate data on actual sets in India difficult to arrive at. (ii) The estimates of radio sets are based on enumerations of households done by the audience research unit at AIR as part of the listernership studies and census data on households.

Source: AIR annual reports.

was politely called a 'dubious social background'. They were invited because there weren't enough musicians from 'good families' to fill in the need for programming hours on AIR. It sounds hilarious now, but it was a serious issue in those days. It meant that many families were not willing to allow their young sons and daughters associate with radio. Luthra illustrates this with an anecdote about Saida Bano, the first woman announcer at the Lucknow station who compèred children' programmes in the early 40s. To overcome the strong opposition from her orthodox family, she lied to them. She said that there was a separate entrance for the 'immoral professional singing girls' and that she never came in contact with them.

Through all of this, the man who had the maximum influence and impact on AIR's functioning was the imperious controller of broadcasting, Lionel Fielden. A programme producer from BBC, he was at heart a man who enjoyed seeing creativity flourish on radio. He worked hard to keep bureaucrats out of programming decisions and make AIR less of a government organisation and more of a creative hotspot for talent. One of the things he did to ensure that all kinds of amateurs came on to AIR was to have payments made on the spot i.e. as soon as the artiste had finished his performance in the studio. This was a big incentive for singers and musicians who were hard up.

All of Fielden's efforts came to naught. This happened because, by the 50s, bureaucracy started raising its ugly head—not only in the administrative, but also in the creative aspects of AIR. Soon many administrative people started coming into programming. They were often brilliant IAS officers. But they did not know anything about broadcasting and they started dictating to people who did. 'The quality of programming started deteriorating,' thinks Sayani. Even Fielden was aware of this. He said in his memoirs, 'I had done my utmost with careful rules of promotion to avoid the rise of clerks who knew nothing about programmes. To keep rewards and prizes for those who possessed originality and vigour however intractable their personalities may be. But I could not stop the growth of red tape or the accumulation of a deadly routine . . .'[4]

The Indian years A classic case of interference during this period almost rendered AIR without an audience. It came from B.V. Keskar, who was the Minister for Information and Broadcasting for about 10 years during 1952–61. Keskar disliked film music because he believed that it corrupted Indian classical music. He decreed that AIR would not play any film music. He then put in motion moves to encourage and nurture classical music on radio, through events like the 'Radio Sangeet Sammelan'. While that was great for classical music, it was disastrous for AIR. 'This happened at a time when Indian film music was the best medium for the spread of the national language and for the spread of togetherness. Banned records were broken or thrown away. This was the golden period when the giants of Indian music were creating some great music. They did not stop producing but AIR was devoid of their talent,' remembers Sayani.

They went elsewhere. In the late 40s, when Ceylon (now Sri Lanka) became independent, some transmitters from the British Southeast Asian command were handed over to Radio Ceylon. It used these to run its commercial service in Hindi and English. The Hindi service had nothing except Indian film music. Within three months, almost everybody had switched to Radio Ceylon. Soon the sponsors of a popular Western music show, 'Binaca Hit Parade', wanted to experiment with a Hindi programme. That is how 'Binaca Geetmala' was born. Keskar's move had given birth to one of the biggest hits on radio. Against an expected 50 letters for the first show, 'Binaca Geetmala' got an astounding 9,000, remembers Sayani who hosted the programme.

Though film music formed barely 10–15 per cent of the total programming on AIR, it was (and is) extremely popular. Finally, in 1957, AIR did respond with *Vividh Bharti*, but it was years before it regained its former popularity with listeners. The period throughout the 60s and 70s were full of incidents like these. Commercials were not allowed on AIR till 1967 because earning revenues was not considered important.

---

[4] Quoted from Luthra (1986) p. 157.

The FM years FM was first introduced by AIR in 1977. But the real thrust came in 1993 when AIR allowed private companies to buy time slots on AIR FM, brand it and make money through commercial time. *Mid-Day, TOI,* Star Entertainment (no connection with Star TV) and Vaishali Udyog acquired the first few slots on the Mumbai station. It did not take off immediately. For every hour of programming, operators were allowed nine minutes of commercial ad time. On an average, even Times FM managed to get only 90 seconds of advertising per hour. These companies had paid Rs 6,000 per hour as licence fees, and were spending anything upwards of Rs 15,000 per hour on programming. Therefore they were making a loss every hour.

Advertisers were not spending money on radio because they had no way of gauging its reach or listenership. There was no rating system for radio and the National Readership Survey (NRS) came out only every four years. It looked like radio's first brush with privatisation would fail. It did not. Listener response in the form of letters and call-ins finally convinced advertisers and FM took off. From the Rs 580 odd million, revenues almost doubled to Rs 930 million in 1997–98. Within a few months, FM was in people's homes and cars.

'Why did FM become so popular?' asks Sayani. He also provides the answers. First, because there was the freedom to do anything as long as one did not violate the programming code. The big advantage was that there was no pre-censorship. The new operators were also playing Western music. It was not available on AIR but was popular with youngsters. The freedom and the lively approach these companies brought to radio created a breezy listening experience.

In spite of all this, unexpectedly and overnight in mid-1998, private FM stations were pulled off air by the then Prasar Bharati chief. Advertisers, media companies (*TOI* and *Mid-Day*) and listeners were stunned. Its popularity and heavy lobbying by media companies meant that the government could not ignore the medium any longer. Especially as private television had been broadcasting for more than six years by then. In March 2000, the government held an open auction for 108 radio licences. Once a company had a licence it could run the station on its own and pay licence fees (with 15 per cent annual escalation as a built-in clause) to the government every year.

The bidding went awry because companies overbid. Against the Rs 800 million it was expecting to collect, the government ended up making Rs 3.86 billion. The highest price for a licence in Mumbai was Rs 97.5 million against a reserve price of Rs 12.5 million. Ten licences were sold in Mumbai, a city that got less than Rs 200 million in radio advertising then, for Rs 975 million. The Mumbai story was repeated nationally. It looked unlikely that a market worth Rs 1 billion could sustain the burden of the licence fees (Rs 3.86 billion) plus operating costs, and yet enable companies to make money.

Many radio operators now admit to being a little carried away in the hype over the 15 days that the bidding took place. The real reason was valuations.

In those days, media companies were being valued at earnings of anywhere between 50–100 times. Many hoped to make up in valuations what they lost in licence fees and operating costs. By the time they got the licences, valuations had plummeted and many companies like Zee and Modi Entertainment withdrew. What was left were a handful of companies with 37 radio stations. Most are losing money.

There are two reasons for this. One, the costs are very high. It takes anywhere between Rs 130–180 million a year to run a radio station in Mumbai. Since most radio advertisers pay for reach only, every station aims for the largest possible mass of listeners. That explains why everyone plays only Hindi film music.

Second, high costs and very few players take away private radio's ability to tap into local advertising and expand the market. Without the money to spend on developing the market, it remains largely a medium dependent on national advertisers for whom radio is of only peripheral importance.

This needs to be emphasised. Radio, particularly FM radio, is essentially a local medium. The signals from an FM radio tower can rarely be received beyond a 60-mile radius. That makes it an ideal medium to reach small, tightly focused groups and communities. As Sayani points out, 'no entertainment can be complete without an element of social relevance' and that is what FM could bring to radio. *Radio City* talks about the condition of the roads in Bangalore or *Radio Mirchi* about the traffic situation in Mumbai. That allows these FM radio stations to tap into local advertising—from restaurants, coaching classes, retailers to every mom and pop store in a given locality—much more easily than TOI's *Bombay Times* can.

This is true globally too. In the US retail (read local) advertisers bring in 80 per cent of radio advertising. In India, one estimate puts all local advertising at over Rs 42 billion in 2005. This is growing at 20–30 per cent, against the national advertising's growth rate of 10–15 per cent. To convince these (usually) first time advertisers, media needs lots of players who can spend money developing the market. As things stand, radio operators in India are unable to do that. One estimate puts local advertising at roughly half of radio revenues. The other half still comes from national advertisers for whom radio will remain a peripheral medium.

THE WAY IT IS

After much lobbying and debate, in 2003, the government finally appointed a committee to look at radio reforms and changes in licensing rules for the second phase. The Radio Broadcast Policy Committee under Dr. Mitra made 19 very sensible recommendations.

If many of them had been adopted in the policy that came out in July 2005, it would have pushed down the cost of operating a radio station. There was one that suggested permitting operators to own more than one station in a city, making local radio networks with different programming on different stations a possibility. Another suggested doing away with the mandatory co-location of radio towers, which had caused no end of trouble so far. Indeed, this had been a major reason for a nearly two-year delay in the launch of the Mumbai and Delhi stations during the first phase of privatisation. The government insisted that radio stations should get together and set up only one tower in the metros. When companies couldn't see eye to eye, delays were inevitable. Many such recommendations of the Radio Committee have been ignored.

There has been some liberalisation of radio, like a 4 per cent revenue share instead of the licence fee. Yet, radio remains a controlled medium since many of the business decisions—such as co-location of towers or content sharing—are dictated by policy. If even 200 of the 337 stations, for which licences were auctioned, are up and running then the shape of the radio industry could change for the good.

With the licence fee knocked out, more players and lower costs, the growth in both variety and advertising revenues could become substantial. When there were less than half a dozen channels, TV was a sub-Rs 5 billion market. At over 160 channels, advertising spends alone on TV were Rs 67 odd billion in 2005. There is a revenue upside for radio. The point is how much of it will become reality.

Besides FM, some other interesting variations of radio are emerging world-wide and in India. Some of them also contain possibilities for subscription revenues.

Satellite radio WorldSpace Inc., the parent company of WorldSpace India, is the pioneer of satellite radio. It is credited with the invention of the medium. Through its two satellites, AfriStar and AsiaStar, the company beams music and information. It is headquartered in Washington D.C., and its Indian operations are run out of Bangalore. It launched direct-to-home digital satellite radio in India in 2001. WorldSpace radio receivers currently cost anywhere between Rs 3,790–8,190, depending on the model. There are various subscription schemes depending on the package that a subscriber buys.

Satellite radio broadcasting operates very much like satellite television. There are channels that are genre or country specific. In India, WorldSpace offers a range of about 40 radio stations across genres—from jazz to classical, to old Hindi film music and rock. These are 24-hour, advertising-free, radio stations in languages ranging from Tamil, Telugu to Bengali, Hindi and even French. WorldSpace also offers news and information channels like NDTV, Bloomberg and CNN, among others. AIR too launched a satellite radio service for the

Indian subcontinent in 2002 on the WorldSpace platform. The WorldSpace service currently has over 60,000 subscribers in India. In the US, the popular satellite radio brands are Sirius and XM.

Internet radio This is radio broadcast via the Internet. It may or may not be over a broadband network. There are thousands of such stations across the world.

Radio over broadband Just like television or telecom, radio signals too can travel via cable or any other broadband network. The stereo or the television can catch a radio broadcast via cable.

There is perhaps a limited upside for subscription radio currently. In most media it is only after audiences have had their fill of a variety of free content, that they feel the need to pay for select, good quality. While TV has reached that stage in India, radio is far from it.

Texting on radio Clear Channel Communications and Infinity Broadcasting, two very large American radio broadcasters, are targeting the market for radio data receivers (RDS) in cars. RDS allows text messages to be displayed on the radio's panel, like the name of the artiste or the title of the song. It can be used to show advertisements too. Some radio stations are being equipped to broadcast these text messages.

THE WAY IT WORKS

Costs The costs for a radio station just starting up in India include:
Licence fees: In the first phase of privatisation, the annual licence fee that private operators agreed to pay after a bidding process, comes with a built-in escalation clause: the fee increases by 15 per cent every year, for 10 years. Under the new radio policy, this has changed to a 4 per cent revenue share or 10 per cent of a one-time entry fee—whichever is higher.
Studio costs: If a company wants to set up a studio, it could cost anywhere between Rs 50–150 million, depending on the location.
Operating costs: This is largely the cost of programming. This would include the royalty paid to music companies, radio jockeys, marketing costs, and overheads. According to industry estimates, these costs add up to about Rs 30–50 million a year, depending on the location.

Revenues
Advertising and sponsorship: These remain the main revenue stream for radio companies. Currently ad spots sell for anything between Rs 400–2,000 per 10 seconds. The mainstay of radio is usually local advertising.

Subscription: For satellite radio companies like WorldSpace, subscriptions are the main source of revenue.

METRICS

AIR began by selling time, through sponsorship and spots, when it was set up as a private company in 1927. In 1934, the government disallowed advertising on AIR and re-introduced it only after the Chanda Committee recommended it in 1967. In that year Vividh Bharti, the film music channel of AIR, began accepting commercials. It made Rs 1.9 million from ad revenue in 1967–68, and the amount kept rising. There was only a fledgling Doordarshan (DD) for competition within broadcasting. Newspapers, in fact, were the main competition to radio. So happy was the AIR experience with advertising that in 1982, even the primary channel started accepting spots.

Sanjay Chakraverti of WPP Media remembers buying time on radio in the mid-80s. Most of the deals were made on contract with the central sales office in Mumbai. To reach the metro audience, advertisers used *Vividh Bharti* and, later, FM. AIR's primary channels, aimed at different cities or areas, were better for reaching semi-urban and rural India. In Gujarat, while Ahmedabad, Baroda and Rajkot could be reached by *Vividh Bharti*, advertisers needed primary channels to go beyond that. If they sponsored a programme they got free commercial time. The contracts were for a period of 13–52 weeks. Since radio hardly had any competition, airtime and even sponsorships on some really popular programmes—like 'Hawa Mahal' or 'Modi Ke Matwale Rahi'—were booked six months in advance. Spot buys or sponsorships rates also depended on the category. Prime time on radio in the 80s, 8–9 am and 7–8 pm, was classified as Category One. If an advertiser wanted a fixed time on Category One, there was a premium of 25 per cent. This is in stark contrast to the current scenario where all the new FM stations put together fill up just about half of their advertising time.

As television began gaining popularity, radio was relegated to targeting lower income audiences that did not have television or could not read newspapers. While a toothpaste company would advertise its toothpaste in newspapers and on television, the tooth powder was put on radio. That changed again from 1993, with FM. 'Radio started fitting,' says Apurva Purohit, a former media buyer and currently CEO, *Radio City*. FM, a largely metro phenomenon has given advertisers another avenue to talk to city audiences.

As more channels get into the game, radio advertising is bound to change in two ways. One, as the number of channels grows they will have to specialise in something and get focused advertising. Most advertisers buy time on radio in monthly contracts of anywhere between 3–10 spots of 10 seconds each, or

177

maybe more, a day. Depending on the station, the time of day and the show, the spots could cost anywhere from Rs 400–2,000 per 10 seconds. As the channels increase in number and specialise in different genres of programming, 'the qualitative calls in buying will come in,' thinks Arpita Menon of Lodestar Media.

Currently, it is all about scheduling the spot at the time when the target audience is listening. It makes for a better fit to advertise Smirnoff Vodka when people are driving home in the evening rather than when they are driving to work. When stations start specialising, advertisers could know that, for instance, listeners of old Hindi film music are most likely whisky drinkers. Or, hard rock listeners are also more likely to buy jeans. They could then advertise only on specific channels and time-bands.

The second change is the cross-media buys that radio, a much smaller medium than print or television, could force. Bennett, Coleman & Company (BCCL) owns *TOI*, India's largest selling English newspaper, plus *Radio Mirchi*. Or *Mid-Day*, a local Mumbai paper owns Go 92.5, a local FM station. These 'combos' as media planners call it will turn out to be more interesting and will offer more value to advertisers. If a good deal in *Mid-Day* also gets you spots on Go 92.5 at an attractive rate, advertisers stand to gain. Alternatively, a buyer could combine it with television from a media company like Living Media that owns TV news channels as well as radio stations.

Currently the options available are:
AIR has an in-house Audience Research Unit. It conducts research on listening habits. The unit, which is spread across India, uses interviews, panel studies and other regular research tools to arrive at numbers on listenership and patterns. Since 1937 it has been the only source of information on radio listenership or even radio sets in India; till NRS came along in the 80s. In 1998, under pressure from advertisers, AIR evolved a system for measuring ratings of programmes on radio—radio programme listenership (RPL) ratings.

NRS came in with a radio listener study in 1983–84 also offered an alter-native to media planners who wanted to buy time on radio (see Figure 5.3).

IMRB and ORG-MARG and A.C. Nielsen also did some syndicated studies. A.C. Nielsen runs the Indian Listenership Track or Wave series, which focuses on radio listenership.

AdEx India, a division of TAM Media Research, entered into a technical collaboration with AirCheck, a wholly owned subsidiary of the US-based RCS. Radio AdEx provides monitoring data and analysis of advertising expenditures in Radio across four metros covering 13 radio stations.

While most of these services do not provide ratings, they offer listenership data. This could be according to demographics, city, advertiser or station.

Private radio stations When radio licences were auctioned in 2000, the following regulations were applicable:

- The licence fee to be paid to the Ministry of Information and Broadcasting shall be increased by 15 per cent every year (compounded)
- Ban on news and current affairs programming
- Advertising has to follow the advertising code
- While a company can own any number of stations, each station should be unique in content. That means the same show cannot be broadcast over, say, all of Radio City stations, at the same time

In 2003 the government set up a committee under Amit Mitra of the Federation of Indian Chambers of Commerce and Industry (FICCI) to look into radio licensing and other issues of the radio industry. The committee was also supposed to suggest ways out of the problems that had cropped up during the first phase. The new radio policy or policy for expansion in phase two was formed on the basis of this committee's recommendations. It was announced in July 2005. These are some of its salient features:

- It marks the shift from the annual licence fee regime to a 4 per cent revenue share or 10 per cent of the reserve one-time entry fee limit—whichever is higher. Gross revenue for this purpose would be the gross revenue without deduction of taxes.
- It offers 337 new FM Radio licences in 91 cities. These licences would be granted on the basis of a closed bidding process. The cities would be categorized as A, B, C and D with metros being put under the A category and relatively backward cities in other three categories. The number of operators in each category of city would vary from 10–11 in the A category to only two in the D category.
- The new policy also permits foreign direct investment (FDI) in FM radio within the existing cap of 20 per cent for FIIs, OCBs and NRIs.[6] It would certainly go a long way in growing the industry. One Indian individual or company should own more than 50 per cent of the paid up equity (excluding the equity held by banks and other lending institutions).
- A radio company is allowed to run only one channel per city provided the total number of channels allocated to the entity is within the overall ceiling of 15 per cent of all allocated channels in the country.
- A radio company cannot outsource, through any long-term production or procurement arrangement, more than 50 per cent of its total content, of which not more than 25 per cent can be outsourced to a single content-provider.

[6] Foreign Institutional Investors, Overseas Corporate Bodies and Non-Resident Indians.

- A radio company cannot hire or lease more than 50 per cent of broadcast equipment on a long-term basis.
- It cannot enter into any borrowing or lending arrangement with other permission (licence) holder or entities, other than recognised financial institutions, which may restrict its management or creative discretion to procure or broadcast content.
- No news and current affairs programmes are permitted under the Policy (Phase two).
- The licence holders under Phase one can migrate to the Phase two regime, under certain conditions.

ACCOUNTING NORMS[7]

The concept of private radio is new to India. After the introduction of the FM band, private radio stations emerged, came close to collapse and are starting to take off again. Radio stations by their very nature have to depend on sponsored programmes or advertisements since the programmes are aired free. Listeners generally do not pay for the right to receive the programmes unlike TV channels structured as pay channels. The exception is satellite radio. Compared to the lack of specific standard here, the US GAAP provides a specific standard to deal with some of the issues of radio accounting.

Revenues

Advertisement This money is received in advance but is meant for a specific number of insertions aired. The income from ads can be recognised only for the insertions that have been aired; the balance is carried forward as advance. It will be taken to revenue after the ad has appeared.

Sponsorships Advertisers sponsor specific programmes, and such shows might then carry the name of those advertisers. These sponsors might be required to pay in advance for a specific number of shows. The amount payable is determined after taking into account the expenses like remuneration to the anchor, cost of running the show and so on. The amount received will normally be treated as an advance and taken into the income account in proportion to the number of shows aired.

Subscription This revenue stream is similar to that for pay channels in cable or DTH. The user is allowed access to a radio station on payment of subscription. If the subscription expires, the software automatically denies access. In such cases the subscription is amortised on a time basis.

---

[7] Ramesh Lakshman of Ramesh Lakshman and Company has put together the section on accounting norms.

Costs

Licence fee Licences are granted for a period of time say three to five years or longer. The fees might either be a single payment for the entire period or an annual licence fee. If it is a single payment, it would have to be amortised over the period of the licence. An annual licence fee is charged to revenue.

Royalty Radio stations buy the right to broadcast material (songs, a piece of music) over a specified period of time. This might be restricted to the number of times it can be aired or can be for an unlimited number of times over a certain period. If the right is for unlimited airing over a certain period of time, the amount paid will be amortised over the period. If the payment is for limited airing, then the amount will be amortised over the number of airings permitted. In any case, the unaired component is not refunded. Therefore it will have to be written off after the contractual period is over.

Programming If a radio station records programmes on its own, the money spent on it should be dealt with as per expectation of revenue. If the programme is likely to be repeated, then the amount will be amortised over the number of times it is likely to be repeated. Otherwise it will be charged to revenue once the broadcast is over. Special performances by reputed artistes will always have value for repeat broadcast. Hence the rights to that programme can be kept as an asset and charged to revenue on some suitable basis.

Taxes No special tax concession is available to radio stations.

VALUATION

There are no valuation benchmarks on radio businesses in India since there have been very few deals so far. A Canadian Financial Institutional Investor, CPDQ, picked up a 20 per cent stake in *Radio Mirchi*. In 2005 GW Capital picked up a 75 per cent stake in Music Broadcast Private Limited's (MBPL's) *Radio City*. The details on neither are available. In late 2005, Entertainment Network Limited, the BCCL subsidiary that owns *Radio Mirchi*, announced that it would be raising funds through an initial public offer (IPO) soon. Since all the numbers will be in the public domain this primary issue should be interesting to watch from a radio valuation perspective.

Radio valuations are done using the same metrics as in television broadcasting. Listenership, reach, the number of stations a network has, management bandwidth, and the ability to scale are the factors that investors look for. Unlike television there is no library valuation involved in radio, unless a station creates in-house programming.

6 telecommunications

*Telecom will eventually be to media what television
already is*

SHOULD A CHAPTER on telecommunications (telecom) appear in a book on media? Well, if the future of telecom was about plain phone calls, perhaps not. The future of telecom, as evident in several markets, is television. Across the developed world, traditional phone companies are being forced to change their businesses by three trends that are eating into their 'voice' revenues: Cable firms that offer 'voice'; mobile firms that encourage people to give up their landlines (many of us in India have); and lastly voice-over-Internet-protocol or VoIP. Literally that means using the Internet as a phone network. This allows people with a broadband connection, with or without wires, to use the Internet to make cheap phone calls anywhere in the world. All they have to do is download free software such as Skype or Vonage, and start talking.

This means that telephone companies have to quickly de-risk, diversify—do whatever it takes to keep users hooked onto the expensive networks that they have created—if they are to continue making money. What they are increasingly turning to is entertainment, mainly TV. A little tweaking and a phone network can carry television signals. That has been known for years. It has also been known that IPTV, or Internet protocol television is a possibility.[1] Because of the price pressure created by cable operators, mobile phones and VoIP, moving quickly on to television has become a business imperative for almost every major telecom company in the US and Europe. Making simple phone calls, or 'voice' as analysts call it, will eventually become a free service, with the revenues coming from IPTV according to some predictions.

---

[1] Again literally that means using the Internet protocol, that is the Internet's method of delivering data in packets, which CDMA uses, as a way of distributing television signals. See footnote 11 for details on CDMA.

As the silos that the Internet, telecom and TV occupied collapse into one another, hybrid businesses that we cannot yet define are being created. Therefore it would seem logical to look at where telecom is in India and what it could possibly do in the future to TV. You could argue that some of this has been evident for some time now. May be. But the thing about both, telecom and the Internet, is that we have tended, for years, to treat them like technology industries rather than consumer oriented businesses.

By way of comparison, broadcasting is very high-tech too. But we never talk of it as a technology business. Nobody wonders how many amplifiers are needed every few metres for cable wires to transmit signals well. Why then do we discuss the network of a telecom operator, how many towers he has and whether these are outsourced or owned? To my mind a telephone line is as much media as a television screen—it is a means of selling information, education or entertainment—which is essentially what the media business is all about. If it has a wire attached then it can do that by offering all these services in your home, through a fatter pipe, called broadband. If it is a mobile phone, it can offer these services on the run with wireless broadband.

That is a realisation driving the growth of telecom markets across the world. Football fans downloading Beckham's goals on their mobile phones or Koreans using broadband for gaming are all signs of the future. By using something that was used so far only to talk, telecom companies are adding one more thing to the list of industries that define the term, 'media'. It is not going to eat into any other media's share. It will co-exist with newspapers and radio and TV and whatever else we have. Telecom, like cable or DTH, will become another platform to distribute entertainment.

Telecom in India has astounded analysts and investors with its growth. At over 80 million mobile-phone users, we are one of the fastest growing mobile-phone markets in the world.[2] 'The growth in the last 3–4 years has surprised even us,' says Sanjeev Sharma, managing director, Nokia India. With a total of 130 million telecom connections, the medium is almost as well-penetrated as TV. You could argue that at 12 telephone lines per 100 people, by January 2006, we still have one of the lowest tele-densities in the world. Even Bolivia had a higher tele-density compared to India in 2003, according to one TRAI (Telecom Regulatory Authority of India) paper. Sure, but we are getting there, and getting there fast. The Ministry of IT and Communications has set itself a target of 250 million phones by December 2007.

At over Rs 760 billion in annual revenues, going by TRAI's estimates, the telecom industry is over five times as large as the television business, which stood at Rs 185 billion.[3] More importantly, unlike TV, the telecom industry is

---

[2] As in January 2006 according to TRAI statistics.
[3] TRAI paper 16 June 2005.

not fragmented. So while some players may need to wipe out accumulated losses, on a cash flow basis the industry is profitable. There is an incentive for investors, who have already pumped in close to Rs 225 billion into the sector, to put in even more money.[4]

Figure 6.1: India's Leading Telecom Companies

Company	Revenue (Rs Billion) Mar-05	Subscribers (million) Jan-06
BSNL	314	52.74
Reliance Group	53.87	18.1
Bharti Tele-Ventures	80.348	18.61
Hutch	41.2	15.07
Idea	25	6.73
MTNL	60.841	5.58
Tata/Hughes	na	8.12
Spice	na	1.71
HFCL	4.355	0.31
Shyam Telecom	2.747	0.2
Others	na	2.83
Total (landline plus Mobile)		**130**

Note: (i) BSNL, Hutch and Shyam Telecom revenues are for the financial year ending 2004. (ii) The subscriber numbers are total of mobile plus landline for each of these companies as in January 2006. However in BSNL's case the landline numbers were available only till December 2005. (iii) Hutch figures include the subscribers added through its acquisition of BPL Mobile. (iv) NA – not available.

Source: TRAI, company websites and industry estimates.

We are a mobile-phone savvy country. As we become broadband savvy as well, we will be going on the same path as the rest of the world.[5] In fact quicker than anyone would think, since we have many years of catching up to do. Also, unlike the US telecom market, we have little historical baggage of old networks. Most of the wiring done by private and even public sector companies comprises optic fibre. In consequence, very little additional work is needed before new private operators like Bharti or Reliance can offer TV signals over their telephone wires.

It will take regulatory jugglery and vision, however—more on that, later. To my mind, the wonder is that we are talking of mobile TV and visual radio and broadband in a country that, until ten years ago, had a waiting list for telephone

---

[4] Source Ministry of Communications and IT 2003 and TRAI (2003 a). The investment figure appears in Dr. Ashok Desai's study on the telecom sector, discussed below in footnote 6.
[5] Even as I write, broadband prices have been falling and penetration rising. According to TRAI the number of broadband connection stood at over one million in January 2006, that is up from about 47,000 or so in January 2005. That incidentally was a number it had been stuck at for years.

connections. For as long as anyone can remember, there has always been a shortage of telephone lines. My father paid Rs 8,000 in the mid-80s to buy someone else's landline connection, after almost a decade of waiting for a landline application to go through the state-owned monopoly. Such stories were the norm; though they may seem incredible to a lot of the younger people reading this book. Today there are mobile phone companies that bundle a phone along with airtime at great prices. There are landline companies that bundle a broadband connection with a telephone. Most of them offer free talktime as well as ringtones, songs and news clippings, astrological predictions, and other such downloads. Clearly, we have left the past behind.

Much of the action on mobile phone penetration and usage in Asia is taking place in China and India (see Figure 6.2). With about 700 million telecom subscribers in China (December 2005) and over 130 million in India (January 2006), it is bound to be.

Figure 6.2: A Comparison of the Telecom Markets in China and India

Particulars		China	India
Fiscal Year	Unit	Dec–04	Mar–05
Total Revenue from Telecom services	US$ in bn	65.3	17.78
Total Subscribers, at the end of March	Mn	674.5	98.08
Fixed Line	Mn	325.4	45.9
Mobile	Mn	349.1	52.17
ARPU – Basic	US$	9.14	15
ARPU Mobile (GSM+CDMA)	US$	9.69	9.04
ARPU Mobile – CDMA	US$	10.31	5.74
ARPU Mobile – GSM	US$	9.62	8.89
ARPU Mobile – GSM – Post-paid	US$	20.18	20.34
ARPU Mobile – GSM – Pre-paid	US$	6.77	5.25
MOU – GSM – Total	Minutes	297	330
MOU – GSM – Pre-paid	Minutes	194	233
MOU – GSM – Post-paid	Minutes	517	599
Capital employed per subscriber-basic service	US$	169	362
Capital employed per subscriber-mobile service	US$	163	167
Opex per subscriber-Basic	US$	4.30	5.92
Opex per subscriber-Mobile	US$	2.41	4.18
RoCE-Basic	%	14.79	10.92
RoCE-Mobile	%	22.87	7.83
Subscriber Growth in Basic	YoY	15.50%	8%
Subscriber Growth in Mobile	YoY	23%	55%
Rental–Rural per month	US$	1.20	1.11
HHI Index in Basic Service	–	0.58	0.67
HHI Index in Mobile Service	–	0.40	0.16

Note: (i) ARPU–Average revenues per user. (ii) GSM and CDMA are mobile phone technologies. (iii) Opex–Operating expenditure. (iv) MOU–Minutes of usage. (v) RoCE–Return on capital employed. (vi) HHI–Household Index. (vii) YoY–Year over Year.
Source: TRAI Study Paper; June 16, 2005.

In fact in 2004, two major mobile phone handset makers, Elcoteq and Nokia, announced their plans to set up manufacturing facilities in India to meet the demand in the local market. Almost every major airtime operator is in India, and riding on the growth. When voice growth plateaus, the imperative to offer more and more data will drive mobile companies. That is when the fun will begin in earnest. More so because telecom, in large measure, is finally free of all the regulatory and political intrigue that has been dogging it ever since privatisation began in the mid-80s. There is also a clearer sense of the technologies that will drive growth. There is, let us say, a sense of comfort about where we are. Now that the broad regulatory and technological para-meters in which the game is being played is clear, hard business is the centre of attention.

THE PAST[6]

The pre-liberalisation years Telecommunications is the process of con-veying information with the use of electrical energy. It evolved out of an earlier system involving optical energy. Until less than 250 years ago, the transmission of information was limited in reach by the speed at which it could be conveyed and the distances it could cover. The first primitive communications system based on an electrical technology was invented in 1747 in England. That is when William Watson demonstrated electrical transmission using an electro-static source. George Lesage showed a primitive telegraph in Switzerland in 1774 but it was not until the early part of the nineteenth century that the first practical systems began to emerge to meet the needs of commerce and industry for more advanced forms of communication. The modern age of telecom began in 1839 when Samuel Morse developed an effective system for coding signals and completed the electric telegraph system from Baltimore to Washington DC. Guglielmo Marconi's transmission of signals by radio demonstrated the

---

[6] A large part of the portion on past history have been put together by Kanchan Sinha of Amarchand & Mangaldas & Suresh A. Shroff & Company, a New Delhi-based law firm. Some of it has been sourced, with lots of gratitude, from Ashok V. Desai's study on the Indian telecom industry for The National Council for Applied Economic Research. Dr. Desai, who is my colleague at Businessworld, was kind enough to share this study with me while it was at draft stage. The third important source on the past history and evolution of the business was a paper put together by Lara Srivastava of the Strategies and Policy Unit of the International Telecommunication Union (ITU) and Sidharth Sinha of the Indian Institute of Management. This study is part of a series of Telecommunication Case Studies produced under the New Initiatives Programme of the Office of the Secretary General of the ITU. It was downloaded from the Internet for the research on this chapter.

potential of wireless technologies and since then the basic technologies on which the early systems were built have been extended and improved to create the worldwide telecom network.[7]

The first telegraph network was set up in India in 1856.[8] Its initial use was during the First War of Independence the following year. For many years, therefore, the development of telecom was driven by military and governmental concerns, rather than by consumer issues or commercial factors. Originally, telecom was part of the Post and Telegraph (P&T) ministry. Telegraph lines existed till the 50s, but gradually the telegraph came to be abandoned and telegrams were transmitted by telephone and tele-printer. The ministry ran two businesses, post and telegraph, and telephones. The postal service was much more widely used than telephones. Although the telephone service was highly profitable, it was used to cross-subsidise postal services. That is why very little of the money that telephones earned went into expansion and consequently there was a long waiting list for telephones. Shortages have marked the Indian telecom history all along.

The first whiff of liberalisation came with the prime-ministership of Rajiv Gandhi in 1984. Sam Pitroda, a telecom engineer returned from the USA and became his advisor. Pitroda set up a Centre for Development of Telematics (C-DOT), an R&D organisation to develop electronic switches. In January 1985, two separate departments were created for Posts and for Telecommunications. This ended telecom's cross-subsidy to postal services. In 1986 a new ministry of communications was created. In the same year, two businesses were separated from the ministry. Mahanagar Telephone Nigam Limited (MTNL) was set up to manage telecom in Bombay (now Mumbai) and Delhi, and Videsh Sanchar Nigam Limited (VSNL) to run international services. However, the rest of the telephones remained with the ministry; the service was run by the Department of Telecom (DoT). Paradoxically, it remained in charge of the regulatory role in telecom. So a Telecom Commission was created in 1989 to formulate policy, regulate implementation and also prepare the budget for DoT. However, none of these moves meant anything to consumers. The waiting period for a telephone line just grew longer and longer. Like any incumbent, for years together DoT continued to dominate, force and mutilate telecom policy in India, to the detriment of consumers.

The liberalisation years In January 1992, DoT invited bids for mobile services in the four metros. ' When the bidding took place, all hotels in Delhi were overflowing and everybody overbid,' remembers S.C. Khanna, secretary general of the Association of Unified Telecom Service Providers of India.

---

[7] David Gillies & Roger Marshall, *Telecom Law*, Butterworths, London, 1997,

[8] In all the different sources the dates for when the first system was set up are different. For the purposes of this book I am going with the one in the ITU paper.

The Himachal Futuristic Communications Group (HFCL) bid a crazy Rs 850 billion for nine circles.[9] In October 1992 the licences were announced. Soon, four of the rejected bidders went to court. By the time the legal process ended, it was October 1994. By this time the number of people waiting for a telephone line had risen from 7 million on April 1, 1992 to 10.5 million two years later. Private investment was crucial to feed this need and hence the National Telecom Policy of 1994 was born.

In May 1994, the government opened local basic and value-added telecom services to competition. Mobile services were introduced on a commercial basis in November 1994. India was divided into 21 'Telecom Circles.' Circles correspond approximately to states and are categorised as either 'A,' 'B' or 'C' —according to size and importance. Category A includes the heaviest volume areas such as Delhi, Uttar Pradesh, Maharashtra, Gujarat, Andhra, Karnataka and Tamil Nadu. As part of the licence conditions, traffic could be routed to VSNL's international gateway only by passing through DoT/DTS's network. Basic service was planned as a duopoly between the DoT and a selected service provider in each of the telecom circles. The bidders were evaluated on financial and technical parameters and only one private service operator was to operate in a service area apart from the DoT. However, owing to various reasons such as very high bid amount in some cases and certain legal issues, only six licences could be granted in basic services i.e. for the service areas of Andhra Pradesh, Gujarat, Madhya Pradesh, Punjab, Rajasthan and Maharashtra. The first mobile telephony service in the metros started in August 1995.

And it is from here that the regulatory mess, which was to mar the growth of telephony in India, began. For perspective, contrast this with private TV broadcasting where no regulation existed for over 10 years after cable TV took off in India in the mid-80s. The first law governing cable came in 1995 long after consumers had tasted private fare. There was no licensing involved to start with (refer to the chapter on 'Television'). There was only one state-owned broadcaster as a fairly passive, rather ineffectual competitor.[10] A few months after the arrival of satellite TV in India, by the time the first Hindi satellite channel was launched in 1992, it was evident that private broadcasters could offer much better variety. Now add the fact that a private cable network, owned by thousands of entrepreneurs, was already in place. Most new channels just rode on it by selling their signals to these operators. In the case of telecom, the onus of service was put on private operators but they were forced to use the network of the incumbent and price their services in line with the incumbent.

---

[9] Eventually HFCL exited the telephony business.

[10] Later advertisers were not allowed to buy airtime in dollars on foreign uplinked channels broadcasting into India, ostensibly to protect Doordarshan. However this was done away with in 2004. (See regulation portion in the chapter on television broadcasting.)

DoT did everything to ensure that private telephone operators could not make money. The wrangles over subsidies, access-deficit charges, interconnect-rates and calling party pays (CPP) standards, are well documented. Frankly, they are also tedious to read. Unlike broadcasting, if you read the first 10 years of the history of Indian telecom it doesn't seem as if there was light at the end of the tunnel. According to Dr Desai's study, most private operators ended up making losses not only because they had paid high licence fees and inter-connection and other charges to DoT, but also because the business was un-viable. In anticipation of the launch of private services, DoT started meeting the pending demand. As a result, the projections made by private operators went awry.

By 1998, eight mobile service operators and all the landline operators were in default of their licence fees. An ICICI study of 22 mobile service operators found that only one, Bharti Tele-Ventures, had made a small profit of Rs 25 million in 1997–98. Seventeen per cent of the subscribers had not used their phone at all, and 37 per cent had bills of under Rs 500 per month. Another TRAI study in 1999 found the same problem of low user off-take, low ARPUs (Average Revenues Per User) continuing. The recommendations of these studies generated debate in the media and legal wrangling followed. Finally, the Group on Telecom, an inter-ministerial committee, resolved the issue.

The result was the New Telecom Policy 1999. This brought about four major changes. One, all circle operators were required to pay 2.8–2.9 years' licence fee at the old rates before migrating to a revenue-sharing formula. Two, DoT and MTNL were allowed to enter the mobile phone business. Most mobile operators were already offering services below the Rs 8.40 per minute maximum set by DoT. With two more players in the fray, a price war was imminent. Three, private landline operators were allowed to give CDMA mobile connections. So far cell phone technology in India had been based on GSM.[11] Finally, it was

---

[11] CDMA is Code Division Multiple Access. According to the CDMA Development Group's website, CDMA is a technology that allows many users to occupy the same time and frequency allocations in a given band/space. It assigns unique codes to each communication to differentiate it from others in the same spectrum. In a world of finite spectrum resources, CDMA allows many more people to share the airwaves at the same time, than any other technology.

GSM is Groupe Speciale Mondiale or Global System for Mobile Communication. GSM is an open, non-proprietary system and is one of the most widely used telecom standards in the world today. According to the GSM world website, GSM differs from first generation wireless systems in that it uses digital technology and time division multiple access transmission methods (against code division in CDMA). Voice is digitally encoded via a unique encoder, which emulates the characteristics of human speech. Both these technologies compete with each other currently, though eventually they will become one. In March 2005 there were more than 1.3 billion GSM phone subscribers in 210 countries across the world. In June 2005 the total number of CDMA subscribers stood at 270 million worldwide.

no longer necessary for private operators to route intra-circle calls through DoT and MTNL. They could build their own networks. The government monopoly in domestic long-distance traffic was abolished in April 2001, and in international traffic in April 2002. By all accounts it looked like telecom was finally getting on with it after shedding a decade of nitpicking, losses and regulatory hassles.

Landline companies began using CDMA wireless connections to push costs down and mobile phone operators were free of the licence fee. As call charges fell, the market expanded. This was when TRAI began experimenting with tariff regulation. In 1996 it cost Rs 16.80 per minute to make a phone call. Even this fell by half in 2000, one year after the New Telecom Policy.

The boom years 'The real surge began only after 2002,' says Sanjeev Sharma, managing director, Nokia India. There were several factors, which contributed to it. The total cost of ownership, that is the cost of the phone as well as the airtime costs went down as a result of the New Telecom Policy of 1999. By 2002, the government brought down the duties on handsets from 72.5 per cent to about 14 per cent. These came down further to 4 per cent, allowing hardware companies like Nokia to offer mobile phones for as little as Rs 5,000.

To this add the launch of Reliance Infocomm's mobile service, in December 2002, at never-before prices. A subscriber could pick up a Reliance phone for an upfront payment of Rs 3,000 and monthly installments of Rs 600 over 36 months. While the response was huge to start with, about 100,000 new customers a day, it fell because the quality of the first CDMA service was patchy. Then, in mid-2003, Reliance launched what is now referred to as the famous 'Monsoon Hungama.' It offered a mobile phone plus connection for an upfront payment of Rs 501 in addition to Rs 449 a month, over three years. The market never looked back after that. 'The realisation that telecom is infrastructure and therefore a driver for GDP, happened only in 2002–03. The emphasis shifted to doing whatever it takes to push penetration,' thinks Sharma of Nokia. The effective rate of making a mobile phone call dropped to under Rs 2 per minute and the number of users kept jumping.

At some point in 2005, the number of mobile phones finally overtook landlines. The landmark is crucial. Everybody—the regulator, the industry and the investment bankers—knows that. It is time for broadband to take off in India.

THE WAY IT IS

According to a study done by US-based Pyramid Research, it is when a country's mobile telephone population overtakes landlines that broadband takes off.

Korea and Taiwan are prime examples. This happens because at this point landline phone companies start offering set top boxes (STBs) as a carrot to hang on to subscribers who might want to disconnect their landlines. So just like cable operators are offering Internet access and cable radio as value-added goodies, telephone companies can offer TV signals as an add-on service. India is right now at that stage. It has a stagnating landline population. The evidence was also there in the price cuts in broadband prices by everyone, from cable companies like Hathway to telecom ones like Bharti. The result has been galloping penetration. According to TRAI, broadband connections in India went up 21 times from a mere 47,000 in January 2005, to one million in January 2006. It doesn't compare very well with telephony penetration in general, but remember that the number had been stagnating ever since 2001 or so, when the first rush of broadband subscribers was witnessed. Yet India is some way from seeing IPTV.

That is because for both hardware manufacturers and airtime companies, the next level of growth is now coming from smaller towns and lower income groups. That explains the Rs 200 per month plans that some companies announced in 2005. There is a lot of juice to be extracted on sheer penetration in India. There is a lot of pressure expected from VoIP, though it has not yet manifested itself. There is a TRAI study paper and some suggestions from the government on using VoIP for rural development. TRAI expects, 'VoIP will have a big impact on the traditional circuit switched telephony, initially fixed line followed by mobile, driving prices and margins down, forcing far-reaching changes in industry and consequently in the regulatory and licensing regimes.' The only way telecom companies can fight the dual forces of falling prices due to VoIP and saturating markets is by offering something that subscribers cannot refuse.

The markets in the US and Europe, where Skype and Vonage and cable operators are eating into telephony revenues, companies are already coping with this reality. VoIP is expected to penetrate over 50 per cent of broadband households in mature broadband markets like the UK, Japan, France, Hongkong, Korea, Austria, Taiwan, and Malaysia, among others. In the US, six large cable companies control 90 million homes. They have spent about $80 billion over several years to make their cable carry two-way communication. They now control 70 per cent of broadband net access in the US, according to one estimate.

The result: SBC Communications Inc., a US-based telecom company, announced 'Project Lightspeed' in mid-2005. The idea is to enable millions of residential customers to access integrated digital TV, superhigh-speed broadband access, and voice over IP (Internet Protocol) services via a fibre-rich network. The UK will be moving to an entirely new IP-based network by 2008–09. According to estimates by British Telecom this would save it one billion pounds annually. In India, the infrastructure for broadband is almost ready. Various operators have laid about 670,000 route kilometres of optical fibre in India, even in the interiors, and the process continues. BSNL has connected 30,000 of its 35,000 exchanges with optical fibre.

The question marks There is little doubt that IPTV over broadband and other value added-services—say, gaming—is what will hook and keep telecom subscribers. But even internationally there are some issues on IPTV that will be resolved only after there are at least a few countries that have experimented with it. First is a question mark over the ability of the technology to cope with broadcasting. Telecom pipes have copper that can just about carry voice and data. Even DSL[12] -enabled copper wires may not be able to carry concurrent video. If 40 people in a housing society are all watching the TV serial *Astitva*, and if it takes one mbps (mega bites per second) of bandwidth to watch it, then each of those homes should receive *Astitva* at the same speed at the same time. If the bandwidth is shared, as in the case of telecom operators offering broadband, chances are the signal will be pixilated or break. So you might see Dr Simran's face (the serial's female protagonist) before you see the rest of her. This is because data travels in packets on a fibre network unlike a co-ax cable that is built to carry video.

The second issue is the packet-monitoring technology (like CDMA). While telecom firms are using it to enhance security and quality, it can also, arguably, be used to make rivals look bad. According to reports, telecom firms are building —into their residential gateways—new technology that will help them identify traffic from third-party rivals.[13] This then could end up at the back of the queue rendering a rival's service slow and patchy.

The third issue, telecom companies are used to selling a plain vanilla product that is largely commoditised. There is also the question of what telecom companies can give beyond what DTH or cable TV operators are already offering. Can they survive in the hurly-burly of television broadcasting, pay huge amounts of money to acquire rights for film and sports, or create new channels? Will they, in the first place, get a broadcasting licence? These are questions that time and competition will be able to answer. The way the industry is structured currently, the business imperative to get into IPTV will happen sooner rather than later. Remember that DTH itself will eat up a lot of potential IPTV homes, so telecom companies will have to move fast.

At one point in 2004, a TRAI paper, put together by IBM and CII (Confederation of Indian Industry), had suggested unbundling. That would have implied both the state-owned telecom majors throwing open their last mile access into the 40 million odd landline homes that they have. That would have accelerated broadband penetration because not everyone would have had to build wires

---

[12] DSL—Digital Subscriber Line is a modem used to increase the capacity of copper telephone wires.
[13] The War of the Wires, The Economist, July 28, 2005.

that lead into every house. They could have leased—on a revenue, or profit-sharing basis—infrastructure that was already in place. However, the recommendations never saw the light of day in the final broadband policy that was unveiled in mid-2004. There was also talk (not in the report) of allowing cable operators to offer voice. None of this has happened, so the business imperative to offer high-end services on fixed line networks is as yet not so great. Therefore, while there is the odd project that is being announced, it could be at least three years before there is a serious IPTV rollout.

When SMS (Short Messaging Services) first appeared on the horizon, many operators were reluctant to introduce it because they thought it would cannibalise voice. However, SMS has proved to be a big revenue generator by itself. That is why most operators now have an open mind on value-added services. The challenge is to take consumers to the next level, where they feel the need to use features like clippings (news, songs, etc.), stock trading applications and games before pushing TV services. The usage for most of the other things is as yet low in India. There are two barriers to these services, not enough applications and inadequate consumer understanding.

Take the first. Most operators have just started using mass media and figuring out what they can offer subscribers. Currently telecom's interaction with mass media is limited to being used as a promotional tool. Media companies are using SMS contests, ringtones, wallpapers and others ways to interact with viewers, listeners or readers. These fall roughly in the area of promotions or mobile entertainment. In this area companies like Activemedia Technology, Mobile2win or Hungama act as a link between media companies wanting to use interactive marketing and mobile companies seeking to offer content and generate revenues. Many of these companies design the contest, host it and collate the data. If Ten Sports is running a contest during a WWF match, everything from the number to the backend comes from Activemedia. Ten Sports generates the buzz by using its channel to publicise the contest. 'Currently we are constrained by two things. One is the data networks and the other is the screen size,' says Raj Singh, executive director, Activemedia Technology. That, says he, is the complexity since the real estate on which the message can be displayed is limited. 'The key thing that will change the situation is bandwidth and speed,' believes Singh. That is correct. What will make both mobile and wireline data run is the ability to carry more and more either over the airwaves or on wires. As broadband prices drop, the numbers are already jumping.

The second barrier to pushing video and other value-added services on telecom networks is consumer comfort. Unless consumers are comfortable with all the non-voice aspects their phones offer, the next level of growth will be difficult to achieve. 'The barriers are lack of knowledge on how to use an application,' thinks Sharma of Nokia. Mobile phone companies may be ready with products that the market will not yet accept. As they shed their licence-fighting gear and get into their woo-the-consumer mode, these are challenges telecom companies will learn to deal with. Television did that many years ago, and is now getting consumers to accept a new way of watching television—DTH. Maybe that is where telecom companies should look, for inspiration.

THE WAY IT WORKS

In January 2006, the Indian telecom market stood at 130 million connections. There are ten major telecom service providers and several 'vendors.' These are companies such as Ericsson, Nokia, and Motorola, which sell handsets and the backend equipment for mobile networks. Telecom companies, that is the service providers, make their money through voice and data services:

Voice—rental, airtime and other services Rental is the fixed amount that telecom companies charge irrespective of whether or not a subscriber uses the service. It could range from nothing, to Rs 399 or more—depending on the package opted for. Most companies bundle their services in different packages. These may include free calls to a frequently called number, roaming services and so on. Most telecom companies charge higher rates if a subscriber uses the (mobile) phone outside the geographical area in which it has been bought. A user travelling from Mumbai to Delhi is 'roaming' and will be charged a higher rate to make or receive phone calls. A bulk, maybe more than 80 per cent, of the revenues for most Indian telecom firms comes from voice.

Data or value-added services This could include SMS, ringtones, caller tones, song downloads, and any other services that telephone companies may offer.[14] These services are usually more profitable since the demand is price elastic. Downloading a song as your ringtone could cost anywhere between Rs 5–30, depending on how popular it is. Generally speaking, the lower bandwidth services, such as ringtones, can be easily sold on existing networks. There are, however, services that require a higher bandwidth. It is these services that will ensure the survival of telecom companies as discussed earlier.

METRICS

The metrics normally used in telephony to measure popularity, profitability and make decisions on whether to expand, invest or create more services are:

---

[14] Short Messaging Services, whereby you could use the mobile phone or a WLL landline to send short text messages to another number.

Usage refers to average time users have spent on the phone. This could be either for talking or using the data services—such as SMS or Internet access—that phone companies offer. The more the average minutes of usage per subscriber, the more money a phone company makes, assuming that it is not discounting heavily.

ARPU stands for Average Revenues Per User. This is by far the most important metric. The higher the ARPU, the more profitable a company is. However, this is dependent on the state of the market. In the year 2000 ARPUs were Rs 1,319 per subscriber month but almost all the mobile phone companies were losing money since the subscriber base was just about 1.88 million, according to TRAI statistics. In March 2005, ARPUs had plummeted to Rs 405 per month, but most companies now make anywhere between 20–40 per cent in gross margins. That is because the figure for mobile subscribers has climbed to over 50 million people.

Churn is the number of people who give up on a telecom service or fall out of the subscriber-list. There could be various reasons for this. In the course of market expansion, a company may have picked up subscribers who can barely afford the service and have therefore dropped out. On the other hand, poor quality of service may be a reason for subscribers opting out. Whatever the reason, operators usually keep track of churn rates. Since the cost of acquiring a subscriber is pretty high, it is important to retain them. It impacts everything from the image of the company to its valuation (discussed later in this chapter).

REGULATION[15]

197

The legal framework governing the telecom sector in India is provided by:

- The Indian Telegraph Act, 1885.
- The Wireless Telegraphy Act, 1933.
- The Telegraph Wires (Unlawful Possession) Act, 1950.
- The Cable Television Network (Regulation) Act, 1995.
- The Telecom Regulatory Authority of India Act, 1997.

'Telecom' falls under the Seventh Schedule of the Constitution of India. The Centre—and not the States—can formulate laws regulating this sector. This control over the telecom sector is embodied in the Telegraph Act, 1885 and

---

[15] The section on regulation and foreign investment has been put together completely by Amarchand & Mangaldas & Suresh A. Shroff and Company, a New Delhi-based law firm.

the Wireless Telegraphy Act, 1933.[16] The Central Government has the exclusive right of establishing, maintaining and working telegraphs; it has the ability to grant a licence to any person to either establish or maintain or work a telegraph in any part within India. The provision of any and every telecom service will necessarily involve the working of a telegraph whether it is Internet or fixed telephone lines. The Telegraph Act vests the Centre with the power to regulate all telecommunication services.[17]

The Wireless Telegraphy Act regulates the possession of wireless communication apparatus, use of frequencies and the place of establishment of wireless equipment. The Act mandates that no person shall possess wireless telegraphy apparatus unless he has a licence issued under this Act. These licences are to be issued by the telegraph authority set up under the Telegraph Act subject to such conditions and payments as the authority thinks fit.

The Telegraph Act and the Wireless Telegraphy Act have always left the sector open to private participation but subject to the Government granting a licence. As the policy changed, the numbers of licencees has increased over time. This necessitated the setting up of an independent regulatory body along with a free and fair dispute redressal mechanism. As a result a bill passed in 1995 envisaged the creation of an independent and autonomous agency for the regulation of telecom. In 1997, the Telecom Regulatory Authority of India (TRAI) was established under an act of the same name. It was set up with a view to strengthen the regulatory mechanism, provide an expeditious dispute resolution method and boost investor confidence.

Currently TRAI performs several recommendatory and regulatory functions for the telecom sector. It makes recommendations on:

- The need and timing for introduction of new service providers.
- Terms and conditions of the licence to a service provider (It cannot grant or renew licences. This remains the DoT's responsibility.)
- Revocation of licence for non-compliance of terms and conditions.
- Measures to facilitate competition, efficiency, growth and technological improvements.

---

[16] Section 4 (1) of the Telegraph Act, 1885 states that *Within India, the Central Government shall have the exclusive privilege of establishing, maintaining and working telegraphs: Provided that the Central Government may grant a licence on such conditions and in consideration of such payments as it thinks fit to any person to establish, maintain or work a telegraph within any part of India.*

[17] Indian Telegraph Act, 1885 defines 'telegraph' as *any appliance, instrument, material or apparatus used or capable of use for transmission or reception of signs, signals, writing, images and sounds or intelligence of any nature by wire, visual or other electro-magnetic emissions, radio waves or heritzian waves, galvanic, electric or other means.*

- Type of equipment to be used by the service providers.
- Measures for the development of telecom technology.
- Any other matter related to the telecom industry in the general and efficient management of the available spectrum.

The TRAI may also set rates for telecom services. Its decisions can only be challenged in the High Courts or the Supreme Court of India.

Later in 2000 the adjudicatory functions of TRAI were vested in a separate body called Telecom Disputes Settlement and Appellate Tribunal (TDSAT). The TDSAT consists of a Chairperson and not more than two members who are appointed by notification by the Central Government.[18] It adjudicates disputes between a licensor and a licencee, two or more service providers, as well as a service provider and a group of consumers. It hears appeals against any direction, decision or order of the TRAI. TDSAT, therefore, exercises both original and appellate jurisdiction.

Foreign investment Currently, in basic, mobile phone, value-added services and global mobile personal communications by satellite, FDI up to 74 per cent is permitted. It is subject to adherence to licensing and security requirements by the companies that are investing, and the companies in which the investment is being made. The licence conditions include a lock-in period for transfer and addition of equity and other licence provisions. There is no equity cap in telecom manufacturing. In the following 100 per cent FDI is allowed:

- ISPs not providing gateways (both for satellite and submarine cables).
- Infrastructure providers providing dark fibre.
- Electronic Mail.
- Voice Mail.

However, FDI in the telecom sector is permitted subject to the following conditions:

- FDI up to 100 per cent is allowed subject to the condition that such companies will divest 26 per cent of their equity in favour of the Indian public in five years, if these companies are listed in other parts of the world.
- The above services would be subject to licensing and security requirements, wherever necessary.
- The Foreign Investment Promotion Board (FIPB) shall consider proposals for FDI beyond 49 per cent on a case-to-case basis.

---

[18] Section 14-B (1), TRAI Act, 1997.

ACCOUNTING NORMS[19]

Revenues All subscription revenues are recognised on a time basis. If they pertain to the number of calls made, then they are accounted for in proportion to the calls made. All specific services are recognised to revenue as and when the customer consumes the service. Telecom companies sell prepaid cards where the customer can prepay the subscription for a specified duration. It is possible that the customer is not allowed to return any unused portion. Nevertheless, the revenue is recognised on the basis of the use of the prepaid card over the period of its use in proportion to the actual. Since the hardware and the software that track it also control the usage of the prepaid card, it is possible to generate the required information from the system and account accordingly.

Taxation As per section 80-IA of the Income Tax Act, 1961, deduction of 100 per cent of the profits from business for a period of 10 consecutive assessment years is allowed. This is granted to companies that have started or are to start providing telecom services—whether basic or mobile, including radio paging, domestic satellite service, network of trunking, broadband network and Inter-net services—on or after 1 April 1995 but before 31 March 2005.

VALUATION[20]

Pure telecom Earlier, when the sector was just beginning to take shape in India, valuations were based *on subscriber numbers*, just as for cable TV or DTH. But today they are not longer relevant says Nitin Gupta, vice president, transaction advisory services, Ernst & Young. At one point before subscriber numbers really grew, telecom companies got a valuation of $1000 per subscriber. This had fallen to $300–400 per subscriber by mid-2005, says Gupta. While it looks as if the valuation has fallen, the fact is that the subscriber-base has grown. If the valuation of Bharti has gone up by several times since its initial public offer (IPO), the per-subscriber valuation has declined. The per-subscriber measure makes sense only when the market is stable, as in the US or the UK. In a rapidly growing market like India, it loses relevance.

---

[19] The accounting norms for all chapters has been put together by Ramesh Lakshman and Company.

[20] This entire section has been put together courtesy Ernst &Young and especially Nitin Gupta. The firm, and he have done a lot of work in this area. Both have been part of valuing some of the biggest telecom companies in India.

Then there is the *EBITDA multiple*, the most popular measure in capital-intensive industries like broadcasting and telecom.[21] The usual practice is to multiply the EBITDA by a factor to arrive at a valuation for the company. The multiple or the factor by which EBITDA is multiplied is essentially dependent on the negotiations between the investor and investee as well as the market conditions. It is also dependent on the benchmarks in that industry, locally and globally at times. EBITDA or operating margin is popular as a base because it is directly indicative of how much cash the business is generating. If the company is investing a lot of money in expanding telecom networks it will not reflect in net profit, which will be depressed because of interest, taxes and depreciation. Gupta suggests taking some things into account before applying a multiple of EBITDA to a telecom company. These are:

The growth of the industry: The multiple used to value a company in a market growing by single digits, say Singapore, cannot be applied to a company in India, which is growing in double digits.

ARPU: Again, the multiples in two countries with completely different ARPUs are not comparable. In June 2004 Australian mobile, ARPUs were $43 per subscriber per month. This cannot be compared to India's $9 per month per subscriber.[22] Therefore, using Telstra, the Australia state-owned telecom major, as a benchmark or reference point would not be correct.

Market dynamics and competition: There is usually comparison between the Indian and Chinese telecom markets. But that may not be entirely fitting, even ignoring the difference in sizes—China had close to 700 million telecom subscribers in December 2005, compared to India's 130 million in January 2006. The market structure there is totally different. There are just four telecom companies, all owned by the Chinese government, with their areas and businesses defined. In India there are more than 10 major service providers. There is a planned duopoly in most areas in China. That means prices are stable and margins better. While ARPUs are comparable, EBITDA margins for most of the Chinese firms are in excess of 50 per cent compared to the 30 odd per cent that Bharti, one of India's largest telecom players, has been averaging since 2003. Any comparison with the valuation of an international company may work for Bharti maybe three to fours years later when the market is more stable and some amount of consolidation has taken place.

Management and efficiency of operations: This is a fairly subjective parameter, but is also obvious in many ways. Bharti or Hutch could get a higher EBITDA multiple against MTNL even if they are in the same country, the same market and battle the same competitors. These differences arise out of what investment

---

[21] EBITDA—Earnings before interest, taxes, depreciation and amortisation.
[22] ARPUs for GSM and CDMA combined , March 2005 sourced from TRAI's study paper dated June 16, 2005.

bankers and analysts perceive of both their abilities to scale their businesses, to manage it efficiently (within given cost and timeframes) and so on. It could work the other way round too. Hutch could command a multiple equal to Bharti, even though it is a smaller company. It could be either because it is doing something differently, that makes it earn more money or because the quality of its subscribers is better or its attrition rate is lower. Reliance Infocomm is known for its ability to set up a network in a short time, and cost-efficiently. The company would, therefore, be valued higher when it goes out to raise capital. 'Using multiples in an ad hoc manner does not help. They don't mean anything until they are applied in the correct context,' emphasises Gupta.

A third way of valuing a company could be *discounted cash flows* (refer to 'Valuation' in the chapter on Television). However, the discounted cash flow was a difficult measure to use in India since nobody knew how regulation— on interconnection, technology and a whole lot of issues that have dogged this business—would pan out. 'After the dispute between CDMA and GSM players has been sorted out, the risk (of regulation changing) has been reduced. It is a more level playing field,' says Gupta.

Gupta, however, prefers to use a hybrid or a combination. He prefers to look at the differences in the valuation arrived at by the discounted cash flow method versus the one by EBITDA multiple. If there is a significant gap between the two, may be two times or more, then it might be important to know why that occurs.

Broadband 'Valuing a telecom (company) is not a challenge, since we know where the market is headed. It is valuing a broadband company that is challenging. It is not yet profitable, the growth is yet to take off, the user base is small,' reckons Gupta. If the broadband operation is part of a large telecom company such as Reliance or Bharti, it becomes easier. Even so, a discounted cash flow or EBITDA multiple may not be appropriate. That is because predictions on how much the market could grow by might go awry. This is typical of any nascent industry. After over five years and more than Rs 500 billion worth of investments by all sorts of players, broadband penetration remains at about a million users. Therefore, predicting cash flows based on future revenues, which in turn are based on some assumptions on the numbers of users, is pointless. And since most broadband operations are not yet profitable, again EBITDA multiples won't be pertinent. That is why a pure broadband company, like Sify Broadband, is valued-based on revenue multiples. That means Sify's revenues will be multiplied by a factor of whatever the investor deems fit, say 5, and that will be the valuation.

7 internet

The future of the Internet lies in its ability to connect with other media

THE NET SITS at the crossroads of almost every buzzword being bandied about today. Broadband, mobile content, convergence, are terms that find their meaning in a world that the net has created.[1] Broadband, currently, is a way of accessing the net faster. Mobile companies use the Internet to generate revenues and cross-leverage content. This could be through cross-promotions, downloads of ringtones, video clips or entire films among scores of other things. There is this hybrid world emerging where the internet, mobile, TV, and even newspapers are crossing into one another's territories and creating new and, as yet, unnamed businesses. These are sometimes referred to, loosely, as New Media.[2]

Its ability to aggregate everything, from information to products and services; to sell, promote these; to enable people to communicate, either by plugging into any other media or by itself has been the net's biggest triumph so far. It could be used to buy a car, a camera, see your mum's picture or research a paper. The Internet is today exactly what the newspaper was more than a century ago; an aggregator of almost every kind of information, a communication tool and one for entertainment as well. It goes several steps further. Unlike a newspaper it allows you to talk back, respond, revert and participate in the goings-on—or interact. That makes it an 'interactive medium.'

---

[1] Broadband is an Internet connection that delivers a relatively high bit rate—any bit rate at or above 100 kbps. Cable modems, DSL and ISDN all offer broadband connections. In India TRAI has defined broadband as data speed of 256 kbps or above.

[2] If we think of television, print, Internet or mobile as separate circles, then the point at which these circles intersect each other or converge is the point at which they form a new business. Therefore selling ringtones on mobile phones, though a portal is as much convergence and new media, as possibly IPTV will be in the future.

The fact that we take it for granted, the fact that it exists on most media plans, tells you that the mainstreaming of the net is almost complete. At 7.5 million subscribers and over 38.5 million users, it is a significant medium. The net generated a little over one billion rupees in advertising in 2005. Then there are the revenues from access. These amount to roughly Rs 17 billion.[3] Add classifieds, e-commerce and the total Internet business revenue in India is closer to Rs 22 billion. This does not include numbers for a host of paid-for services that the Internet provides—broking and mobile content—among others. It is even bigger if we add what business-to-business companies make. According to investors they are among the more profitable Internet companies though the numbers for most are difficult to access (see Figure 7.1).

Globally, Internet advertising and access spending was set to touch $145 billion in 2005.[4] In the US, the leading market for online advertising and marketing, adspends were estimated at over $9.2 billion on the Internet in 2005. Most of it is spent to reach out to the 70 per cent US homes that have Internet access. Every major Internet brand, from *Google* to *Amazon* to *Yahoo!* is making money and taking away more and more from traditional media companies.

Yet, it is by becoming more like traditional media that the Internet has achieved this. *Google* allows surfers to search for anything on the web and then gives you targeted classified advertising, something that newspapers usually aggregate. *Yahoo!* offers everything from search to news that has been carefully selected and put together by its battery of editors. These are now frequently referred to as media rather than technology companies.

Even if we forget the profitable Internet businesses across the world, there is enough evidence of the medium's success in India (see Figure 7.2). Some very large turnover websites like Indiabulls.com have already gone public. Others have given their venture capital firms handsome exits. Some more are very profitable and are the target of private equity investors.

Indiatimes.com promoted by the Bennett, Coleman & Company (BCCL), *Nazara.com*, *Indiabulls.com*, and *naukri.com*, among others, have been valued very well recently. Times Internet, the digital arm of BCCL is seen as a media—not technology—company. Mahendra Swarup, Ex-CEO, Times Internet, defines his target group as the mobile plus Internet user base of over 120 million or so. *Indiatimes.com* makes money from song downloads, from selling airline tickets, from promoting films and from advertising. It runs a mobile dating service and several others centred on the number 8888. More than two-thirds of its profits in 2004–05 came from mobile services.

---

[3] This is based on an assumption of average access charges of Rs 200 per month for 7.5 million net connections. The actual rates vary between Rs 200–1,000 a month, depending on the schemes that access providers offer and actual usage. See Figure 0.3 for ad revenue figures.

[4] PricewaterhouseCooper's Global Entertainment and Media Outlook 2004–08.

Figure 7.1: The Shape of the Indian Internet Industry

Internet Industry	Retail	Jobs	Matrimonial	Travel	Advertising	Broking	B2B Marketplaces
Size (India) in Rs billion	1.5	1.35	0.40	7.5	1.62	5	1.8
Growth in 2005(%)	25	35	35	100	60	100	100
Current leaders	Rediff	Naukri, Monster	Shaadi, Bharatmatrimony	Makemytrip, Indiatimes	Rediff, Indiatimes	ICICI Direct, Indiabulls	Metaljunction, Agriwatch

Note: (i) All figures are estimates for 2005–06. (ii) Broking figures refer to the commission earned by the online arms of the broking firms. (iii) B2B does not include e-procurement sites. (iv) Travel figures are billings. (v) Advertising and retail figures are revenues.

Source: *Businessworld* magazine.

Figure 7.2: Top Indian Internet Companies

Company Name	Sector	05–06 Revenues (Rs million)
Indiatimes	portal	1750
Indiabulls	broking	1260
Rediff	portal	1140
Naukri	classifieds (jobs)	750–850
Shaadi	classifieds (matrimonial)	200–300
Bharatmatrimony	classifieds (matrimonial)	200–300
Sify	portal	250
Makemytrip	travel	200

Note: *Sify* and *Indiabulls'* revenues are for their online business only.
Source: *Businessworld* magazine.

Indiatimes stands at the crossroads of almost every media—mobile, television, films, print, and the Internet. When I last spoke to Swarup, it was testing a beta site for downloading films.

It is now an accepted fact that VoIP or voice over Internet Protocol and broadband will bring about the big change in both telecom and the Internet. It will force landline companies to drop the access rate, maybe even make it free and charge for other things like entertainment. (Much of this has been discussed in great detail in the chapters on Telecommunications and Television.) There is some debate on whether the Internet will kill telephony. Even if it doesn't, the Internet, especially its access, will move more and more to companies whose future revenues are dependent on entertainment rather than voice or plain net access. These could be cable, DTH or broadband companies. This is evident in the interest with which the broadband rollouts of companies like Reliance, Bharti or Hathway are being tracked. In that sense, India is in tandem with the rest of the world on its vision of the net's future.

The question mark, if any, on the Internet's future is how quickly penetration can increase to deliver the same numbers as, say, mobile telephony. In January 2006, on the back of falling prices, broadband subscribers in India had grown from 47,000 at the beginning of 2005, to 1 million, according to The Telecom Regulatory Authority's (TRAI) numbers: this, after years of stagnation. Most of these subscribers typically use a broadband connection to access the net. That means that the people accessing hi-speed, hi-quality Internet had jumped 21 times in the course of one year. They will continue to use it for that, till VoIP and then IPTV take off.[5] But those are still some way off. The total Internet subscriber base of 7.5 million is a very small proportion, just about 12 per cent, of the total cable TV homes or 10 per cent of mobile phones.

---

[5] VoIP is Voice over Internet Protocol. IPTV is internet protocol television.

And that is the first problem with the Internet. It is coming into its own when almost every other media—newspaper, television, radio—is also booming. This is unlike say the US, where first newspapers took off, then radio, then TV and so on. It gave every media the time to evolve. In India the new media, mobile, Internet or even radio, have little breathing space to make mistakes and go through their evolution cycles. This simultaneous boom across media also means that the competition for capital is intense. Even if you argue that the quantum of money needed for Internet businesses is not on the same scale as say manufacturing, the fact remains that it is significant. The Internet lost a disproportionately high amount of money to start with, which makes investors wary. The dot-com crash of 2000 almost killed the Internet. But as Rajesh Jain, one of the first few Indian dot-com entrepreneurs puts it, 'There has to be failure, nine out of ten businesses (on the net) have to fail for the big idea to emerge.' Even he agrees that, 'Things have stagnated with respect to the net. The companies that could spend money on it are now doing it with mobile phones.'

That second problem, thinks Jain, is that there isn't enough innovation of services or things-to-do happening on the net, for advertisers and users to flock to it. Of the three screens that dominate consumer lives these days—the PC, the TV and the mobile screen—the PC gets short shrift in non-office time. While there is a problem, its magnitude could be debated. Later on in the chapter, I have talked about the kind of things happening (refer to 'The way it is').

The fact remains that world over the medium is seeing a resurgence based on investor confidence and rising consumption numbers. Since the Iinternet took off in India roughly along with the rest of the world, chances are that we will catch up on the numbers pretty soon.

207

THE PAST

The early years The 'Internet' is a global group of connected networks that allows people to access information and services. It includes the World Wide Web, electronic mail (e-mail) file transfer protocol (FTP), Internet relay chat (IRC) and USENET (news service).[6] Today, the Internet is a network of millions of computers allowing constant communication throughout the

---

[6] Anyone can apply for an e-mail address and send and receive messages from their computer. The main benefit is the almost instantaneous delivery of messages. E-mail to the other side of the world takes a mere 60 seconds. One can also sign up to automatically receive newsletters and other information, delivered directly to one's computer. Web pages are transferred between computers using the HTTP protocol, with other types of

world. It is a worldwide mechanism for information dissemination, collaboration and interaction between individuals through their computers irrespective of their geographic location. It works by taking data, breaking it into separate parts called packets and then sending them along available routes to a destination computer. The packet switched network uses available wire space for only fragments of a second as it transfers a digital message in one direction. To connect to the Internet, one has to subscribe to the services of Internet Service Providers (ISPs).

Four computers located each at the University of California at Los Angeles, the University of California at Santa Barbara, the University of Utah and the Stanford Research Institute, were part of the early beginnings of the Internet. The work was initiated and funded by the U.S. Department of Defense through the Advanced Research Project Agency (ARPA). This network was designed to be a centralised system, which could divert communications in the event of an attack on an individual network. It was intended as a military network of 40 computers connected by a web of links and lines. The ideas that created this network, which later became the Internet, were floating around long before that.

In August 1962 J.C.R. Licklider of the Massachusetts Institute of Technology (MIT) first discussed a 'Galactic Network,' or a globally interconnected set of computers to access data and programs from any site. Licklider was the first head of the computer research program at DARPA starting October 1962.[7]

files sent using FTP. Users can share files, such as music and videos between themselves and the rest of the world by uploading them to a server and then allowing others to download them to their own computers. IRC is a service allowing one to connect to his/her chosen channel and talk to others with the same interests. By downloading an appropriate programme, one can start chatting right away. USENET (Unix User Network) is a system of bulletin boards whereby messages and points of view can be posted to be read and replied to. USENET contributed enormously to the Internet's rapid expansion and is considered to have begun in 1979. Its spirit of information sharing and discussion was the hallmark of its system and was reflected in the Internet as a whole. When personal computers were introduced in the late 1970s, a huge new and ever-expanding computer population was introduced to the Internet. E-mails were increasingly used, network discussions took place and in the 80s and communities were formed in chat rooms c.f. *www.trai.gov.in.*

[7] A brief history of the internet, Barry M. Leiner, Vinton G. Cerf, David D. Clark, Robert E. Kahn, Leonard Kleinrock, Daniel C. Lynch, Jon Postel, Lawrence G. Roberts, Stephen Wolff. From the Internet Society website, *www.isoc.org.* Kanchan Sinha of Amarchand & Mangaldas & Suresh A. Shroff & Company, a New Delhi-based law firm, has also put together large portions of the history. The Advanced Research Projects Agency (ARPA) changed its name to Defense Advanced Research Projects Agency (DARPA) in 1971, then back to ARPA in 1993, and back to DARPA in 1996. The ISOC website refers to DARPA throughout the history portion.

There he convinced his successors, which included MIT researcher Lawrence G. Roberts, of the importance of this networking concept. Leonard Kleinrock at MIT published the first paper on packet switching theory in 1961 and the first book in 1964. Kleinrock too talked to Roberts about how feasible it was to use information packets, not circuits. That became one step along the path towards computer networking. The second was to make computers to talk to one another. By August 1968, Roberts and the DARPA-funded community had refined the overall structure and specifications. By the end of 1969, four host computers were connected together into the initial ARPANET; the Internet was off the ground.

It was based on the idea that there would be multiple independent networks of different designs with the ARPANET as the pioneering packet switching network. Later, others like packet satellite networks or packet radio networks could join in. Transmission Control Protocol/Internet Protocol or TCP/IP was adopted as a defence standard in 1980. By 1983, ARPANET was being used by a significant number of defence R&D and operational organisations. By 1985 both the Internet and e-mail were being used across several communities, often with different systems.

Englishman Tim Berners-Lee introduced the World Wide Web in 1991. In 1993 the first web-browser, Mosaic, was developed at the US-based National Center for Supercomputer Applications (NCSA).[8] The web-browser can be understood as a graphical user interface to the Internet. It is that part of the Internet that most users see and use—Internet Explorer or Mozilla Firefox are the common ones. It has led to tremendous growth both in terms of the size as well as the use of the Internet.

On October 24, 1995, the Federal Networking Council passed a resolution defining the term 'Internet'. This definition was developed in consultation with members of the Internet and intellectual property rights communities.[9]

India goes online It was around this time that India discovered the Internet. In 1995 Internet access in India was restricted to a few major cities and

---

[8] According to the Internet Advertising Bureau's glossary, a browser is a software programme that can on request, download, cache and display documents available on the World Wide Web. Browsers can be either text-based or graphical.

[9] The resolution read—The Federal Networking Council (FNC) agrees that the following language reflects our definition of the term 'Internet'. 'Internet' refers to the global information system that—(i) is logically linked together by a globally unique address space based on the internet Protocol (IP) or its subsequent extensions/follow-ons; (ii) is able to support communications using the Transmission Control Protocol/Internet Protocol (TCP/IP) suite or its subsequent extensions/follow-ons, and/or other IP-compatible protocols; and (iii) provides, uses or makes accessible, either publicly or privately, high level services layered on the communications and related infrastructure described herein.

everything was in the hands of the government.[10] The state-owned Videsh Sanchar Nigam Limited (VSNL), which was responsible for providing Internet services, did so with erratic connectivity and very little bandwidth in a market where phone lines were in perpetual shortage. It was normal for users to be cut off while surfing the net. The rates for this level of service were among the highest in the world at that time. Indian users paid approximately $2 per hour and leased lines ranged over $2,000 per month for a 64 kpbs line. Only a few companies could afford to have leased lines. As a result, by the end of 1998, there were barely 150,000 Internet connections in India.

None of this however dampened the enthusiasm of dozens of entrepreneurs who jumped into the fray. Just as with cable TV, these entrepreneurs led India's first steps into this world and its subsequent growth. There were people like Ajit Balakrishnan (*Rediff.com*), Rajesh Jain (*IndiaWorld.com*) or Haresh Tibrewala and Sanjay Mehta (Homeindia.com) who gave in to the lure of a net-worked world. Take the story of three different portals, the men or companies that set them up and where they are now to get a sense of the Internet history of India.

The first story is that of Rajesh Jain, a techie who set up a portal IndiaWorld.com and within four years sold it at a price that seems preposterous today. The second is of an ad agency chief and serial entrepreneur, Ajit Balakrishnan, who went on to set up one of India's largest portals *Rediff.com* that is now listed on Nasdaq. The third story is of *indiatimes.com* that BCCL, India's largest media company, launched as an extension of its newspapers.

The IndiaWorld.com story Rajesh Jain was one of the earliest ones into the game. I remember meeting him in a cramped office in Mumbai's business centre, Nariman Point, in 1998. His interest and knowledge about the net and its possibilities was infectious. Jain was the progenitor of IndiaWorld.com. It was launched from a server in the US in March 1995, five months before net access was available formally in India. He reckons it was the first portal from India, though he is not sure if it was the first website. Jain's writings are on his blog, *emergic.org*, and he says his own story rather well.[11] So what follows is bits and pieces from *emergic.org* and from an interview I had with him for this book. 'The IndiaWorld story begins in September 1994. I was in the US, try-ing to figure out a good business to do in an area other than software exports. It was the time when the Internet and the World Wide Web were just about beginning to catch people's fancies. I spent a few weeks at a friend's place, browsing the Web on a 14.4 kbps dial-up modem with Netcom's Netcruiser

---

[10] Some parts of the India background have been put together by Kanchan Sinha or Amarchand & Mangaldas & Suresh. A Shroff & Company.

[11] Large chunks of Jain's journey are reproduced from his blog in own words. I also interviewed him for his insights on where the medium is headed.

account. The experience was absolutely amazing. It was quite evident then that the Web as a medium would have a significant impact on how information was disseminated. The Web offered a good business opportunity: attract the NRIs (non resident Indians) and then look at offshoots in electronic commerce.'

On his return to India in November 1994, Jain wrote to various publishers and talked to a number of companies and individuals to participate in the venture by offering their content. 'It was tough explaining the Internet and the Web to people in India then: there was no commercial Internet access provider. Most thought the Internet to be another variation of a satellite channel! I would take a notebook with NCSA Mosaic, and show them the power of hyperlinks,' he writes on his blog.

IndiaWorld.com started as a news and information service with content from *The Indian Express, India Today, Dataquest, Reader's Digest,* Kensource, Crisil, Centre for Monitoring the Indian Economy (CMIE), DSP Financial and several others. 'When I was looking to aggregate content there was no real Internet,' says Jain now. Emails to friends and postings in newsgroups were some of the ways in which he tried to popularise the site initially. Two days after launch, *IndiaWorld.com* covered the Union Budget live. It had a group of analysts and journalists watch the TV in one room and give their comments. Then someone would type it all up and put it up on the site. 'We were very keen to charge a subscription fee for sections of *IndiaWorld.com*. We started at $49, then dropped it to $29, then to $20 for a year, and then in November 1996 dropped it altogether. This was a flawed model and it probably drove some people away.'

For the first two years of its existence, *IndiaWorld.com* generated almost 95 per cent of its traffic from outside India. By 1997, as the Indian traffic numbers started increasing it altered course. *IndiaWorld.com* started creating specific non-news sites. Starting with *khoj.com*, a search engine, the portal had several other sites, Khel (cricket), Man Pasand (favourites), IndiaLine (Internet), Samachar (customised news), Dhan (personal finance), Bawarchi (food), Itihaas (History) and newsASIA (a Samachar variant for the Asian region). In November 1999 when it had 13 million page views a month, Satyam Infoway bought it out for Rs 5 billion or about $115 million at that time.[12]

The Rediff.com story Ajit Balakrishnan, who set up *Rediff.com*, was the co-founder of the advertising agency, Rediffusion.[13] In the mid-80s the personal computer (PC) fascinated him; he joined hands with a friend to set up a PC-making company in Bangalore. He eventually sold it to a French company in 1989–90, at what he modestly describes as a 'good price'. 'The market in India

211

---

[12] This is according to the dollar rate of that time.
[13] Balakrishnan is now chairman *Rediff.com*. The entire *Rediff.com* story is Ajit Balakrishnan's account shared with me in an interview for this book.

was not a place for hardware makers,' says Balakrishnan. His friend went off to the Silicon Valley while Balakrishnan hung around in India mulling over what he wanted to do. It had to be something that combined computer technology and media, his two loves. 'Standing on those crossroads it was easy to see the Internet when it came by,' says Balakrishnan. In 1992–93, he set up an online information service. But the user interface was clunky and the technology underdeveloped. He soon gave it up.

When his wife enrolled in a programme at Oxford in the early 90s, Balakrishnan accompanied her. It was in Oxford that he discovered the joys of logging onto *CompuServe* using Mosaic, one of the first browsers. 'That is when I knew exactly where we were headed,' says he. He spent a lot of time on *CompuServe* chatrooms. He then migrated to the Internet Explorer and later to Netscape. At that time Netscape was an incredibly light browser to use since it had figured out a way of caching or putting in the PC's temporary memory the page a surfer visited regularly; that made the pages open easily. When Balakrishnan came back to Mumbai he took a two-year break to figure out what to do. In 1995 he set up *Rediff-on-the-net* (later renamed *Rediff.com*), on a small lease line server. He financed it by selling a portion of his stake in the agency, Rediffusion, to Young & Rubicam.

Balakrishnan had earlier requested *Yahoo!* to carry *Rediff.com* on its site directory. That resulted in a million hits the next day, all from the US, he remembers. Almost all of them were Indians working in computer science labs in the US, and therefore having net access, a rare thing then. When they saw an Indian site on *Yahoo!* they logged on to it enthusiastically. In the first few years *Rediff.com* also built sites for other people, learning a lot in the process. Yet, by 1997 revenues were negligible and Balakrishnan had exhausted his capital.

While he was still scouting for capital, he was invited to speak at a seminar in his capacity as one of the few net entrepreneurs in India. In the audience sat the then 70-year-old Bill Draper, a venture capitalist from the US. He had just set up Draper International to focus on venture investments in India.[14] He heard Balakrishnan and approached him. Draper wanted to invest in *Rediff.com* and eventually he put one million dollars in 1998. 'I told him it was a lot of money and he said you will need it,' remembers Balakrishnan. What helped *Rediff.com*—more than the money—were the connections that Draper, based in Silicon Valley, brought. He was sitting in the middle of the action and that helped *Rediff.com* learn and grow.

---

[14] The Draper name is well known in the venture capital industry. Bill Draper's father too was a venture capitalist. Bill was a founding investor in Apollo Computer (acquired by Hewlett Packard), Dionex, Integrated Genetics (Genzyme), Quantum, Qume (I.T.T.), Activision (Mediagenic), Xidex (Eastman Kodak) among several other companies. Draper International was set up in 1995 to look at India focused investments.

Rediff.com commenced trading on the Nasdaq, June 14, 2000, raising net proceeds of US$49.8 million.[15] During the years 2001 and 2002, it made a number of acquisitions in the US to strengthen its NRI offerings. First, it acquired *thinkindia.com*, an Internet portal that serviced people of Indian origin in the United States, for $3.4 million. In March 2001, it acquired ValuCom, a provider of online phone cards, for US$3.7 million. In April 2001, it acquired *India Abroad* and *India in New York*, two weekly community newspapers based in New York, for approximately US$10.7 million. *India Abroad* was an established weekly newspaper, nearly four decades old, focused on the Indian community in the United States.

Between 2001–04, *Rediff.com* consolidated most of the editorial and production functions of *India Abroad* in Mumbai to achieve cost savings and greater efficiencies. Produced by the editorial staff in Mumbai, the paper is transmitted electronically to printers for publishing in New York and Toronto every Friday. Besides these products, *Rediff.com* currently offers e-mail in English, Hindi and a dozen other major regional languages, as well as news, blogs, shopping, radio, information on jobs, movies and sports, and its own matchmaking services. It made Rs 541 million in revenues in March 2005 and had 37.5 million registered users.

The indiatimes.com story In 1996, soon after *Rediff.com*, BCCL decided to get into the net space. At that time the idea, says Sunil Rajshekhar, director, BCCL, was to simply explore what the company could do with this medium. There was some notion that *indiatimes.com* could get classified advertising by putting its brands online. 'We looked at it purely to see whether there was any money in it,' remembers Rajshekhar. To start with, *Femina* and *Filmfare* were put online. *The Times of India* (TOI) and *The Economic Times*, two of its largest selling newspapers were added later. Though it carried stories from the print edition only, the site was a big draw in the US, just like *Rediff.com* and *India World.com*. That is when BCCL started marketing the advertising space on the site to banks and financial institutions, which were targeting non-resident Indians (NRIs). For two years the website continued to function, at a small—though profitable—level. Then BCCL managing director Vineet Jain became interested in the medium and the business got a champion from within the top management.

The US-based traffic made BCCL realise that the portal it created then would have to reflect both, the fact that it was from the *Times* stable and that it was India-centric. That is how *indiatimes.com* was created in 1998–99. 'It was fun talking to people. Nobody was clear what the Internet was all about. Everyone used to think it is a tech game, we had an issue internally convincing people that it is a media game,' says Rajshekhar.

---

[15] Later the underwriters of Rediff's offering exercised their over-allotment option and it issued additional equity shares that netted US$7.5 million.

213

The boom and bust years What made things easier was the availability of money for setting up Internet businesses. Many foreign venture capital firms had set shop in India. India's software successes made them think that the Internet would give them similar returns. By 2000 positive investor sentiment about the net was fuelling the growth of all kinds of websites—on marriage, games, gossip, work, cooking, working women and so on.[16]

Journalists quit their jobs for Internet companies that paid them three times or more plus a fancy designation. A plain reporter could become 'head of content' in a website selling plumbing pipes or office stationery. There were several dozens of people who left perfectly good jobs to set up Internet businesses. Some because they believed in the medium and others because they thought they would get a good valuation and make money. A lot of the capital coming in, which fuelled these rising salaries and overheads, was based on dodgy valuations since there were no profits or revenues that could be used as a base. Anything from hits to pages were used to judge the popularity of a website and value it. 'In that sense valuation was completely de-linked from the financials,' says Sanjiv Agrawal, partner, transaction advisory services, Ernst & Young.[17] Between 1999–2000, more than 100 dot-com valuations happened according to Agrawal. The media, including magazines like *Businessworld* and others, joined enthusiastically in cheering on what looked like the birth of a medium.

Many companies got in because of the fear of being left behind. It was clear in several cases that they either hadn't understood the medium (fair enough, considering it was new) or they hadn't thought through what they wanted to do with it. This is true not only for Indian companies but even for American corporations. Walt Disney spent billions of dollars on *Go.com*, which did not, well, go anywhere. News Corporation wrote off more than $300 million worth of investments that it had made on Internet businesses during this period. Almost one-third of this was spent buying or setting up Indian portals.

Everybody got a little carried away and later because they felt silly, many dismissed the medium. The 'dot-com crash' as it has now been branded, happened over 2000–01. It was about bloated valuations and share prices of internet companies finally falling to reflect the companies—many non-revenue generating, non-profit making, non-businesses that had hitched a ride on the back of investors who were supposed to know better. But the fact is that the investors, many of them looking at the Internet at the same time as the entrepreneurs they were funding, were equally clueless.

---

[16] During 1998–2001, I was writing on information technology and specifically on the internet, so I saw some of this excitement first hand.

[17] The section on valuation has been put together based on an interview with Agrawal and with a lot of help from E&Y. Agrawal was also involved with internet valuations during the boom and bust periods.

There was no 'big' crash in India, but it affected us. The venture capital sentiment turned against Internet companies and finally the flow of capital dried up. Dozens and dozens of web businesses disappeared overnight or ran out of funds. But the ones that survived did so either because they were solid businesses to start with or because they changed business models.

THE WAY IT IS

There is now a sense of solidity about the Internet. There is a shape emerging, of an industry with its own genres, people, business models and so on. One probably cannot classify net businesses very easily right now but broadly there are three trends that are evident.

One is the emergence of focused business-to-business (BtoB) Internet companies. In areas like technology, lifestyle, writing, promotions, advertising or even media, there are focused portals that talk to a specific audience. *Hungama.com*, for example, only does promotions, online and offline across media, be it the net or mobile. It then uses this ability to connect with marketers trying to find solutions to the clutter in mass-media. *Agencyfaqs.com* talks only to advertising, media and marketing professionals and then uses this audience to get advertising from people wanting to talk to this community. A bulk of the advertisers on *agencyfaqs.com* is media companies wanting to reach out to advertisers and advertising agencies. The others are direct marketing firms, design consultants or others who offer services to this community. It has a magazine (*The Brand Reporter*), an image monitoring service (Cirrus) and is looking at getting into other magazines and services.[18] What is true for *agencyfaqs.com* is true for almost every other Internet company, especially in the BtoB space. Most have a presence in another media, some in more than three. Most are very profitable because the audience they offer to advertisers is sharply targeted so the premium they can charge on advertising is higher.

The second is the way large portals, like *Rediff.com* or *indiatimes.com* or any of the others have morphed to become businesses that do things far beyond the net. They have become media companies. *Rediff.com* has a radio service in the US, weekly newspapers, is into e-commerce and so on. Indiatimes.com too is less Internet and more media.

The third is the sheer variety and amount of experimentation that we are seeing in net businesses now (in spite of what Jain says). Whether it is an existing company trying to de-risk and is therefore experimenting, like *Hungama.com* or new genres emerging that are totally India-centric and profitable, like *Shaadi.com* or *Bharatmatrimony.com*. These are matrimonial sites, a totally Indian product idea. Employment, which is a global revenue source for newspapers, has also

---

[18] My husband Sreekant Khandekar is a promoter and shareholder in agencyfaqs.com.

215

shifted to the net for low to middle level jobs with sites like *naukri.com*. There are profitable sites for commodity trading, for organising your travel, for personal finance and a host of activities built around the way you would spend your time and money.

The Internet is now a robust, thriving industry. Where we have stumbled is on both telecom and broadband policy, thinks Jain. He reckons that even now our sights are set too low. '10 million (broadband connections by 2010) is a ridiculously small target. Why can't we make India the wireless test bed of the world, why don't we allocate 3G spectrum? We are debating all this and losing time,' he says. What will bring those changes is VoIP or voice over Internet protocol, a development that has pushed Internet companies and phone companies to actively encroach on each other's turf or to collaborate.

'The inflection on the net will come because of mobile. The mobile will become a sampling mode for what you can see on the big screen,' thinks Swarup. He thinks that going into the future the net will need other media less. 'The next big thing is convergence, my belief is that it will first happen on mobile and TV screens, on highly penetrated media. If convergence happens then Internet companies are best equipped to make the most of it. You could watch a video on the net or take a test,' thinks Swarup. The more bandwidth that is available on both wireless devices like phones or on television through satellite broadband, the faster convergence will happen, he thinks.

THE WAY IT WORKS

The main revenue streams for an Internet company are not as tightly defined as, say, for publishing. As the medium evolves many streams are being born out of hybrid businesses. The revenues could come from:

Access This is the monthly charge that users pay to access a website or to use the services of an Internet service provider. Access charges could vary between Rs 200–1,000 per month depending on the package bought, the hours of usage, the bandwidth used, the number of phone calls made and so on.

Subscription This could come from fee-based services like paid e-mail and others. Rediff SMS2India allows subscribers to send text messages (SMS) from a personal computer to a mobile phone in India or the U.S. The mobile user can reply by SMS back to the subscriber's personal computer. A three-month subscription with a maximum of 400 messages is currently priced at US$9.99. Rediff Radio in the US gives subscribers access to two channels of radio with Indian music. A one-month subscription to Rediff Radio was US$4.95 and a three-month subscription came for US$11.95 in 2004.[19]

---

[19] A lot of the *rediff.com* data is from its 2004 filing with the Securities and Exchange Commission in the US.

Advertising This is an important, though not necessarily, the largest chunk of revenues for Internet companies. It is, however, a large contributor to the revenues of a BtoB site. That's because a BtoB site is more focused, so the advertiser pays a premium to reach that audience. If a media company advertises on *agencyfaqs .com* it is reaching out to its key target group of advertisers, agencies and media buyers since they comprise the audience this site addresses. Advertising rates differ based on several parameters discussed later in the section on metrics.

Selling This is the margin made by selling goods and services like any other retailer. Both *indiatimes.com* and *Rediff.com* earn a nice sum from selling everything from airline tickets to cameras. On *Rediff.com*, buyers can use all leading U.S. dollar and rupee credit cards, debit cards and online money transfers for payments.

Partnerships The revenues come from joining hands with mobile, TV, print or other companies to sell services. Many websites sell ringtones, logos, picture messages, wallpapers and games available from a third party provider. They usually share an agreed percentage with the telephone operator and the company, which owns the rights to the music or the other visual elements of a film, painting, pictures etc.

Others Most Internet companies now have an offline revenue stream. Some have magazines or newspapers; like *Rediff.com* has *India Abroad* or *agencyfaqs. com* has *The Brand Reporter*. These make money from subscription and advertising like any other print product. Others may make money from events, hosting websites, designing websites.

METRICS

While TV has the ratings system and Press the Audit Bureau of Circulations (ABC) there is no such metric for the Internet in India. There are companies like Mediaturf that serve ad banners for websites. However, there are no companies that certify net traffic in India, yet. Much of this is a function of the size of the industry and its ability to pay for the service. The lack of data and certified reach hampers radio too. Just like the Internet industry, it hasn't got around to doing something about it. The recent formation of the Internet and Mobile Association of India (IMAI) suggests that eventually the industry will move towards having a formal body to certify traffic in India. The Indian ABC has debated offering a website audit, but nothing has come of it though there is a Digital ABC in several countries. Most Indian websites do not get their traffic numbers certified. Many claim whatever traffic and impact figures they want to.

This seems paradoxical. The Internet is the one medium that is the easiest to measure, both in terms of reach and impact and in terms of advertising effectiveness. That is because almost every click on every website is recorded on the servers that host the website. Unlike say ABC (for newspapers) which uses several chartered accountants to look at print company books or TV ratings, which use a box that just records basic stuff, the net can offer much sharper data. An advertiser or investor can know, very easily on who came onto a website, when, what did they read or search for, how long were they there, when they went away and so on. It is this transparency that *Google* uses to sell targeted classified ads to websites across the world. Therefore it is surprising that the Internet industry has not managed to harness this to its advantage.

To be fair to the Indian market it is largely in line with international ones on this. The Interactive Advertising Bureau (IAB) was founded in 1996 as a non-profit organisation in the US. It represents over 200 leading companies in the space, like MSN, AOL or Yahoo! Its members account for over 86 per cent of online advertising in the United States. Yet, it was in November 2004 that the IAB along with other global advertising, marketing and Internet associations, first published measurement and audit guidelines. These are essentially the definitions of various metrics like 'page impressions' or 'clicks'. These have come almost eight years after it had been formed. So India is alright.

The IAB's website claims that its new guidelines are a 'global' measurement standard that has been accepted by all the key industry stakeholder organisations in the U.S., Europe, Asia and Latin America. This is unlike television, radio and magazines that have different bodies using different techniques to measure reach and impact in different country markets. The IAB's guidelines cover both the technology and the processes for executing ad buys. Everybody involved, the publisher and the agency, need to get audited and certified. Some of the common metrics and terms, which may or may not be defined by IAB, but are used while doing business on the net are:[20]

Page is the starting point of every measurement of things on the net. A page is a document having a specific URL.[21] It is made up of a set of associated files. A page may contain text, images, and other elements. It may be static or dynamically generated. It may be made up of multiple frames or screens, but should contain a designated primary object which, when loaded, is counted as the entire page.

---

[20] A lot of the data on the definition of metrics is sourced from the IAB's website, especially the glossary of terms.

[21] URL stands for Uniform Resource Locator. It is the global address for documents and other resources on the web. The first part of the address indicates what protocol to use, the second specifies the IP address or the domain where the resource is located. For example *http://www.businessworldindia* is a URL. Http refers to the protocol and 'businessworld india' to the domain name.

Hits were earlier a very popular measure. When users access a website, their computer sends a request to the site's server to begin downloading a page. Each element of a requested page (including graphics, text, interactive items) is recorded by the site's server as a 'hit'. If a user accesses a page containing two graphics, those hits will be recorded once for the page itself and once for each of the graphics. That means that everything on a web page, a picture, a graphic, a text box, all of which are different files will be counted as a hit, even if just one person has been to that page. While hits were the first metric used when the net took off, they were soon discarded. Since page design and visit patterns vary from site to site, the number of hits bears no relationship to the number of pages downloaded. Hits, now, are acknowledged as a bad measure of traffic. They are used by the websites only to check the workloads on their servers.

Page impression is the number of times a page was requested by a user. 'Page views' are referred to when a web page is actually seen by the user. This is not measurable today; the best approximation is provided by page displays. There are several questions even on page display or impression. Does the server record it when a user downloads a page or when it is requested? It could also be when a tracking pixel, a tiny file placed on a page for counting page views, finally reaches the surfer's screen. If you ask for a page, but lose patience if it is taking time to download, chances are that it will be recorded as a page view though you left the site long back.

Click is a metric that measures the reaction of a user to an Internet ad. There are three types of clicks: click-throughs, in-unit clicks, and mouseovers. These include following a hyperlink within an advertisement or editorial content to another website or another page or frame within the site.

Reach is defined by the IAB as unique users that visited a site over the course of the reporting period. It is also called unduplicated audience. 'Unique users' could also refer to the total number of people who are 'served' an ad. 'Unique users' are unique individuals or browsers that have either accessed a site or have been served unique content and/or ads such as e-mail, newsletters, interstitials and pop-under ads. User registration or cookies can identify unique users. A cookie is a file on the user's browser that uniquely identifies him. A browser is the tool you use to surf the net, such as Internet Explorer or Mozilla Firefox. There are two types of cookies. Session cookies are temporary and are erased when the browser exits. Persistent cookies remain on the user's hard drive until he erases them or they expire. Heuristic is a way to measure a user's unique identity. If a server receives a new request from the same IP (internet protocol) address within 30 minutes, it is inferred that the new request has come from the same user.

Clickstream is a way for companies to analyse consumer behaviour. There are several analytical software packages that can help analyse where consumers enter a site and where they exit. Many abandon a purchase while on a website.

Companies can use clickstream analysis to determine their drop-off rate, to understand how consumers navigate a website, are they looking for something too often, are they hanging up on the website too often and so on. These have to be supplemented with online consumer surveys.

These are some of the different types of internet ads:
Banner is an image displayed on an HTML page used as an ad.[22] Think of it as the equivalent of display advertising in newspapers.
Interstitial ads appear between two content pages. The user sees an advertisement as he/she navigates between page 'a' and page 'b.' These are also known as transition ads, splash pages and flash pages.
Floating ads appear within the main browser window on top of the normal content, thereby appearing to 'float' over the top of the web page. They are also called floaters.

The pricing of net ads could vary across Internet sites and advertisers depending on the objectives of advertising and the reach of the website. In that sense it operates very much like mainline advertising. The only difference is that the permutations and combination are many. The interactivity of the medium and its inherent transparency lends itself to far more number crunching. There is cost-per-action which is based on a surfer taking some defined action in response to an ad. This could mean buying something or signing up for a service or just clicking on an ad among other things. Alternatively, ad rates could be based on cost-per-click, which is based on the number of clicks received. One of the popular ways of paying for net ads in India is cost-per-thousand impression (CPM).

Even now, over 10 years since it took off, the net is not an easy medium to sell. There are times when agencies are not convinced about the efficacy of the medium and others when their creative departments do not know how to create an Internet ad. Many website publishers usually deal directly with advertisers. It works well currently, reckons Swarup of *indiatimes.com,* because the amounts involved are very small, so someone at a relatively lower level can make the decision. As the net advertising pie grows, the decision-making will shift to higher levels.

REGULATION[23]

ISP Policy To improve Internet connectivity in India, the Government decided to allow private participation in this area and consequently, the Internet

---

[22] HTML is HyperText mark-up language. An HTML page is a document written in that language.
[23] The portion on regulation has been put together, largely, by Kanchan Sinha of Amarchand & Mangaldas & Suresh A. Shroff & Company, a New Delhi-based law firm. Some parts of it have also been sourced from *Rediff.com*'s SEC filing.

Service Provider (ISP) Policy was announced in November 1998.[24] With effect from November 16, 1998 the ISP licences were issued to private companies for a period of 15 years on a non-exclusive basis. The term of the ISP licences may be extended depending upon the discretion of the department of telecommunications (DoT). The government waived the licence fee up to 31 October 2003 and a nominal licence fee of Re 1/- per annum is payable from 1 November 2003. Private ISPs are permitted to set up their own gateways. ISPs are also allowed to set up international gateways using satellite and submarine cable landing stations.

Any Indian company registered under the Indian Companies Act, 1956 is eligible to apply to DoT for an ISP licence. Currently, foreign equity of up to 74 per cent is permitted in ISPs with gateways, radio-paging and end-to-end bandwidth. In ISPs not providing gateways (both for satellite and submarine cables) 100 per cent FDI is permitted in. However, FDI beyond 49 per cent requires prior government approval. All these approvals are subject to the licensing and security requirements. In the event, an ISP receives FDI up to 100 per cent, it is required to divest 26 per cent of its equity in favour of the Indian public in 5 years, if it is listed in other parts of the world.

The application for an ISP licence is required to be made separately for each service area in which the company intends to operate. There is no restriction on the number of ISP licences, which may be granted to one company. The licensee should:

- Commission all the necessary systems to provide the Internet services as per the licence within 24 months from the effective date.
- Comply with all the operations, technical and quality requirements in providing services to its subscribers.
- Set up security monitoring system at its own cost in accordance, with the conditions laid down in the ISP licence.
- Set up its nodes, that is, routers or servers within the geographical area of the service area for which the licence has been granted.

If an ISP licensee is not intending to start its service, it can surrender its licence. The DoT allows the licensee to exit without starting the service, by paying a surrender charge. This amount is equivalent to 5 per cent of the performance bank guarantee to the DoT.

Internet Telephony has been allowed in India by the DoT with effect from 1 April 2002, it defines Internet telephony as an application service, which

---

[24] The details of this policy are available at *www.dotindia.com*.

the customers of ISPs can avail from their personal computers capable of processing voice signals or other IP-based equipment such as:

- PC to PC (both within as well as outside India).
- PC to Telephone (PC in India to telephone outside India).
- IP-based terminals in India to similar terminals both in India and abroad, employing IP-addressing scheme of 'IANA.'[25]

Besides these three, no other form of Internet telephony is permitted in India. Internet telephony services offered by ISPs is different in nature, scope and kind from the real time voice offered by telecom operators. Voice communication by dialling of a phone number, terminating the voice communication to any telephone within India, establishing connection to any public switched network in India, dial up lines with outward dialling facility from nodes, interconnectivity between ISPs which are permitted to offer internet telephony services and the ones which are not permitted to do so are some of the examples that do not fall under the category of internet telephony. TRAI has presently not stipulated any tariff for Internet telephony services offered by the ISPs over the public Internet. It may at anytime fix it and this shall be binding on the licensee. It may even impose the universal service obligation levy.

The IT Act The Internet industry is by turns subject to regulation by the Ministry of Information Technology, which was formed in October 1999, the Ministry of Communications of the Government of India and the TRAI. On June 9, 2000, the Indian Information Technology Act (IT Act) was enacted. It was made effective as of October 17, 2000. The IT Act has been enacted to:

- give legal validity to online contracts
- give legal validity to digital signatures
- make electronic records admissible in court in evidentiary proceedings
- set default rules for time and place of dispatch and receipt of electronic records
- allow for filing of documents with the Government of India in electronic form
- allow for retention of documents, information or records in electronic form
- set up certifying authorities to issue and supervise digital signatures
- set up a controller of certifying authorities to monitor and supervise them

---

[25] 'IANA' stands for Internet Assigned Number Authority. Paragraph 2.1 of the guidelines for issue of permission to offer Internet telephony services, 2002.

- set up Cyber Regulations Appellate Tribunals to act as quasi-judicial bodies with respect to disputes relating to online transactions
- penalise computer crimes.

Although the IT Act has been enacted, clarity on various issues including legal recognition of electronic records, validity of contracts entered into through the internet and validity of digital signatures, needs to be established. The biggest problem with the Internet is its borderless nature. This gives rise to a very big problem: which law does a website comply with? If a server is located in the US and caters to French customers and is accessible from any part in the world (as most websites on the Internet are), the laws of which country does the website follow?

Globally, the trend seems to be that if a website 'affects' a country, then the laws of that country are applicable to that website. The IT Act states that the Act shall apply to offences committed outside India if the offence involves a computer or computer system located in India. With regard to the offence of publishing or transmitting 'obscene' material, the question arises when a computer or computer system in India is involved. While there is no Indian judgment on this point, guidance may be obtained from similar laws in other countries. British jurisprudence (within the framework of similar, though not identical, laws) indicates that the transmission of data to an ISP and from an ISP to the viewer's computer, are acts which amount to the act of publication. Therefore, even if a server is not in the UK but the offending material is downloaded in the United Kingdom, the prohibition contained in the Obscene Publications Acts, 1959 (UK) would apply.

If a similar view is adopted in other countries, entertainment productions that are published on the Internet may have to face the prospect of having to conform to the 'obscenity' laws of all these countries. The laws on publication of 'obscenity' being extremely varied and based on a national concept of public morality, compliance becomes virtually impossible.

New Telecom Policy, 1999 The New Telecom Policy, 1999, deals with the restructuring of the Indian telecommunications sector. It states that ISPs that wish to provide applications such as tele-banking, tele-medicine, tele-education, tele-trading and e-commerce, will be allowed to operate using infrastructure provided by various internet access providers. It also provides that no licence fees will be charged for providing these services, but registration with the Government of India will be required. It prohibits such service providers from offering switched telephony.

The TRAI Established in January 1997 under the provisions of the Telecom Regulatory Authority of India Act, 1997, it is an autonomous body to regulate the telecom industry (refer to the chapter on 'Telecommunications'.)

National Internet Exchange of India (NIXI) It is a 'not-for-profit' company under Section 25 of the Indian Companies Act, 1956 promoted by the Department of Information Technology in association with the Internet Service Providers Association of India (ISPAI). It is entrusted with the responsibility of setting up the Registry for '.in' country code top level domain name. For this the NIXI will create the .IN Network Information Centre (INNIC) to operate as a Registry for .IN domain in India.

ACCOUNTING NORMS[26]

Revenues Internet service providers typically provide access to the net through their pipes. The service is based on usage. Revenue is recognised on the basis of the contract. Initially it is recognised pro-rata on the basis of the hours used. If the user forfeits the balance subscription amount on expiry of the time duration, then, the balance is recognised as revenue. If the unused amount is allowed to be carried forward with the renewal of subscription then the balance is added to the new subscription and amortised on the basis of use.

In the case of a portal, there could be several revenue sources for which accounting will differ based on the contractual obligations.

Advertising revenues: Recognised over the contractual period of the advertisement, starting from the time the ad is placed on the website, these are usually linked to the traffic to a site. If an ad flashes based on the content accessed and the advertising company pays only if the user clicks on the link, then revenue can be billed only on the basis of such number of ads routed from the site. On the other hand there could be a banner ad placed for a fixed duration seen by all visitors to the site. Typically banner advertising includes the guarantee of a minimum number of times that a page is served or viewed. If these are not met, revenues are deferred until the guaranteed impression levels are achieved. In this case the revenue would be amortised over the time of the contract.

Revenues are also derived from sponsor buttons placed in specific areas of a website. These direct users go to sponsor websites. Such revenues are recognised ratably over the period in which the advertisement is displayed, provided that no significant obligations remain and collection of the resulting receivable is probable.

Fee-based services: These include e-commerce, subscription services and wireless short messaging services. E-commerce revenues come from the sale of books,

---

[26] Ramesh Lakshman and Company has put all accounting norms together for this book.

music, apparel, and other things to surfers. Usually a portal pays the supplier of the products after deducting its share of commission and costs. Revenues from e-commerce services also include fees charged to the supplier for creating, designing and hosting the supplier's product information on the website. Such fees are amortized over the hosting contract period. Subscription revenues like paid e-mail, short messaging service-based services, astrology and other services are recognised ratably over the period of subscription.

Website development: It is usually about designing graphics, layout, artwork and content of the other websites. Revenue from such services, if they are large contracts, are recognised upon completion of the targets specified in the contract.

Others: Revenues could be from ringtones, picture messages, logos, wallpapers, e-mail and other related products to mobile phone users. In this case contracts are with third-party mobile phone operators for sharing revenues from these services. SMS based revenues are recognised when the service is performed. A website might also earn royalty from another site for sharing content. In such case, the revenue is recognised on the basis of the agreement.

Costs Since websites are content driven, their creation and development determines a lot of the costs for Internet companies. The content on a website may be updated either by in-house staff or by outside consultants. If the content is semi-permanent and likely to be retained for some extended period, then the cost will be charged over the expected time of their use. Otherwise it will be charged to revenue as and when incurred. Outsourced content updating costs are charged to revenue as and when incurred.

Valuation

225

In 1999, before the dot-com crash, Internet company valuations were done indirectly since there were no benchmarks. The first round of funding was about the idea. The second round was when the product or service was about to be launched.

Sanjiv Agrawal, partner, transaction advisory services, Ernst & Young reckons that in 80 per cent of the companies financed during the boom the valuation in the first round was Rs 40–50 million and second one Rs 100–150 million.[27]

---

[27] The section on valuation has been put together based on an interview with Agrawal and with a lot of help from E&Y. Agrawal was also involved with internet valuations during the boom and bust periods.

In the US these numbers were $1–2 million and $3–4 million in the second round. The third round was the one where everyone made money. In many cases it was an Initial Public Offer (IPO). There were several high profile aberrations, like *Hotmail.com*.

There were other ways of valuing a new company. The investor looked at hits and page views. These were used to arrive at some projections on sales, growth rates and profits in the future. The discounted cash flow method was applied to this and a present value arrived at.

Currently Agrawal reckons that an EBITDA (earnings before interest, taxes, depreciation and amortisation) multiple is more 'scientific' for Internet companies than a P/E (price to earnings) multiple. 'EBITDA is directly related to the operating results of the company, even for normal valuations it is considered to be good,' says he. Typically, in high growth, dynamic industries—like television or even the Internet—investors prefer EBITDA since it better reflects cash that the business is generating. If a company is investing a lot, like Internet companies might, on say distribution, marketing or content, to drive up turnover, it may drag down profits in the short run. That is why operating profits or EBITDA makes sense. There are two things that have be considered:

Growth rate and risk Agrawal reckons that an EBITDA multiple of 5–7 times is good enough in most industries. In very high growth industries, like say software, it could be 10–12. Even in software, in the context of the Indian economy, he reckons that the multiple seven is good enough. It is ultimately a function of the risk. If the growth and risk both are high, then the multiple is lower. If the growth is high but risk is controllable then a multiple of even 20 is good. The rough principle is that if a company is growing at 30 per cent the multiple will be 15, says he. There are many other factors that come into play here. How scalable is the business, how fast it can add new businesses or consumers to push up revenues. This will depend on the segment it operates in.

Segment The valuation also depends on the segment or market the company operates in. BtoB companies are treated as 'normal businesses, not net businesses,' says Agrawal. Since they reach a targeted audience, say 10,000–20,000 companies, the real value is the reach, efficiency and reduction in costs they offer advertisers or business associates. In the growth stage a BtoB company could even command a multiple of 15-20 times. For a BtoB firm scalability may be about offering more services to the same group of consumers. For a website dependent on e-commerce, such as Amazon, it may be about adding more product lines.

annexure 1

Figure A1.1: Global Entertainment and Media Market by Region (US$ Millions)

Region	1999	2000	2001	2002	2003p	2004p	2005p	2006p	2007p	2008p	2004–08 CAGR
United States	443,050	481,869	484,670	501,535	523,159	552,907	580,766	615,634	646,136	680,446	
% Change	8.0	8.8	0.6	3.5	4.3	5.7	5.0	6.0	5.0	5.3	5.4
EMEA	345,454	373,510	388,415	406,582	420,354	439,520	463,068	493,557	519,317	548,514	
% Change	5.8	8.1	4.0	4.7	3.4	4.6	5.4	6.6	5.2	5.6	5.5
Asia/Pacific	183,262	201,105	208,170	216,920	229,058	246,763	269,224	298,476	332,341	365,925	
% Change	6.2	9.7	3.5	4.2	5.6	7.7	9.1	10.9	11.3	10.1	9.8
Latin America	30,502	32,492	32,729	31,898	32,621	34,076	36,028	38,931	41,674	44,671	
% Change	0.0	6.5	0.7	-2.5	2.3	4.5	5.7	8.1	7.0	7.2	6.5
Canada	18,079	19,712	20,831	22,276	23,588	24,971	26,508	28,076	29,764	31,373	
% Change	5.9	9.0	5.7	6.9	5.9	5.9	6.2	5.9	6.0	5.4	5.9
Total	**1,020,347**	**1,108,688**	**1,134,815**	**1,179,211**	**1,228,780**	**1,298,237**	**1,375,594**	**1,474,674**	**1,569,232**	**1,670,920**	
% Change	**6.6**	**8.7**	**2.4**	**3.9**	**4.2**	**5.7**	**6.0**	**7.2**	**6.4**	**6.5**	**6.3**

Note: (i) EMEA—Europe, Middle East and Africa (ii) p—projected.
Source: PricewaterhouseCoopers Global Entertainment and Media Outlook, 2004–2008.

Figure A1.2: Global Advertising (US$ Millions)

Segment	1999	2000	2001	2002	2003p	2004p	2005p	2006p	2007p	2008p	2004–08 CAGR
Television	101,988	114,851	108,629	113,671	119,898	131,221	136,422	146,386	152,693	163,888	
% Change	5.3	12.6	–5.4	4.6	5.5	9.4	4.0	7.3	4.3	7.3	6.5
Radio	25,627	28,522	26,771	27,768	28,848	30,352	31,821	33,720	35,327	37,284	
% Change	11.6	11.3	–6.1	3.7	3.9	5.2	4.8	6.0	4.8	5.5	5.3
Out-of-Home	14,057	15,394	15,384	15,548	16,229	17,067	17,967	18,950	19,913	20,886	
% Change	5.8	9.5	–0.1	1.1	4.4	5.2	5.3	5.5	5.1	4.9	5.2
Internet	5,461	10,319	9,360	8,469	10,410	12,223	13,983	15,719	17,337	18,908	
% Change	153.5	89.0	–9.3	–9.5	22.9	17.4	14.4	12.4	10.3	9.1	12.7
Magazines	44,722	48,747	44,433	42,228	42,908	44,309	46,022	48,286	50,644	52,883	
% Change	4.8	9.0	–8.8	–5.0	1.6	3.3	3.9	4.9	4.9	4.4	4.3
Newspapers	100,726	108,249	101,012	98,284	99,874	102,248	105,532	109,239	113,306	117,753	
% Change	4.7	7.5	–6.7	–2.7	1.6	2.4	3.2	3.5	3.7	3.9	3.3
Total	292,581	326,082	305,589	305,968	318,167	337,420	351,747	372,300	389,220	411,602	
% Change	6.7	11.5	–6.3	0.1	4.0	6.1	4.2	5.8	4.5	5.8	5.8

Note: p—projected.
Source: PricewaterhouseCoopers Global Entertainment and Media Outlook 2004–2008.

Figure A1.3: Global Consumer/End-User Spending (US$ Millions)

Segment	1999	2000	2001	2002	2003p	2004p	2005p	2006p	2007p	2008p	2004–08 CAGR
Filmed Entertainment	49,386	55,002	61,514	68,804	75,325	82,082	89,434	95,898	102,052	106,026	
% Change	3.9	11.4	11.8	11.9	9.5	9.0	9.0	7.2	6.4	5.9	7.5
TV Networks:											
Broadcast and Cable	30,740	32,240	35,015	37,598	39,933	41,943	44,181	46,084	47,873	49,419	
% Change	5.2	4.9	8.6	7.4	6.2	5.0	5.3	4.3	3.9	3.2	4.4
TV Distribution: Station, Cable, and Satellite	67,912	77,468	85,526	92,623	100,203	108,246	116,841	125,361	134,333	143,272	
% Change	11.9	14.1	10.4	8.3	8.2	8.0	7.9	7.3	7.2	6.7	7.4
Recorded Music	37,059	36,553	35,296	32,679	30,476	29,586	29,578	30,208	31,707	33,850	
% Change	1.6	−1.4	−3.4	−7.4	−6.7	−2.9	0.0	2.1	5.0	6.2	2.0
Radio	9,395	9,443	9,819	10,081	10,380	10,679	11,255	11,740	12,308	12,805	
% Change	1.6	0.5	4.0	2.7	3.0	2.9	5.4	4.3	4.8	4.0	4.3
Internet Access Spending	25,084	41,009	58,722	74,924	92,431	110,143	131,551	154,823	180,881	204,970	
% Change	62.6	63.5	43.2	27.6	23.4	19.2	19.4	17.7	16.6	13.3	17.3
Video Games	18,379	17,603	18,675	21,008	22,304	24,564	28,371	36,149	46,862	55,837	
% Change	14.6	−4.2	6.1	12.5	6.2	10.1	15.5	27.4	29.6	18.7	20.1
Business Information	63,943	68,655	68,405	67,592	67,864	70,115	73,333	77,346	81,527	85,301	
% Change	6.7	7.4	−0.4	−1.2	0.4	3.3	4.6	5.5	5.4	4.6	4.7

(Figure A1.3 continued)

(*Figure A1.3 continued*)

Segment	1999	2000	2001	2002	2003p	2004p	2005p	2006p	2007p	2008p	2004–08 CAGR
Magazines	35,973	37,477	37,338	37,665	37,766	38,060	38,479	39,030	39,766	40,504	1.4
% Change	3.1	4.2	−0.4	0.9	0.3	0.8	1.1	1.4	1.9	1.8	
Newspapers	52,178	53,187	53,803	54,291	55,018	55,504	56,158	56,920	57,776	58,751	1.3
% Change	0.9	1.9	1.2	0.9	1.3	0.9	1.2	1.4	1.5	1.7	
Consumer Books	54,167	53,597	53,098	53,628	55,147	55,191	56,622	58,210	59,850	61,492	2.2
% Change	1.7	−1.1	−0.9	1.0	2.8	0.1	2.6	2.8	2.8	2.7	
Educational and Professional Books and Training	211,145	220,940	228,420	231,500	229,376	233,796	241,671	253,371	265,620	278,311	3.9
% Change	4.8	4.6	3.4	1.3	−0.9	1.9	3.4	4.8	4.8	4.8	
Theme Parks and Amusement Parks	16,830	17,760	18,349	19,290	19,779	20,415	21,255	22,470	23,527	24,713	4.6
% Change	4.2	5.5	3.3	5.1	2.5	3.2	4.1	5.7	4.7	5.0	
Sports	55,575	61,672	65,246	71,560	74,611	80,493	85,118	94,764	95,930	102,466	6.6
% Change	9.3	11.0	5.8	9.7	4.3	7.9	5.7	11.3	1.2	6.8	
Total	**727,765**	**782,606**	**829,226**	**873,243**	**910,613**	**960,817**	**1,023,847**	**1,102,347**	**1,180,012**	**1,259,327**	**6.7**
% Change	**6.6**	**7.5**	**6.0**	**5.3**	**4.3**	**5.5**	**6.6**	**7.7**	**7.0**	**6.7**	

Note: p—projected.
Source: PricewaterhouseCoopers Global Entertainment and Media Outlook 2004–2008.

annexure 2
the media buying survey (January 24, 2005)

BUSINESSWORLD

STORY ONE

Pause, young dealer

Media buying has grown breathlessly. It is time to pause, for more growth

It is about 7:30 in the evening. Lakshmi Narasimhan, a big-bull trader, has been negotiating to buy advertising time on the Indo-Pak cricket series all day, and the deals are closing just as I walk in. There is a happy, satisfied air about Narasimhan as he switches off his cellphone and settles down for a long chat. 'I am a hardcore Tam Bram (Tamil Brahmin), but I feel like a trader. If I don't do 2–3 deals a day, I don't feel complete,' he smiles.

Narasimhan is the national director of the central trading group of WPP's Group M, (earlier Mindshare) India's largest media-buying agency. Every year, he buys over Rs 2,200 crore (Rs 22 billion) worth of TV seconds, column centimetres, and so on, or about 40 per cent of the organised media bought in India. There are eight traders like him who buy over Rs 5,500 crore (Rs 55 billion) worth of time and space to reach a billion Indians. (See 'The Big Bull Buyers'.) That is half of the total money spent on advertising in 2004. For over five years now, these eight people have been

The Big-bull Buyers

Holding group	Media agencies
WPP	Mindshare, Maxus, MEC, Fulcrum, Mediacom, TME*
INTERPUBLIC	Initiative Media, Universal McCann, Lodestar Media
MADISON	Madison
MUDRA	Optimum Media Solutions
PUBLICIS	Starcom, Zenith Optimedia
OMNICOM	TBWA Media, Media Direction
HAVAS	MPG
AEGIS	Carat

* TME and Mediacom are not yet part of WPP. There is no accurate source of what each of these media agencies bills, or of their market shares.

deal-making for HLL, Coca-Cola or Samsung among hundreds of advertisers. The deals they make decide where and how these advertisers spend their money.

Should they?

Ten years after media buying started moving out of ad agencies and five years after consolidated buying picked up speed, several people are asking that question: media owners, because thanks to people like Narasimhan, the real cost of media has actually fallen over the last few years, squeezing their margins; advertisers, because they still feel powerless about the way their media money is spent. Many now hire audit firms like Meenakshi Madhvani's Spatial Access Media Solutions to make sense of what their media agencies are doing. And lastly, the media agencies themselves are questioning consolidation. All those brands that shift their media business, the ones you read about everyday on exchange4media.com or agencyfaqs.com, do it because some agency offers them lower rates. So, all that the media agencies have done is build volumes at the cost of margins. For most media agencies, except a few large ones, margins are in abysmal single digit numbers. 'Even a cloth merchant who makes a deal over a phone call makes more than a media agency,' cribs Sam Balsara, chairman, Madison Communications, one of India's largest media buying agencies.

Sure, media agencies help push down costs through bulk buying. They also make sense of a complex and fragmented media world, deal with all the logistics that the buying of 100 channels, dozens of newspapers or radio stations across hundreds of cities and scores of brands, could involve. They bring what Balsara calls, 'a point of view'. Yet, at the end of all this shindig, every media agency head, advertiser and media owner agrees on one thing: deals and rates are all client-specific. There is a 'Lever rate' and a 'Pepsi rate' and a 'Coke rate'. Every major media owner deals directly with the advertiser and discounts are based on a range of factors from share of budget to time of the year. 'Client-specific deals work better and we would like to keep it that way. If an advertiser is spending Rs 20 (Rs 200 million) crore on Star Plus and another is spending Rs 1 crore (Rs 10 million), if the deals are different, they both get what they deserve according to their spend size,' thinks Punitha Arumugam, COO, Madison. 'Whether consolidation happens or not doesn't impact us because we don't do agency deals. I don't treat the advertiser differently because he comes through Mindshare (now Group M),' says Rohit Gupta, executive vice-president, SET India (Sony). 'Nobody buys to plan because rates change the plan; so what is the point of planning?' asks Raj Nayak, CEO, NDTV Media.

The Market Metrics

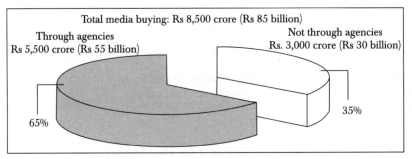

Total media buying: Rs 8,500 crore (Rs 85 billion)

Through agencies
Rs 5,500 crore (Rs 55 billion)

Not through agencies
Rs. 3,000 crore (Rs 30 billion)

65%

35%

Why Inflation Doesn't Matter

	Share of Ad-ex (%)		Inflation by media		Weighted Inflation	
	2003	2004	2003	2004	2003	2004
TV	45.2	44.8	11.8	12.0	5.2	5.4
PRINT	42.5	42.5	13.4	12.5	5.7	5.3
RADIO	2.2	3.0	3.0	11.0	0.1	0.1
CINEMA	0.1	0.2	0.0	5.0	0.0	0.0
OUTDOOR	9.3	8.9	10.0	8.0	0.9	0.7
INTERNET	0.6	0.7	5.0	5.0	0.0	0.0
TOTAL					11.96	11.87

Note: Figures 2003—Actual and 2004—Projected
Source: Group M estimates.

The fact is, a parallel market of advertisers and media sellers still thrives. So, while organised buyers have a chunk of the market, there is still about Rs 3,000 crore (Rs. 30 billion) or more worth of buying that does not come a media agency's way. Some very large advertisers—like Paras, Nirma or Cavin Care—do not use an agency. 'I am better off negotiating by myself as a large regional player. My 40-crore (Rs 400 million) spend may mean nothing in Mumbai, but since I buy out of Chennai and deal with the regional offices here, I am a large player in terms of the channel's regional targets, (and) I do get good discounts,' says Mahima Bhanukumar, vice-president (media), Cavin Care.

Then there are several 'new media' categories where growth rates are high like mobile telecom or dotcoms or local newspapers, which deal directly with advertisers. As a result, while the total media buying in India is closer to Rs 8,500 crore (Rs 85 billion), agencies get only 65 per cent of it. It is a large chunk, but constantly splintering and fast becoming unprofitable. Says Ashutosh Srivastava, Narasimhan's boss and CEO (South Asia) for Group M: 'Nobody has competition, it is a nascent market. The adex to GDP ratio is nothing, we are doing all this intellectualisation, but this is not a market-share game at all, currently.' That is because, at $2.2 billion or so, India is not a patch on the $337-billion-odd global ad market. Compared to China's $25 billion, the Indian market for advertising is a fly on the wall. Our ad to GDP ratio is one of the lowest in the world, and therefore, media spends, despite all the noise, remain tiny. And it looks like they will remain that way till double-digit GDP growth really pushes ad spends upwards. Till then, as Manish Porwal, general manager (investment and new initiatives), Starcom says: 'More and more growth (for media agencies) will come from shifting of accounts, not from consolidation.'

So, has consolidation failed?

No, it hasn't. It just hasn't worked quite the way it was supposed to. We will get into the reasons in the next story. The fact is that we have reached a low point in rates beyond which, considering the size of the market, it is going to be self-defeating for agencies, owners and advertisers to squeeze more on the rate front. More efficiencies are not going to come from there. If agencies insist on pushing rates down further (and we speak not as a media company, but as a dispassionate observer of the business), all they will do is breed corruption. It has already reared its ugly head in the form of over-invoicing or incentives to buyers, and so on. That means, eventually, advertisers

Lexicon

TRP	Television Rating Point: A time-weighted average of the time people spend watching a show
CPRP	Cost Per Rating Point: A measure of buying efficiency
GRP	Gross Rating Point: The total rating points that a network or channel offers—used to look at money spent versus what you get from it
Media buyers	The people who buy airtime and newspaper space
Media planners	They make the plan they may or may not have anything to do with the buying
Ad sales	The people who sell space in newspapers or time on TV
AOR	Agency of Record: Essentially an agency appointed to buy media for all the brands that a compnay has

end up paying the price—in bad media buying. 'At 2.5 per cent (commission), quality is going to be 100 per cent compromised,' thinks Nayak. 'Planning and buying is very driven by reach. But impact is also important. Is it better to reach a million people or impact 10,000?' asks Balsara. What he means is that it can't be all about numbers. As Jasmin Sohrabji, president, Mediacom India, puts it: 'So much of buying is gut.'

Precisely. Over the years, media buyers have somehow squeezed out all the joy of using a 30-second commercial or a newspaper ad. The buying game is as much about reaching out to people and giving them a compelling reason to remember or to buy a brand, as it is about the high of a great deal.

This is the fatal flaw that several agencies are now attempting to fix. For example, some of the more profitable Indian agencies, like Lodestar Media (a division of FCB-Ulka), insist on having a common balance sheet for media and creative, even though, operationally, they are different. The idea is to be able to invest in tools and research which help the consumer connect better, without the pressure of margins that being a separate profit centre involves. Combined balance sheets—which mean bringing media back into the creative fold—is an idea that is gaining ground in Europe and it keeps bottomlines healthy, reckons Shashi Sinha, president, Lodestar Media. Others like Madison and Group M find that diversifying into other media helps. Group M's Srivastava has built eight specialist divisions doing everything from consumer research to entertainment and sports advertising. When he speaks about growth, Srivastava refers to these divisions with more conviction and enthusiasm than of the mainline media division. Balsara's Madison has seven specialist divisions. In September 2004, it acquired an in-film advertising firm.

The déjà vu is evident. Most of these agencies are offshoots of advertising agencies and now they are going down the same path that ad firms went in the late 1990s in their quest for growth, when media unbundling happened. Yet, strangely enough, the debates on the good or bad that media specialists have done are being raised at roughly the same time in India, as they are in Europe and or the US. The reason they are cropping up so early on in India is because both media and media buying have grown without a pause for over 12 years now. Over this time, we have grown from two channels to two hundred, from a few newspapers to hundreds fighting for advertiser attention. In just under seven years, media has quickly shifted from about 50 agencies to the hands of just eight major holding companies. So India has raced through several decades of evolution at a breath-taking speed in 12 years. As the industry catches its breath, it is becoming evident that this growth ignored glaring deficiencies in the way the market is built. It is now time to pause and figure out just how and where growth will come from. As Sandeep Vij, president, Optimum Media Solutions, puts it: 'Maybe this is just the turmoil of transition.'

Maybe it is

STORY TWO

TAKE THE BLINKERS OFF

Rates have driven media buying for too long. Maybe it is time to look at ideas

There is some debate on the first company to unbundle media from creative. But most agree that it was led by MNCs like HLL and P&G (Procter & Gamble) in the mid-90s, two of the biggest advertisers in those days. The process was not called anything. HLL, for example, simply referred to Lintas as its 'Agency-of-Record' (AOR). Consolidation happened because several creative agencies typically handled different brands. So if HLL has 30 brands, it could have anything between 8–15 agencies, each doing the creative and media buying for the brands it handled. When there was one newspaper and one TV channel to buy, it did not matter. As the options increased, so did the complexities. Today, if you are HLL, you need to choose between 100 channels, several dozen newspapers, half-a-dozen radio stations, outdoor, cinema, multiplexes, mobile and other options for advertising. Clearly, buying separately for each brand brings no economies of scale. They come when you are a big bull buyer, like Lakshmi Narasimhan of Group M, who dangles all his 30 brands in front of the media owner. Also, remember that creative agencies made 15 per cent on the amount that HLL spent on media, which means the agencies had very little incentive to negotiate or cut costs.

So, in 1994 HLL started experimenting by having one agency, say Lintas or O&M, for six months each, to do all its buying. 'That straightaway made a difference. Otherwise, the Lifebuoy team would go and talk, and then the Lux team would go and talk, and then Liril, and so on (to the same media owner),' remembers B. Venkataramanan, group media manager, HLL. Then, in 1995 it invited all its three agencies for a pitch and HTA (now JWT) set up Fulcrum, which to-date manages all of HLL's media business. P&G, Coke and most other major multinational AORs happened around the same time. By 1997 Carat, the first independent media agency came in. All of them changed the texture, form and structure of media planning and buying in many ways.

Numbing numbers Till then, while numbers were very important, buying and selling was also about relationships, intuition, gut feel and all those soft words which media audit firms and management theorists sneer at. The planner at the creative agency used to bring an understanding of brands, markets and media to the table. 'He was like the Brahmin of advertising, a highly cerebrally endowed man whose biggest strength was his neutrality,' says Sandeep Vij of Optimum Media Solutions. Then came the media agency with its focus on efficiencies, rates and numbers. As media options were exploding all around them, this was what advertisers needed. Also, advertising is one of the largest items of costs on most company balance sheets and any attempt to push it down was encouraged.

So, over the last five years, media buying has become about rates, rates and rates alone. That was the best way for agencies to show that they are good; that they get better GRPs for the same money, or more efficiencies, the measures of which have been simple and suspect for long. There is a popular example floating around on how this rate obsession can go awry. A couple of years back, a large chunk of airtime bought on behalf of Tata Motors was in afternoon slots on television. It turned out that it was a bulk buy for Tata Tea and Tata Salt which was being used for Tata Motors, too. Bulk buying is the way agencies get lower rates and show greater efficiencies. But the buying totally ignored the fact that Tata Tea and Tata Salt talk to women who watch soaps in the afternoon while Tata Motors is a male product. That was when Tata Motors left its Agency-of-Record and went to FCB-Ulka's Lodestar Media.

So despite the obvious differences, technically there is no difference between the way media and *aloo-pyaaz* is being bought and sold. Every buying agency shared half a dozen tools and presentations with us, but the fact is that almost every one of them will take the first opportunity to steal an advertiser, using lower rates, if they can. Most agencies are not fighting on the fact that they offer a better, more impressive way of reaching the consumer, but on rates. It is routine for agencies to take lower rates from media and use it either to pitch for a business or to earn brownie points with advertisers. They take great pride in knowing the rates competitors offered, and then scuppering that deal. One buyer showed us the rates of all his competitors. He had managed to source these for a recent pitch. 'The turnover of media planners is so high, they are always moving from one agency to another, and agencies hire them because they bring information,' says Raj Nayak of NDTV Media.

And if it is not about rates, it is about numbers—in all their hair-splitting glory. Numbers that justify rates and buys and plans and, generally, confuse advertisers into approving plans. Each agency has hundreds of overworked and underpaid planners who crunch thousands and thousands of numbers from ABC, NRS, IRS, TAM, among about a dozen other sources, on endless Excel sheets, to arrive at the optimum media plan. Most of these planners do not read the magazine they buy or see the shows they junk. They simply do not have the time, points out Nayak. 'These days everything goes *chane ke bhav mein*; a spot is a spot is a spot. So 'when I enter my optimiser, I hope that it will gurgle out the numbers of GRPs needed to make my brand a success', it is death by numbers,' says a sarcastic Sameer Nair, COO, SGI. Any planner can show that, say, Zee TV is the leading channel in the Hindi category—in the 8 a.m.–8:30 a.m. band on Thursday morning, if you check the fine print. Almost every news channel claims to be number one; only Aaj Tak is. Recently, a website carried the news that Sony's Indian Idol had beaten *Kyunkii...* a show on Star Plus.

But the fact is Indian Idol did it on one day in one week. *Kyunkii...* has been averaging ratings between 13–17 for four years now.

The game of nitpicking, cherry-picking and bamboozling with numbers is now so strong in buying that sellers are getting into the act to combat it. Most media owners—Star, Sony, and even language newspapers—have at least a planner or two on their ad sales team. 'Now we have a sense that if you have an optimiser, so do we; if you can do analysis, so can we. It is not so complicated; ultimately everyone is using the same TAM numbers,' says Nair. So if a planner knocks, say, Star Movies in favour of HBO from a plan, Star Movies can arrive at the perfect reason why it is irreplaceable based on the same data that the buyer has. Then, if the advertiser thinks that Star Movies has a case, it is on the plan. 'In many of these things, it is a matter of who blinks first,' thinks Nair.

Those little pieces Doesn't all this happen when buyers become bigger buyers, and aren't negotiations supposed to be about who can squeeze whom? Sure they are. But there are some differences in the way consolidation of buying happened in India versus mature markets like the US and UK. It also explains why it is not working quite the same way here. The biggest one is how fragmented both the Indian consumer and media markets are. Remember that consolidation happened in the US or UK because media companies were becoming bigger and bigger with acquisitions while advertisers remained single. Viacom, Walt Disney, Newscorp, all command respect and rates by sheer size. When they negotiate, it is the buyer who blinks first, usually. In India, there are no large conglomerates that sell dozens of dominant brands of newspapers, TV stations, films, radio, and so on. There are very few media owners with some negotiating power; the rest are all small players. Even the big ones are largely one-brand wonders. A Star India still relies on Star Plus and a Bennett, Coleman & Co. still flogs The Times of India, Mumbai. So in India, even while buying has consolidated, media remains fragmented, making it a 'beautiful buyer's market', as Ashutosh Srivastava of Group M puts it.

Now add a fragmented consumer market to it. 'Media buying is complex because of too many languages and diversity,' says Vivek Prakash, vice-president, Samsung India. The estimated Rs 3,800-crore (Rs 38 billion) Samsung is one of the largest ad spenders in India. It has 800 products which include mobiles, TVs, scanners, IT equipment, and others. Every year it launches about 150 models in IT, 20 in phones, 50 in audio and video, and about 30 in household appliances. The scale of its business, and of India, means that Samsung spends three times the money it did three years back to reach the same audience. So while he has more options to reach different audiences, 'more fragmentation has increased the cost of reaching my target audience,' says Prakash. So earlier if, say, 1,000 GRPs gave you 80 per cent reach, it now takes 1,200. Now it is not just about one or two channels. It is about a few national channels, news, regional, music, business, and any other genre that reaches out to your target audience.

This fragmentation, at both the market and the media end, also changes the texture of the market in two crucial ways.

One, it makes it much more volatile. To understand why, take a look at Europe or the US, where about 50–60 per cent of airtime is sold in bulk deals at the beginning of the year—called 'upfront' buying. But the rates, the discounts, the slabs within which they fall are all very clear. What upfront deals do is take the revenue pressure off media owners and agencies, a bit. They can then price the remaining inventory according to demand. So if there is a hot event on Fox or ABC, it can actually price it higher than the upfront rates. This 'variable pricing' makes the market for media inventory far less volatile and more profitable than it is in India. It is also a good way to make the bulk game work.

Two, fragmentation kills margins, for everybody, because the costs of doing business go up. 'Our (Indian media buying) productivity is very poor because the number of transactions is massive and the unit size is small,' says Srivastava. He is right. India is a very small ad market, just about $2.2 billion against $25 billion for China or the $102-odd billion for the US. Then there is the complexity. In India, HLL, for example, will buy spots on every TV channel, in every language, for all its 30-45 brands, and we are still talking only TV. The amount of effort, time and money taken to buy the same amount of advertising in India versus, say, the US is simply far more. According to Group M calculations, on a $10-million spend, a 3 per cent commission yields $125 in India versus $3,000 in the US. Now factor in the mad discounting that happens on commission. That means, unless you build scale, a la Group M, life isn't worth living as a media buyer, even in what is a buyer's market.

It is in this fragmented mess that agencies brought order, and advertisers acknowledge that. 'When I launch a handphone, I may need a 12-city footprint if it is a promotion, I need 60 vernacular publications. That number (of 60) is what the buying agency brings,' says Prakash. But it has also created an atmosphere of mistrust taking away something intangible in the way media was bought and sold. Tariq Ansari, managing director, Mid-Day Multimedia, reckons that the entry of big buyers has actually harmed advertisers in one crucial way. 'The whole thing of a relationship, fuzzy as it sounds, worked well for both us and the advertiser,' says Ansari. For example, Sheetal, a store in Mumbai, wanted to tap into the rich Muslim women in the area it was located in. While talking to Dhiren Shah, the owner of Sheetal, a Mid-Day ad sales representative came up with the idea of doing a *Mehndi* contest in *Inquilaab*, a group paper. It worked and walk-ins into Sheetal jumped.

That kind of thinking on each advertiser is now impossible, says Ansari. 'Now creative is taking a call on creative, media buyer is talking rates, and PR is pushing us to do articles. What was earlier a warm, fuzzy relationship is (now) over, leaving media owners like me feeling cheated,' he says. What he means is that as the relationship changed from a one-point thing (between, say, Mid-Day and Samsung) to a three-point one (between Mid-Day, Samsung, Cheil, Mudra and Triton). 'We are coming to the conclusion that we need to deal with the advertiser directly. If you have an innovation or a co-branding idea, where do you go? The media buyer is not interested because he says it is too much work and the creative agency sticks to its brief, so a lot of good ideas just fall through the crack,' says Ansari. Balsara agrees: 'Younger people treat the numbers and the technique as an end to itself. They cannot do without numbers. They get so consumed by the process that they forget to look at the big picture. You need to balance ideas with the numbers.'

Rates and more That the game has to move beyond rates is now clear. 'As a media owner, I would be mad if I offered a lower rate to an advertiser every time he shifted agencies. If an account moves three times, I would go bankrupt if I reduced rates every time,' points out Nayak. To combat the numbers game, media owners are striking back in several ways. One, by hiring the number crunchers.

Second, by getting hold of the numbers. So *Jagran*, a newspaper company, tracks all the TV channels that get local ad spends from the markets it operates in. TAM, for example, gets requests even from language newspapers which want to buy reports on how regional channels are eating into their share. 'Lot of people are trying to look at perception versus science, data pushes the science to create a difference,' thinks L.V. Krishnan, CEO, TAM Media Research.

There are other ways too. For example, Cartoon Network operates in the Rs 200-crore (Rs 2 billion) children's category. Three years ago, it decided it had to fight the Stars and Sonys for a share of the Rs 3,000-odd-crore (Rs 30 billion) general entertainment ad pie. This means comparing the ratings that Cartoon Network's primarily child audience gets versus Jassi or anything else, and also proving that moms form a big slice of the audience. Every niche genre, from news to music, has done the same thing.

'It makes the game bigger,' says Monica Tata, vice-president (advertising sales), Turner International, which owns and runs Cartoon Network. From October 2004, Cartoon Network started bundling shows like Star Plus does. Its top-rated shows like Pokemon are part of Blockbuster Toons, with the highest ad rates. Then come Super Toons, Prime Toons, and Wonder Toons. Average rates have now gone up by about 100–120 per cent or so, unheard of in TV, definitely unheard of by smaller channels. As the three players try different tricks to deal with lower rates, the shape and texture of media buying is changing.

Dangerous liaisons

The anecdote goes that in its financial year ending July 2003, Star started its annual, what one insider calls, 'orgasmic negotiations' with HLL. Three months and about 16 meetings later, they were still stuck. Typically, HLL was trying to use the weight of its higher volumes to push down rates, and Star being Star refused to budge beyond a certain point on what everybody calls its 'high rates'. A 10-second spot on Star Plus costs a whopping Rs 680,000 in prime time. Its status as India's numero uno broadcast network just makes its negotiating power stronger and the famous 'Lever rate' was not happening. During this period, the brand managers at HLL were breathing down the media buyer's back (egged on by Star Plus' ad sales guys) and asking for TV time for their products. For almost three months, there were no HLL ads on Star Plus. Finally, when the launch of a Brooke Bond product hung in balance, the deal happened. Brooke Bond is a classic female product. It simply couldn't launch without Star Plus.
Welcome to the inside world of media buying.

(*Box continued*)

(Box continued)

Forget the science. The politics of it reads straight out of a spy thriller. So, for example, the industry buzz goes that Group M makes it a point of not supporting the leading brand in any category or market. Star and Group M keep each other at arm's length and, given the smallest opportunity, hit at each other. The rivalry has its uses. 'The Indian market would have completely crashed if *KBC* had not happened. The only reason the market hasn't gone the Group M way is because Star Plus has held on and not given agency rates,' says Sandeep Vij, president, Optimum Media Solutions. That, in turn, has meant that both Sony and Zee too have had the flexibility to hold on. So buyers cannot easily play one against the other. That is unlike the fun they have with *TOI* and *HT* in Delhi. If an agency wants a good deal from *TOI*, Mumbai (usually very difficult), it goes and offers more than half of an advertiser's money to *HT* Delhi. That prompts Times to bend on Mumbai in order to get the Delhi budget.

Spend a few weeks meeting buyers, sellers, agencies and auditors and you will come out with a basketful of such stories. You will also realise that the distrust in this industry runs deep. That is natural. Airtime and newspaper space are perishable things, just like airline seats. They have to be used fast, otherwise they are gone. So desperation is expected. Now add the languages, the spread, the brands and the conflicting interests of the three main parties. It is a recipe that makes for an excessively complicated, opaque and intrigue-ridden market with planners being hired and re-hired only for the information they bring.

What works in this Machiavellian market? Trust. Ironically, after all the number-crunching and reams of data, what people look for is reassurance and trust in their buys. 'People who do the best buys are owner-driven companies, Paras, Liberty Shoes... and I am not afraid to reduce my rates with these guys because I won't lose the business and I can build a relationship with them,' says Raj Nayak, CEO, NDTV Media. What was that about life coming full-circle?

240

STORY THREE

Let the Fun Begin

It's easy to connect to people if you simply look past those Excel sheets

Sometime in 2002, P&G launched Hugo Boss fragrances for women in India. Since it is a premium brand, the thinking was that it should be advertised to a premium audience. This is usually defined as English-speaking types in the age group of 15–30 years who are best reached through English magazines like *Verve* and *Elle*. Most high-end watch and perfume brands like Omega or Christian Dior are advertised in such magazines.

Starcom, Leo Burnett's media agency, however, decided to first use research to figure out if the target audience they were intuitively looking at was right. It wasn't. The relationship between the ability to read English and spend on premium products was not strong. These consumers believed that good fragrances hit overseas markets first, and usually asked friends to get them. What's more, they used the fragrances only on special occasions, so their consumption was less.

The real consumers, the people who would spend freely on the stuff and use it liberally too, were (surprise) the wives of rich traders and brokers from a 'certain ethnic community', as Manish Porwal of Starcom puts it. (Read wives of Gujarati and Marwari businessmen.) Starcom then used a proprietary tool called Passionfinder to figure out their key pastimes and passions. Their main passion was soaps and films. More than half these women watched a *Kyunkii...* or *Kahaani...* at night, as well as its repeat telecast the next afternoon. They met in groups to discuss these soaps and films. Many claimed to have written to Balaji Telefilms, the producer of these soaps, at least once. That is when the media plan did a U-turn from what Starcom would have done based on the traditional definition of consumers. A bulk of Hugo Boss' money was spent on mainline Hindi general entertainment channels.

The result: within three months of Hugo Boss' launch, it became the largest-selling foreign premium fragrance brand, making India P&G's third-largest market for the brand outside of Europe, and a case study in the P&G network.

It seems a simple enough thing to do. Yet, this connection with consumers rarely happens in media planning and buying. As the rate madness settles a bit, as media owners react cleverly, and as agencies themselves start believing in the words 'value add', the connection with consumers is beginning to happen. The three players are now making their own little attempts to connect. The result: a sharpness and precision in consumer targeting that is scary at best and impressive otherwise. But these are sparks that fly on and off. The transition from a numbers- and rate-oriented media market to a consumer-focused one is happening. Not by design, not very fast, but it is happening. There are three steps that agencies, owners and advertisers are taking that are driving the impact bus forward.

Getting into the show One of the best ways for advertisers to get impact is to inject the brand within the editorial pages of newspapers and magazines or within TV shows or a film or a radio programme. Globally, in-programme advertising or 'soft' advertising is emerging as a way to beat personal video recorders (PVRS) that allow viewers to avoid ads. In India, though the market structure is not the same as that of the US, clutter is making in-content advertising an imperative. The question is how to do it subtly. 'We are not keen to do product placements because unless we can do it in style, it is like prostituting the channel,' thinks Sameer Nair of SGI. So Star has done the odd one like WHO's Oral Rehydration Solution on *Kyunkii....* But rival Sony Entertainment Television (SET) has managed to crack in-content better. It does special deals with companies like LG, Hutch and P&G which commit over 50 per cent of their money to Sony. For example, 90 per cent of P&G's spends on general entertainment are with Sony. For advertisers like these, 'we go beyond mere airtime,' says Rohit Gupta, executive vice-president, SET.

Last year, for instance, Sony ran the Shiksha campaign along with P&G and used its hit show *Kkusum* to promote it. During the promotion period, all P&G products like Tide, Ariel, Whisper, and so on carried scratch cards. The winners of these, who could get anywhere between Rs 5,000–200,000 as scholarships for education, were announced on *Kkusum*. It increased the ratings for the serial by 15 per cent and also gave P&G mileage. When Maruti started increasing its spends on Sony, the relaunch of Zen was integrated into its hit show *Jassi*... Newspapers too have started doing the same thing, albeit in a slightly secretive fashion. Medianet, a division of The Times of India Group, offers to do paid-for articles for lifestyle products. Magazines do it through advertorials. At roughly Rs 200 crore (Rs 2 billion), in-film advertising is the hottest-growing segment of the entertainment business. Then there is SMS marketing, and so on and so forth. The idea is to either intrude the entertainment or become part of it; ads intrude, in-content works by becoming part of it. Earlier this year, TAM even won a European research award for figuring out how to measure in-content or soft advertising in TRP and rate terms.

Walking all around The best way for media agencies and owners to deliver impact is by offering the very things advertisers are looking for—whether it is inside a programme or outside. These could be in-content services (films, sports, print), outdoor, events, direct connect or anything else. Take HLL. Its focus is now on reaching consumers wherever they are. Venkataramanan of HLL points out that 50 per cent of the rural audience cannot be reached by any media and only 40 per cent of it is touched by TV. 'National media is like a sledgehammer. There is huge wastage. I need to reach the consumer in Dharwar. So we have to use local media and entertainment, temple activation, beach, restaurant, trade, in-film,' Venkataramanan says.

The media he mentions are the areas that media agencies are getting into, one by one. Last year, non-traditional businesses grew at 100 per cent at Group M, against the 5–6 per cent growth in its regular media buying and planning business. Madison now gets half its revenues from its non-media units. These include creative, Anugraha (for rural marketing), MRP (for retail) and PR. While most of these decisions are driven more by the need to retain advertiser spends or get a larger share of them, it eventually means better consumer connect if the agency does a really good job of it. Even media owners now try to offer 360-degree services. Jagran Solutions offers outdoor and event support to clients. The idea, says its CEO Sanjay Gupta, is less about revenues and more about being able to keep the advertiser interested in *Dainik Jagran* and prove its capabilities in the Hindi belt that the newspaper dominates. CNBC, MTV, Nick Jr, and even Cartoon Network do events, shows, promotions, school contact programmes, merchandising and what not, to offer 'value adds' to advertisers. These also help in maintaining rates or even pushing them up at times. Samsung, for example, is targeting SMEs through CNBC's events. The bottomline, 'let us get more well-rounded in what we offer,' is great. It makes media buying less obsessed with rates and more interested in getting the point across to the right people.

Try a combo A third more obvious and long-term solution is to make media buying an investment centre, not a profit centre. That means combining creative with media buying. Part of the problem is that most media agencies are now separate profit centres with their own profit and loss (P&L). So, the pressure on margins takes away any incentive to build the research tools and skills, which could in turn bring in higher commissions. With a common P&L , the media agency's ability to negotiate better fees and invest in knowledge improves. So the benefits that flow from one to the other go far beyond financial flexibility. It gives the agency a better topline overall. A look at Lodestar's evolution makes the point clearer.

'We are in the business of providing business solutions. If that is so, then everything in the intellectual space should be under one roof. Whether you address creative or media, the consumer is still the same,' thinks Shashi Sinha of Lodestar. So somewhere in 1992, Lodestar came up with the idea of an 'integrated planner', someone who would examine the consumer from a creative, account planning and media angle, and plan media strategy. 'Unfortunately, this was the era of consolidation and therefore, rates became more important. So the idea did not work,' he recalls. Now, Sinha says its time has come. 'Today, advertisers realise that rates have become hygiene. There are no incremental gains left to be made,' he says. When he heard the global murmurs for combining media and creative, Sinha decided that it made sense to invest in media research irrespective of whether clients pay for it or not. As a result, Lodestar Lab Centre was set up in 2000. The whole idea is to just look at consumer and media research using commissioned studies like NRS or TAM data to understand trends, find insights, and to develop media planning and buying tools. Now, Lodestar tools like Media Graphics are exported to parent FCB's other agencies in the Asia-Pacific region. Lodestar has also won the 'Agency of the Year' award at the Ad Club, Emvies (for media efficiency) in 2002 and 2004.

The investment pays off in several other ways. One, a media agency can be the way for a group to get the creative business. For example, 'We got into Castrol eight years back through media. A year later, we were doing everything,' says Sinha.

Two, it makes for a stable relationship. The lack of one is a big cause for the root-lessness of media buying decisions, their total disconnect from what the brand needs. It also eliminates the turf wars that usually erupt between media and creative. Lodestar has one of the lowest client turnover ratios in the business. 'You must understand that the cost of acquiring a business is very high. So we hang on to the business we get. You can't do that because you are friendly but because you deliver something,' says Sinha. Lodestar has had the Amul account for 17 years, Tata Motors for six, and Whirlpool for eight, among others. So if creative screws up, media makes up and vice versa. But the point is that all the buys on, say, Amul go with the collective knowledge of what the brand has been through and needs.

Three, it delivers better consumer connect and saves money. When Zodiac launched Zod, a line of clubwear for men in 2002, the brand needed to delink Zodiac from its more sedate grown-up image to a younger, hip and happening one. But its budget was a fraction of that of competitors like Allen Solly, Provogue or Colour Plus. The pressure on the media planners at Lodestar was to pinpoint accurately who the target was and hit, without any misses. Roughly, the agency knew that the Zod man would be a *Dil Chahta Hai*-type trendy man, SEC A, 25–34 years. It also knew that using traditional media research would not pin him down. It used a proprietary FCB tool, Mind and Mood. This uses focus groups (much like Starcom's Passionfinder) to draw insights into the minds and moods of similar consumers. These are then clustered, irrespective of what media they buy and target. A 'Youth Leisure Mind and Mood' threw up achievers, strivers and so on, which were split further into other groups. Out of these sub-groups, the 'Party Animals' emerged as Zod's target group. They could not be reached at home simply because they were party animals. They had to be reached in discos, pubs, through music or celeb-shows, through Page 3, the Internet and films. That is where Zod went. The result: the brand did 30 per cent over its targeted sales.

You could argue that most of what these tools for consumer-connect throw up seem fairly obvious. Weren't agencies doing it? Yes, but not seriously, not with their heart and soul in it, not as if their life (and business) depended on it. 'We are not an investment-driven business. We are good at thinking but bad at taking risks. We are only willing to take risks with clients' money,' thinks Sinha. A combined balance sheet takes away some of the risks attached to having margin-pressured media agencies making bad decisions. It is a point that other agencies, advertisers (sometimes) and even media owners subscribe to. 'If you did a survey of media buyers and planners today, most would tell you that they wish they could go back to a full-service agency,' says Raj Nayak of NDTV Media.

The ugly truth Maybe their holding companies will consider re-bundling creative and media buying, eventually. Keeping media agencies as profit centres and the margin pressure it creates is particularly dangerous in one way. If agencies work for a pittance, they will try to make their money elsewhere. The commission and amounts of money involved mean that corruption is a real problem. The ways in which buyers can be tempted or buying agencies can be remunerated for recommending a channel or newspaper are discussed openly. Media agencies can commit fraud in a million ways because the process is so complicated. How would an advertiser know which hoarding appeared where in which city, whether or not it carried an ad for the entire period, whether it carried the right brand and so on. There is a famous example in Mumbai these days of an outdoor agency which had committed its hoarding to a car major. However, while pitching to a new client, it happily removed the car ads and put in those of the new client. Since the car company is based in Delhi, it was unaware of the episode. In fact, agencies usually get great rates using their bulk, but they may or may not pass on the lower rates to advertisers. Then there are payments, either in the form of incentives or discounts, or half a dozen other ways that can easily be slipped in. 'There is growing concern that media owners could be tempting agencies with discounts and credit notes,' says Balsara.

Of course, there are two caveats to this. One, corruption will happen only when the media owner has no strength or confidence in his numbers and reach. Two, eventually if the media doesn't deliver what the advertiser needs, he will notice it. Precisely because there is too much money at stake.

That is what is beginning to happen. Not necessarily because they do not trust their agency but because they feel a total sense of alienation from this business of trading in seconds and column centimetres that advertisers are beginning to hire media auditors.

STORY FOUR

ENTER THE AUDITOR

It's been an eventful first year for media auditing

Nobody likes Meenakshi Madhvani. Mention her name or the words 'media auditing', and almost everyone has a snide remark to make. Last year, Madhvani set up Spatial Access Media Solutions, India's first media auditing firm. Within 11 months, she had signed on 38 clients ranging from Hutch in Mumbai to Cavin Care in Chennai. She questions and evaluates media planning, buying, implementation and processes, besides offering consulting services in these areas. She is disliked because what she does evokes fear.

Run through one audit by Spatial, and you will know why. Its team takes weeks to arrive at benchmarks for everything—from the price of a spot to plans and the processes of buying. For example, if Spatial does audits for Millennium Alcobev (MABL), a spirits company, it first casts an eye at processes for buying, scheduling, planning, rates and everything else for alcoholic beverages across media to arrive at benchmarks. If MABL launches Zingaro beer in the South, it checks on what it spent, how and what it got for the money. So if Zingaro got the targeted say 600 GRPs on TV, did it get 400 in one week and 200 in others, by actually reducing the frequency? Did that spread of GRPs meet the objective? How much money was lost to noise made by say, Kingfisher or Haywards, around the same time? If Zingaro and Haywards both advertise on BBC's Wheels one after the other, it creates dissonance. So, how much of Zingaro's reach was duplicated? Did it advertise on the same type of newspapers and TV channels, losing money by reaching out to the same set of people more than once?

Then, the extra, wasted, null GRPs—the ones where people forgot the ads or which were not visible at the right time or place—are eliminated, and Spatial arrives at the new GRPs or new audiences reached by the brand. It then looks beyond reach into awareness, momentum and other impact parameters. Mind you, this is just one brand and one media. Imagine the complexity of an audit across all of MABL's brands. The point, Madhvani reckons, is that many times the solution to a marketer's problem may be in bad media planning and buying; not in bad distribution or pricing or any other variable. The audit helped MABL shave off between 20–25 per cent on media costs. The company now uses that money on events and promotions. Hear Girish Shah, general manager (marketing), MABL, on why he hired an auditor: 'As a medium-sized advertiser (Rs 10 crore–12 crore [Rs 100–120 million]), our exposure is only through the buying agency. So it is a question of who will guard the guard.' He is bang on.

As things stand, marketers need auditors like they need a crutch. To make sense of the bewildering maze of options, where someone they just hired is deciding how they will spend their money. Some form of corruption, therefore, either in the quality of buys or in the actual money spent, is inevitable like we mentioned in the previous story. So enter the auditor.

But to 'guard the guard' or figure out whether media is the problem, Spatial needs to know the plans, rates and almost every detail of every deal that MABL's buying agency signs with every media-owner. It needs to get into the innards of actual buying. And this is what bothers buyers. 'The most confidential thing is our rates and our tools. The moment we have to share it, we get worried. Auditors collect a lot of information from us to create a benchmark,' says Punitha Arumugam of Madison Communications. Adds Lakshmi Narasimhan of Group M: 'As a process, we welcome audits and as a buyer they need to know what I am doing in a positive and productive way. But the pooled benchmark, on which the audit is based, is hearsay. It has to be constant and positive.' His CEO, Ashutosh Srivastava, agrees: 'In any audit system, there have to be some basic guidelines and benchmarks which have to be arrived at between the client and the agency. In the absence of that, all decisions on what is or is not efficiency become rather subjective.'

Ad time can be bought when spots are being sold cheap by TV channels in distress, or because advertisers want to push up depressed sales with a cheap, quick-fix high frequency campaign, or for scores of other reasons. In the absence of this knowledge, all an auditor can do is raise a lot of heat and dust, says Srivastava. 'Nobody likes auditors because essentially the relationship is between the agency and the client,' he says. As one major buyer puts it: 'Auditors look good only if we look bad.'

Madhvani is sanguine. 'In all markets, media auditors have faced initial resistance from media agencies. Over time, this changes and becomes acceptance,' she says. She is right. Even now, more than a decade after media audit took off in Europe, there is intense bitterness about auditors' questioning. In the US, where auditing is more recent (just five per cent of radio and TV spends there are audited), specialist magazines and websites are full of articles questioning auditors or justifying media audits. In mature markets, media audit was born from finance heads worrying about all those costs on the balance sheet and questioning them.

That is true for India as well. The opacity of the process and money involved, roughly 5–15 per cent of revenues, means finance heads are now increasingly involved in the media audit game. 'The thought is whether they can squeeze 5–7 per cent savings out of it,' says Srivastava. 'We find MDs and CFOs very open to the concept,' says Madhvani. The reason is also, partly, distrust, thinks Sandeep Vij of Optimum Media Solutions. 'In a close, non-transparent market, what the agency brings is neutrality and that is also being questioned. Madhvani's business will run because there is distrust,' he says.

Already, the growth of audit services is aided by what Madhvani calls 'environmental issues'. 'This market (media auditing in India) can absorb three firms at least,' she says. Of these, two already exist. Earlier, it was the plain paperwork of media that was audited by firms like Ernst & Young; now Spatial audits the strategy, the plan and the actual buy. 'If Ernst & Young does full-fledged auditing, it will be good because there is no individual-driven agenda,' says Srivastava, tongue firmly in cheek.

He has touched upon the first of two reasons for the collective dislike for audit services—the fact that Madhvani herself was a buyer earlier. She set up Carat, India's first independent media buying agency. 'MM has herself done all these things, so who's talking what,' asks one big buyer. Another worries that she will get everyone's rates and deals, then return to buying and outwit everyone with the inside information she has. Madhvani refutes this: 'We would never have made the kind of investments we have made in the business if it wasn't for the long haul! My media buying days are dead. My media auditing days are alive. Why should I go back in time?' Besides, she adds: 'Rates is one part of what we do. We advise clients not to focus on rates because it is distorting media solutions. We would rather focus on 'value', what is the value you get for the rate you pay.' But since 'value' is difficult to establish, the ruckus is natural. Still, there are buyers who claim that auditing doesn't bother them. 'We have been through planning and process audits, and the experience has been good because it happened with mature clients who know how to use audits,' says Srivastava.

You could put down most of the nastiness to a clash of personalities which is getting magnified because the industry is so small. But the other thing that bugs buyers is more objective and real. 'International experience tells me that there is no resolution between auditing and planning and buying. The way auditing is done here, the auditor is not aware of the 25,000 emails and phone calls between plan and buys. That in-between thing is what you are audited for. The client might say stop the spot, and put this on cricket,' says Jasmin Sohrabji of Mediacom. For example, a buyer may decide to bet on a new show not because he thinks it will give him more ratings but because when a channel promotes a new show, the advertiser gets huge mileage from the promos. 'These things happen all the time. I am there and the auditor is not. So, much of everybody trying to rationalise a decision impacts the gut and fun of planning,' says Sohrabji. 'Post buy, it is easy to pick holes. You have to start from day one,' agrees Rohit Gupta of SET India. There is a valid point there.

Madhvani reckons a few audits that set planning and buying processes in order will fix most of these things. It's early days still. Once the processes are in order, Spatial may not need to be as involved as it is now. For her, the ruckus is clearly part of the evolution. When specialised media agencies happened in India, almost every agency chief questioned the idea. Her contention is when media buying agencies stop treating auditors as adversaries, they themselves will reap its benefits. Her job is to audit and then streamline processes. In the process, if she thinks that poor commissions to an agency is making for bad buys, she will say so. 'In one case, we told the client that they should be paying the agency one per cent more in commission, so they took it up to 3.5 per cent,' she says. Sometimes it could validate that the advertiser is actually buying right. 'We have had a one-time audit done so far. The findings revealed that the in-house agency is doing a good job,' says K.S. Ramesh, CEO, Cavin Care.

Such good news is going to be rare in the first few months of media auditing. The big bulls have had a happy run for over five years. As the questioning starts, expect a lot more kicking and screaming.

247

bibliography

A Correspondent (1991). 'Looming Shortage', *Businessworld*, 27 February, p. 52, Vol. 10, No. 22.

A&M magazine, archives (1993–97).

Acharya, Rabi Narayan (1987). *Television in India, a Sociological Study of Policies and Perspectives*, Manas Publications, Delhi.

Ahluwalia, Bharat (1998). 'Too much static on the mobile line', *Businessworld*, 22 May, p. 50, Vol. 18, issue 4.

All India Radio. From the website, *allindiaradio.org*

Anand M. and Kohli, Vanita (2000). 'Cable Wars', *Businessworld*, 13 November, pp. 24–30, Vol. 20, No. 27.

Audit Bureau of Circulations (ABC). From the website, *www.auditbureau.org*

Audit Bureau of Circulations (1998). Code for publicity by publisher members, notification 658, 6 October.

Audit Bureau of Circulations data (2001). July–December.

Bansal, Shuchi (1993). 'A new note', *Businessworld*, 20 October–2 November 1993, pp. 58–59, Vol. 13, No. 15.

Bansal, Shuchi (1999). 'Oh, to be a Hawker', *Businessworld*, 7–21 April, Vol. 19, No. 1.

Bhandari, Bhupesh (1994). 'A paperless chase', *Businessworld*, 30 November–13 December, Vol. 14, No. 18.

Bhandari, M.G. (2001). 'Taxation of TV Channels', in *Entertainment Industry*, by K. Shivaram for The Chamber of Income Tax Consultants, January 1st edition.

Businessworld archives.

Businessworld magazine, archives (1981–2002).

Cable Television Networks (Regulation) Act, 1995.

Chatterji, P.C. (1987). *Broadcasting in India*, Sage Publications in association with The International Institute of Communications.

Confederation of Indian Industry. 'India broadband economy—Vision 2010', A Discussion Paper, supported by the Department of Information Technology and Department of Telecommunications, *Based on Interim Report submitted by IBM Business Consulting Services, India.*

Das, Samar, with Kakkar, Pradeep Dr and Gupta K., Nirmal Dr under the guidance of Athreya M.B. Dr (1993). 'Gramophone Company of India Limited,' Case study by the Management Development Institute, Gurgaon.

Das Gupta, Surajeet (2005). 'Why Indian music's rocking India's mobile business?' *Business Standard*, 22 September. From the website, *www.rediff.com*

Desai, Ashok, V. Ramneet Goswami and Archana Jaba (2004). 'Telecommunications in India, History, analysis and diagnosis'. The study was prepared for the National Council for Applied Economic Research (NCAER).

Desai, M.V. and Ninan, Sevanti (1996). *Beyond those Headlines: Insiders on the Indian Press*. The Media Foundation, New Delhi (Allied Publishers).

Dhawan, Radhika (2003). 'A fine balance', *Businessworld*, 26 May, pp. 54–56, Vol. 22, issue 52.

Doordarshan's Annual Report (2000 and 2001).

Dubey, Rajeev (2000). 'Changing Times', *Businessworld*, 15 May, Vol. 20, No. 1.

Durga Das Basu, Acharya Dr (1996). *Law of the Press*, Prentice-Hall of India Private Limited, 3rd edition.

EnterMedia (2001). A CII-Ernst & Young Report on the seminar on 'The Business of Entertainment'.

Felix Albuquerque (1988). Notes on commercial broadcasting over All India Radio (AIR), Mumbai.

Film Federation of India (2001). Pre-budget memorandum to the Finance Minister.

Film Federation of India, archives.

Ghosh Roy, Mahashweta (1995). 'Man of the Times', *Businessworld*, 22 February– 7 March, Vol.14, No. 24.

Gomes, Janina (2003). *Internationalisation of the Indian film industry*, Indo-Italian Chamber of Commerce and Industry.

Gupta, Sujoy (1986). 'The Paper Industry's Hour of Despair', *Businessworld*, 3–16 February, pp. 62–70, Vol. 5, No. 23.

Hasan Manto, Saadat (1998). *Stars From Another Sky: The Bombay Film World of the 1940's*, Penguin Books, India.

INS (2000–01). Annual Report and website.

International Federation of Phonographic Industries. From the website, *www.ifpi.org*

Internet Advertising Bureau. From the website with a very comprehensive glossary for Internet terms, *www.IAB.net*

Jagannathan, N.S. (1999). *Independence and the Indian Press, Heirs to a Great Tradition*, Konark Publishers, Annexure, Major newspapers, pp. 139–150.

Jayaram, Anup (2003). 'King under attack', *Businessworld*, 13 October, pp. 28–33, Vol. 23, issue 20.

Jayaram, Anup (2004). 'Birth of a new industry', *Businessworld*, 6 September, pp. 102–104, Vol. 24, issue 15.

Jayaram, Anup and Surendar, T. (2003). 'Clever Arithmetic', *Businessworld*, 21 July, pp. 58–60, Vol. 23, issue 8.

Jayram, Anup, Seetha and Bhandari, Bhupesh (1999). 'Murder on the information Highway', *Businessworld*, 16 August, pp. 20–26, Vol. 19, issue 14.

Jeffrey, Robin (1997). 'Indian Language Newspapers', a series of 11 essays, *Economic and Political Weekly*, January–March. Special reference to 'Telugu: Ingredients of Growth and Failure', 1 February.

Jeffrey, Robin (2000). *India's Newspaper Revolution—Capitalism, Politics and the Indian Language Press—1977–1999*, Oxford University Press.

Kalra, Nonita (1993). 'Radio Active', *Businessworld*, 20 October–November 1993, pp. 58–59, Vol. 13, No. 15.

Khanna, Vidhu and Braganza, Wilma (1995). 'These Little Firms went to the Market', *Businessworld*, 22 March–4 April, pp. 140–141, Vol. 14, No. 26.

Khandwala Research Indian Film Industry—An Insight (2001).

Kinnear, Michael (1999). Indian Music History in the earlier part of the twentieth century, downloaded from the internet.

Kohli, Vanita (1993). 'Marketing Comes to the Movies', *A&M*, June 1993, pp. 40–46, Vol. 5, No. 3.

Kohli, Vanita (1999). 'Change in Rhythm', *Businessworld*, 30 August, pp. 30–34, Vol. 19, No. 16.

Kohli, Vanita (2000). 'Sixty Minutes that Saved Star', *Businessworld*, 25 September, pp. 22–30, Vol. 20, No. 20.

Kohli, Vanita (2000). 'The Sound of a Business', *Businessworld*, 20 November, pp. 36–42, Vol. 20, No. 28.

Kohli, Vanita (2001). 'Testing Times', *Businessworld*, 28 May, pp. 28–29, Vol. 21, No. 3.

Kohli, Vanita (2002). 'Agony', *Businessworld*, 9 September, pp. 32–40, Vol. 22, No. 15.

Kohli, Vanita (2002). 'The Rise of the Locals', *Businessworld*, 20 May, pp. 28–33, Vol. 21, No. 51.

Kohli-Khandekar, Vanita (2003). 'License to Kill', *Businessworld*, 24 March, pp. 52–53, Vol. 22, No. 43.

Kohli-Khandekar, Vanita (2003). 'Push for Pay', *Businessworld*, 13 January, pp. 30–35, Vol. 22, No. 33.

Kohli-Khandekar, Vanita (2003). 'The Sun TV Sequel', *Businessworld*, 28 April, pp. 36–40, Vol. 22, No. 48.

Kohli-Khandekar, Vanita (2003). 'The future of broadcasting', *Businessworld*, 15 December.

Kohli-Khandekar, Vanita (2005). 'Breaking News', *Businessworld*, 28 March, pp. 40–52, Vol. 24, issue 44.

Kohli-Khandekar, Vanita (2005). 'The Big Finn', *Businessworld*, 7 March, pp. 36–42, Vol. 24, issue 41.

Kohli-Khandekar, Vanita (2005). 'The broadcasting logjam', *Businessworld*, 16 May, pp. 32–40, Vol. 24, issue 51.

Kumar, Sheila (1983). 'Filmland's High Stake Casinos', *Businessworld*, 28 February–13 March, pp. 38–48, Vol. 2, No. 25.

Leiner, Barry M., Cerf, Vinton G., Clark, David D., Kahn, Robert E., Kleinrock, Leonard, Lynch, Daniel C., Postel, Jon Roberts, Lawrence G., and Wolff, Stephen. *A Brief History of the Internet*, From the Internet Society website, *www.isoc.org*

Lodestar Media Research.

Luthra, H.R. (1986). *Indian Broadcasting*. Publications Division, Ministry of Information and Broadcasting, Government of India, February.

Manorama Year Book (2002).

Mathai, Palakunnathu G. (1995). 'Is this really the final episode?' *Businessworld*, 8–21 March, Vol. 14, No. 25.

Ministry of Information and Broadcasting, Government of India (1982). 'Mass Media in India' (1980–81), compiled and edited by the Research and Reference Division and published by the Director Publications division, November.

Ministry of Information and Broadcasting, Government of India (2000). 'Information Technology and Communications', final draft report of the sub-group on convergence.

Ministry of Information and Broadcasting, Government of India (2001–02). Annual Report.

Ministry of Information and Broadcasting, Government of India (2002). 'Entry of Foreign Print Media and Foreign Direct Investment in Print', Standing Committee on Information Technology, 32nd Report presented to the 13th Lok Sabha, 22 March.

National Readership Survey (2001). Round 2+3, All India. A.C. Nielsen, IMRB and Taylor Nelson Sofres Mode (TNS Mode).

Newspaper Association of America. From the website, *www.naa.org*

Prasad, Shishir (1999). 'Satyam's prize bid', *Businessworld*, 13 December, pp. 44–47, Vol. 19, issue 31.

Prasar Bharati (2000, 2002, 2003). Annual Report, from Doordarshan, Delhi, and the website of the Ministry of Information and Broadcasting, *http://mib.nic.in*

Press Information Bureau (2005). 'Regulation of news and entertainment channels', Government of India, 8 August.

Press in India (2001). Registrar of Newspapers in India (RNI).

Press Institute of India, archives.

Price Waterhouse Coopers (2002–06 and 2003–07). Global Media and Entertainment Outlook.

Rajadhyaksha, Ashish and Willemen, Paul (1994). *Encyclopedia of Indian Cinema.* London: British Film Institute. New Delhi: Oxford.

Radar (2002). IMRB's syndicated establishment plus listenership studies. IMRB International, Outlook.

Radio Marketing Guide and Fact Book for Advertisers (2000–01). Radio Advertising Bureau.

Reserve Bank of India (2004). Foreign Exchange Management Act (FEMA), 1999—Current Account Transactions—Liberalisation—A.P. (DIR Series) Circular No. 76–24 February.

Report of the First Press Commission appointed in 1951.

Report of the First Press Commission. 'Capital Investment and Turnover', Chapter III, pp. 40–48 and 'Economics of Daily Newspapers', Chapter IV, pp. 49–59.

Report of the Indian Banks Association (1999). Working Group on Bank Finance for the Film Industry.

Saregama India (1999–2000 and 2001–02). Annual Report.

Satellite & Cable TV magazine, archives.

Tewari, Santosh Kumar Prof (2001). 'Provisional press councils needed', *Vidura*, (Magazine of the Press Institute of India), pp. 6–7, Vol. 38, No. 3, July–September.

The Economist (2005). 'How the Internet killed the phone business', 15 September.

The Press and Registration of Books Act (1867). From the website of the Ministry of Information and Broadcasting, *http://mib.nic.in*

The Press in India, RNI (2003–04).

TRAI (2005). 'Digitalisation of Cable Television', Consultation Paper No. 1/1005, 3 January.

TRAI (2005). 'Financial analysis of telecom industry in China and India', Study paper No. 1/2005, 16 June.

TRAI (2005). 'Indicators for Telecom growth', Study paper No. 2/2005.

TRAI (2005). 'Next Generation Networks', Study paper, 15 July.

Shekhar, Meenu (1994). 'Enter Big Bucks in the Cable industry' *Businessworld*, 30 November–13 December, pp. 138–143, Vol. 14, No. 18.

Shekhar, Shashi and Vijay, Srinivas (1990). 'Music Mughal', *Businessworld*, 7–20 November, pp. 62–69, Vol. 10, No. 15.

Thoraval, Yves (2000). *The Cinemas of India 1896-2000*, Macmillan India.

Vidura—Press Institute of India's magazine archives.

Vishwanathan, Vidya (1999). 'Masters of the web', *Businessworld*, 24 May, pp. 30–35, Vol. 19, issue 3.

Vogel, Harold L. (1998). *Entertainment Industry Economics*, A guide for financial analysts, Cambridge University Press, 4th edition.

Willmore, Larry (2001). *Government policies toward Information and Communication Technologies; A Historical Perspective*, United Nations.

Zee Television. From the website, *www.zeetelevision.com*

index

257

261